• • • • •

How to Open a Financially Successful

Bed & Breakfast
or Small Hotel

with companion CD

• • • • •

REVISED 2ND EDITION

HOW TO OPEN A FINANCIALLY SUCCESSFUL BED & BREAKFAST OR SMALL HOTEL WITH COMPANION CD REVISED 2ND EDITION

Copyright © 2016 by Atlantic Publishing Group, Inc.
1405 SW 6th Ave. • Ocala, Florida 34471 • 352-622-1825 • 352-622-1875–Fax
Web site: www.atlantic-pub.com • E-mail: sales@atlantic-pub.com
SAN Number: 268-1250

Library of Congress Cataloging-in-Publication Data

Fullen, Sharon L., author.
How to open a financially successful bed & breakfast or small hotel / by Sharon L. Fullen and Douglas Brown. -- Revised 2nd edition.
     pages cm
"With companion CD."
Includes bibliographical references and index.
ISBN 978-1-62023-064-0 (alk. paper) -- ISBN 1-62023-064-X (alk. paper) 1. Hotel management. 2. Bed and breakfast accommodations--Management. 3. Small business--Management. I. Brown, Douglas Robert, 1960- author. II. Title.
TX911.3.M27F8349 2015
647.94068--dc23
                    2015028685

Over the years, we have adopted a number of dogs from rescues and shelters. First there was Bear and after he passed, Ginger and Scout. Now, we have Kira, another rescue. They have brought immense joy and love not just into our lives, but into the lives of all who met them.

We want you to know a portion of the profits of this book will be donated in Bear, Ginger and Scout's memory to local animal shelters, parks, conservation organizations, and other individuals and nonprofit organizations in need of assistance.

– Douglas & Sherri Brown,
President & Vice-President of Atlantic Publishing

Table of Contents

Chapter 8. Marketing And Marketing Literature 179

Chapter 9. Decorating And Renovating 225

Chapter 13. Staff

CHAPTER ONE

· · · · ·

Should You Own A B&B?

*"Owning a B&B brings people from all walks of life into yours.
These different outlooks can greatly enrich the owners' lives."*

– John and Malinda Anderson, Maplevale Farm Bed & Breakfast; Oxford, Ohio

Do you love to throw dinner parties and tend to invite every "stray" you come across over for Thanksgiving dinner? If so, it's very likely that you would do well as a bed-and-breakfast owner.

More and more people are becoming attracted to the notion of owning a bed-and-breakfast (B&B). There are lots of reasons for this. Some people are retired, want to make a little extra money and love the company and stories their guests bring into their lives. Others are fed up with the corporate lifestyle and want to find a more relaxed, retiring way of life. There are also people who mainly want to work from home due to family obligations, or they just simply want to be their own boss. All of these are worthwhile reasons for exploring the idea of owning your own B&B, but it's wise to take a good, hard look at yourself and your expectations before taking the plunge. Oh sure, that couple you stayed with last summer at the country inn seemed so relaxed and carefree that they made it look like a vacation, but owning a B&B is a lifestyle

more than a job, and potential owners need to be absolutely sure it's the right lifestyle for them before sinking their time, money and hard work into this rewarding, yet demanding business/lifestyle.

A survey of bed-and-breakfast owners showed that the reasons people decide to adapt to this lifestyle are varied. Bruce and Lynn Bartlett, the owners of Longwood Manor Bed & Breakfast in Brookeville, Maryland, started their B&B because Lynn wanted to have a home-based business so she could work but still be at home with her children. Sherry and Darryl McKenney of the Murphin Ridge Inn in Adams County, Ohio, bought a country inn to fulfill a personal dream after being restaurant owners for years. Ouida Dickinson, a software engineer by day and innkeeper of The Dickinson in Huntsville, Alabama, by night, bought the inn to build up a business in preparation for when she retires. Joan Bradford of the Yellow Turtle Inn in New Windsor, Maryland, got into the B&B game simply because she loves being her own boss. "Unfortunately," she said, "I can't fire myself. My boss won't let me!"

As you can see, the reasons people buy bed-and-breakfasts are as varied as the innkeepers themselves!

A Little History

B&Bs are still a fairly new trend in the United States, but they have been a European staple for a long time. These B&Bs are generally run out of someone's home and guests enter the family's life for the time of their visit. The attraction for visitors to a traditional European B&B is becoming part of the culture rather than just a tourist experience.

The Professional Association of Innkeepers International's (PAII) most recent edition of *Statistics of Bed-and-Breakfast/Country Inns* estimates that there are about 17,000 inns currently operating in the U.S. with an estimated collective worth of $3.4 billion.

As the B&B industry in the United States began to grow, the industry also grew within itself. Today, you can find a variety of accommodations that refer to themselves as B&Bs. There are many variations on the following types of B&Bs, but these categories will give you a breakdown of the terms and what type of establishment guests expect if a business uses a particular descriptive phrase in their advertising.

Home stay. These accommodations are the closest to the traditional European bed-and-breakfast. In these establishments, hosts generally run the B&B directly out of their own home with probably one or two extra bedrooms in which the guests stay. The owner/operator lives on the premises and guests are able to get a local experience by staying with the family. Usually, guests will stay at a home stay for this kind of atmosphere rather than focusing on an abundance of amenities.

B&B. These establishments usually have three to six rooms, but they may have as many as 25. The owner may or may not live on the premises and, of course, breakfast is included in the price of the room. The number and type of amenities offered at B&Bs varies greatly. There may be private baths, semi-private baths or a combination, there may be fireplaces and/or whirlpool baths, and there may even simply be a snack plate available to guests in the evening.

Inn/Country inn. These tend to be larger than B&Bs, usually more than six guest rooms and, generally, inns operate a full-service bed-and-breakfast as well as serve breakfast. The bed-and-breakfast may only be open to inn guests or it may be open to non-guests as well.

Personality

Owning a B&B is a 24-hour service job, so it's critical that you genuinely like people, and like to be around them! Not only is it important that you like people, but you must be able to constantly demonstrate this in your attitude and interactions with your guests. Do you smile easily or not easily show frustration? Do you feel comfortable striking up conversations with strangers? These are traits a B&B owner should possess or acquire to be successful. You need to be able to be warm with people and treat total strangers like members of your family so that they are confident in choosing you over another B&B, or worse, a hotel chain.

Take a few minutes and honestly answer the questions below to help you see if you naturally possess a B&B-owner personality.

1. At a party you are more comfortable:
   a. Sitting in a corner by yourself
   b. Seeking out new people to talk to
   c. Conversing with a few friends you know
   d. Dancing on the table with a lampshade on your head

2. How do people describe you?
   a. Warm and open
   b. Hard to get to know
   c. Loud and boisterous
   d. A person that clams up around strangers

3. What's your idea of a fun Saturday night?
   a. Taking in a play and a nice dinner out
   b. Dancing till dawn
   c. Staying at home with a good book
   d. Having a few close friends over to enjoy cocktails by the fire

4. What are your optimal work habits?
    a. Do you need absolute silence to concentrate?
    b. Do you prefer to be left alone to do your job?
    c. Do you like to take frequent breaks to gossip around the water cooler?
    d. Do you like to work with a variety of people on a project?

5. What is your ideal Saturday morning?
    a. Laying in bed reading the paper until noon
    b. Laying in bed sleeping until noon
    c. Getting up to leisurely watch the sun rise and sip coffee
    d. Getting up and have no one utter a word to you until you've finished your first cup of coffee
    e. Getting up and having breakfast with your family

6. Which statement best describes your cooking habits?
    a. I prefer to eat out
    b. My freezer is stocked with frozen entrees for each day of the week
    c. I enjoy cooking, but am not very good at it
    d. I love to try new recipes

7. How would you describe your cleaning habits?
    a. Clean? Am I supposed to clean?
    b. I clean once a week
    c. I tidy up every day and do major cleaning weekly
    d. I would prefer a maid

There really isn't any one right answer to the questions in this test, but there are wrong answers. For instance, if you picked answer D for Question 5 or answered B for Question 3, you probably wouldn't be very happy as a B&B owner. If you answered B or C for Question 1 and A for Question 2, however, you have a good chance of being happy and successful at inn-keeping. And let's be honest, why bother adapting to a new lifestyle if it isn't going to make you happy? That's one of the main reasons people dream of opening a B&B — because they think it will make them happy.

Warmth

A good deal of the charm of stay-ing at a bed-and-breakfast is the warmth and friendliness of the host or hosts. Hosting is an art. Some people seem to have a nat-ural knack for it while others can easily learn it. You could think of it as going on stage. No matter what your mood is, you need to convey a happy, caring persona to your guests when they arrive. You should always greet them with a smile and a warm welcome.

The job of host begins when someone calls you for a reservation and ends only when the guests are waving goodbye as they pull away. You want to do everything you can to make your guests feel comfortable in your inn. This may mean spending time with them chatting over breakfast, or it may mean leaving them alone. It's your job to ascertain what your guest needs and then to provide it.

Attention to detail is a very important part of hosting; it's often the small things that will make your inn stand out. All bed-and-breakfasts provide a room, a private or shared bath and some kind of breakfast. Maybe you have soy milk for people who don't drink milk, or you have a diary of past guests' experience and a rating of area restaurants along with restaurant menus. Thinking of all the little things that might improve your guests' stay is a big part of hosting.

Skills

Okay, you've gotten past the first hurdle and you think you'd really enjoy being a B&B owner. Enjoying is one thing; doing is another. If this is going to be a way for you to make a living (or even just add some extra income), you need to think about whether or not you'd be good at the job as well. There are a variety of skills an innkeeper needs. Take a look at this skills assessment inventory and check off the ones that apply to you.

Skill Assessment Inventory

Check if this applies to you.

	Entrepreneur/Managerial
	I am good at resolving conflicts
	I enjoy working hard
	I am able to meet deadlines
	I am able to maintain a budget
	I am a self-starter
	I am a creative problem-solver
	I set clear goals
	I have the ability to follow through
	Organizational
	I'm good with figures
	I keep an updated calendar
	I have to-do lists
	I have the ability to prioritize tasks
	I am good at record keeping
	I have a filing system
	Communication
	I am good at giving instructions/directions
	I am good at writing memos/letters/reports
	I am a good listener
	I speak clearly, making sure people understand

Customer Service	
	I don't get frustrated easily
	I don't lose my temper easily
	I am comfortable with enforcing rules or policies
	I like to solve problems
	I am tolerant of all people, no matter their race, gender or religion
Hospitality	
	I am friendly and open
	I like working with people
	I enjoy pleasing people
	I enjoy helping people get the information they need
	I am optimistic
	I like to entertain
	I like to cook

How did you do? If you were able to check the majority of these, you will probably do fine as a bed-and-breakfast owner. Remember though, this is by no means a comprehensive list! It wouldn't hurt if you were handy, for example. Calling a repair person for every little problem can eat into profits fast. The ability to fix a leaking faucet or broken step can go a long way in making you a more efficient B&B owner! If you're not very good in math, you might want to consider taking a bookkeeping class at your local community college as well. You'll probably hire an accountant for the more major financial issues, but it would be helpful if you could take care of your own daily accounting needs.

You might also have skills beyond the normal ones you'll need day to day that could come in handy. Does it bring tears to your eyes every time you hear a downy woodpecker? Maybe you could add value to your B&B by offering guests a guided bird-watching tour. If you are an expert at canoeing, offer your guests afternoon canoe trips to a cozy little cove for a romantic picnic. Some of these services you may want to charge extra for; others you could include in the price of the room, but we'll get into more on that later when we talk about setting room prices.

Being an innkeeper is a wonderful lifestyle for many reasons, one of them being that you get to use and acquire all kinds of skills. If you like to do a variety of tasks during your workday, owning a B&B is an excellent vocation choice. B&B owners are actually modern Renaissance people, good at so many different things!

Getting Your Feet Wet

You've taken a good, hard look at your wants, goals and skills, and you've decided that you would love to operate a bed-and-breakfast. So how do you get a little real-world experience to make absolutely sure this is the lifestyle for you? First, you need to stay in B&Bs! Make sure before you take the plunge that you stay at several B&Bs as a guest to see what the experience is like from a guest perspective. What is the host like? The rooms? Are there shared baths or private baths? What items are in the rooms and bathrooms? What are common areas like? What types of extra services are offered? What type of breakfast is offered? You may want to tell the host you are thinking of opening a B&B and he or she might be willing to sit and chat with you, offering tips and strategies. Don't be disappointed if this doesn't happen, however. It's just as likely that the host may feel threatened by the competition and be unwilling to talk. When trying this approach, you'll have to rely on your judgment of people to decide if letting your host know your intentions is the best idea.

You can also develop your own survey to take along and fill out so you can compare all the bed-and-breakfasts you visit (you probably should fill these out in the privacy of your own room — walking around with a clipboard like an inspector is bound to ruffle many a host!).

The following box shows a sample bed-and-breakfast survey sheet. Use it as a jumping off point to develop your own survey form.

Bed-And-Breakfast Survey

B&B Name _____

Location _____

Area attractions? _____
_____

What are the major roads in vicinity? _____

Is there an airport/bus station nearby? _____

Is there a sign? _____ How much parking is there? _____

How many guest rooms are there? _____

What are the check-in/check-out times? _____

What is the general appearance of the building exterior? _____
_____

What is the general appearance of the building interior? _____
_____

Do the rooms have private or shared baths? _____

What are the room rates? _____

What amenities do the rooms have? _____
_____

Describe the dining area (are there booths, tables, type of tablecloths, etc.?).
_____
_____

Number of guests weekly:

Mon _____ Tues _____ Wed _____ Thurs _____ Fri _____ Sat _____ Sun _____

Is alcohol served? _____

Do they serve any other meals besides breakfast? _____

If so, what meals and what are the prices? _____

Describe the common areas and general décor: _____

What does the typical guest profile seem to be (i.e., are they catering to families, business travelers, etc.)? _____

_____

Are pets allowed? _____

Smoking? _____

Another way to investigate the bed-and-breakfast lifestyle is to inn-sit. There are many opportunities to inn-sit for hosts looking to take a vacation. Many bed-and-breakfast associations offer listings of hosts looking for temporary inn-keeping help. The Interim Innkeepers Network has a list for members, and they go as far as offering an Interim Innkeeper Certificate Program. You can obtain more information on this resource at **www.interiminnkeepers. net/index.php/certification-program2**. Bed & Breakfast Inns Online (**www. bbonline.com**) offers a listing of innsitter services as well.

Bed & Breakfast Inns Online also offers a list of seminars and consulting services. One of the organizations shown as offering seminars is the wonderful The B&B Team. This group has workshops, apprenticeships and consulting services. They can be reached at **http://bbteam.com/home/contact-us**.

Several inns also offer a chance to intern. Check out the following inns for these "innternships."

David Caples

Lodging Resources
98 S. Fletcher Ave.
Amelia Island, FL 32034
800-500-9625
www.lodgingresources.com
Email: djcaples@lodgingresources.com

Carl Glassman

Wedgewood Inn School
111 W. Bridge St.
New Hope, PA 18938
215-862-2570
www.wedgwoodinn.com/for-aspiring-innkeepers.html
Email: stay@wedgwoodinn.com

Barbara Notarius

Alexander Hamilton House
49 Van Wyck St.
Croton-on-Hudson, NY 10520
914-271-6737
www.alexanderhamiltonhouse.com
Email: alexanderhamiltonhouse@gmail.com

The B&B Customer

Your particular location and your individual style as a bed-and-breakfast will be the best determinant of what type of guest to expect, but, in general, people who stay at bed-and-breakfasts are seeking more of a "local" than a "tourist" experience. They want to immerse themselves in the local flavor. The trend today is for more business customers to stay at bed-and-breakfasts, but again, this will partially be determined by your location. Young couples and retirees make up a large number of B&B guests as well. According to industry research, approximately 77 percent of bed-and-breakfast guests are between the ages of 25 and 54. Approximately 92.8 percent have attended college, and almost 50 percent of the guests make an average household income of $75,000 and up. You can find more information on the profile of bed-and-breakfast customers on the PAII website at **www.paii.com**. An especially good source of this kind of info is the PAII 2013 Industry Study of Innkeeping Performance.

A Day in the Life (a.k.a. Keeping it All Organized)

Betty owns a B&B in a small town in Missouri. She also works part time as a graphic designer for a small company in town and has two school-aged children. She and her husband have owned the B&B for about two years. They have a total of four rooms and offer a full buffet breakfast from 7:30 to 9:30 a.m. Today is Tuesday; the inn is full and she has to be at work at 1 p.m.

6 a.m. Betty gets up, showers and dresses.

6:30 a.m. Betty wakes her husband and the boys so they can get ready for work and school.

6:45 a.m. Betty starts making breakfast and the kids' lunches. Last night around midnight, she made an egg strata that has been sitting overnight. She pops that into the oven so it will be done by 7:15 and begins getting out an assortment of rolls, croissants, muffins and bread. She sets them on top of the oven to warm while she takes the butter and orange juice out to the dining room. (Luckily she remembered to set the table last night before retiring.)

7:15 a.m. Betty puts the finishing touches on the table in the dining room, including some fresh-cut flowers from her garden, and starts the coffee.

7:20 a.m. Betty's husband loads the kids in the car and they are off.

7:30 a.m. The guests in the Rose Room and the Oriental Room arrive for breakfast. Betty greets them with a smile and a pot of coffee in hand. The woman in the Rose Room reminds Betty that she is allergic to wheat so Betty heads back to the kitchen to make her a quick omelet since the strata has bread in it.

7:40 a.m. Betty returns with the omelet and refreshes coffee for the guests.

7:45 a.m. The other guests have not come down for breakfast yet, so Betty takes the opportunity to clean up some of the breakfast dishes in the kitchen and she prepares the final bill for the guests in the South Room.

8 a.m. The guests from the South Room come down, pay their bill and then sit down for breakfast. Betty pours their coffee and buses the dishes from the earlier diners.

8:10 a.m. The phone rings and Betty talks to a potential guest. The woman has never been to a B&B before so Betty spends some extra time going over the services and policies. Ten minutes later, the woman decides she'll think about it and will call back later.

8:20 a.m. Betty runs upstairs and strips the linens from the three guest rooms that have checked out. As she is dusting these rooms, she hears the couple in the suite head downstairs. She takes the back stairs and meets them in the dining room with more coffee. After she goes back to the kitchen to retrieve a glass of milk for the man, Betty heads to the laundry room to wash the sheets. She has three new guests checking into these rooms tonight.

9:00 a.m. The nice old couple staying in the Garden Room arrive for breakfast. All the other diners have been quick because they have to be in town on business, but the Reynolds want to sit and chat with Betty; this is the reason they stay in B&Bs — they love talking to the inn owners and making new friends. Betty sits and has a cup of coffee with them while she tells them about how she and her husband first decided to be innkeepers, and she gets them a map of a historic walking tour of the city.

10 a.m. The Reynolds have returned to their room to get ready to go out and Betty clears the dining room and cleans up the kitchen.

10:45 a.m. By this time the laundry is done, but Betty puts her other set of sheets on the beds and finishes cleaning the bathrooms and empties the trash in these rooms. She'll leave the sheets in the dryer for now and air fluff them later so they don't wrinkle.

11:45 a.m. The Reynolds have left for their walking tour, and Betty changes the towels in their room and empties the garbage.

12:45 p.m. Off to work, which, luckily, is only a few blocks away.

4 p.m. Back to the inn to check in the Taylors who will be staying in the Rose Room. The Johnsons arrive shortly after, and Betty checks them in as well. The Johnsons plan to dine out that night and ask Betty if she would mind suggesting a restaurant and making the reservations for them. Betty also spends some time with each of the guests showing them the premises and going over the B&B's policies.

5 p.m. Betty makes a cheese, fruit and cracker platter and puts it in the common room as an amenity. As the new guests come down and explore, Betty offers them a glass of tea or wine.

6 p.m. Her last guests arrive and get checked in.

7 p.m. Betty's husband makes dinner for the family while Betty gets together items for the next day's breakfast.

9 p.m. After tucking the boys in for the night, Roger, Betty's husband, runs to the store for some more eggs and apricot marmalade while Betty goes over the weekly receipts.

10 p.m. Betty does a house check just to make sure everything is okay.

10:30 p.m. Betty and Roger retire for the evening and try to catch up on each other's day.

You can see how important it is to be organized! If you own a small B&B, it is likely you will be doing all the work — at least for the first year or two. Even if you own a larger B&B and have employees, you'll need to be scheduling and organizing their time as well.

How Much Can You Expect to Make?

Obviously the answer to this question is dependent on how many rooms you have to rent. Let's say you have five rooms: two doubles with private baths, a suite and two queens with a shared bath. Let's say you charge $150 for each of the doubles, $225 for the suite and $75 for both of the queens. If you can book all these rooms 100 nights per year, you stand to make $67,500 a year.

According to the PAII's 2000 Bed & Breakfast/Country Inns Industry Study, B&Bs with one to four rooms can expect an average room revenue of $43,147, and inns with five to eight rooms can expect an average of $121,125. The  study also concludes that inns with one to four rooms will have $33,306 in operating expenses and a B&B with five to eight rooms comes in at $83,657 in expenses. So, the profit you can see would be $9,841 for a B&B with one to four rooms and $37,468 for an inn with five to eight rooms. These numbers are only averages; your real profits will vary due to any number of factors including location, amenities and the amount of advertising you do.

While you should not expect to make a large profit in your first year of operation, the PAII's study shows that inn-keeping can be a profitable business.

How Much Money Do You Need?

The following worksheets, provided courtesy of the Small Business Administration, will aid the bed-and-breakfast owner in estimating start-up costs and expenses.

To help you estimate the amount of financing you will need to get your venture off the ground, use the following checklist. Keep in mind, however, that not every category may apply. You should estimate monthly amounts.

Salary of Owner/Manager (if applicable)	
All Other Salaries and Wages	
Mortgage/Property Taxes	
Advertising	
Delivery Expenses	
Supplies	
Telephone	
Utilities	
Insurance	
Taxes, Including Social Security	
Interest	
Maintenance (Facilities/Equipment)	
Legal and Other Professional Fees	

Dues/Subscriptions	
Leases (Equipment/Furniture/Etc.)	
Inventory Purchases	
Miscellaneous	
One-Time Start-Up Costs	
Fixtures/Equipment/Furniture	
Remodeling	
Installation of Fixtures/Equipment/Furniture	
Starting Inventory	
Deposits with Public Utilities	
Legal and Other Professional Fees	
Licenses and Permits	
Advertising and Promotion for Opening	
Accounts Receivable	
Cash Reserve/Operating Capital	
Other	
TOTAL	

*Your total amount will depend upon how many months of preparation you want to allow for before actually beginning operations.

FURNITURE / FIXTURES / EQUIPMENT

LIST OF FURNITURE, FIXTURES & EQUIPMENT					
	If you plan to pay cash in full, enter the full amount below and in the last column.	If you are going to pay by installments, fill out the columns below. Enter in the last column your down payment plus at least one installment.			Estimate of the cash you need for furniture, fixtures & equipment.
		PRICE	DOWN PAYMENT	AMOUNT OF EACH INSTALLMENT	
LINENS					$0.00
STORAGE SHELVES					$0.00
DISPLAY STANDS, SHELVES, TABLES					$0.00
CASH REGISTER					$0.00
SAFE					$0.00
COMPUTER					$0.00
SPECIAL LIGHTING					$0.00
OUTSIDE SIGN					$0.00
KITCHEN EQUIPMENT					$0.00
DINING ROOM FURNITURE					$0.00
MATTRESSES					$0.00
OTHER BEDROOM FURNITURE					$0.00
COMMON ROOM FURNITURE					$0.00
					$0.00
TOTAL FURNITURE, FIXTURES & EQUIPMENT					**$0.00**

CHAPTER TWO

· · · · ·

Selecting The B&B Location

One of your first decisions is to determine where to set up your B&B. If you already own a lovely Victorian home, you may just be considering using your current property for the venture. If you are in the general market for a B&B, however, you'll need to take many varying factors into consideration when choosing your location. After determining a likely area best suited for the B&B, be sure to obtain as many facts as you can about it. For example: How many inns and hotels are located in the area? Can you find out something about their sales volume? What attractions might bring people to the area? Is the B&B located where you could expect a good volume of business travelers? families? couples? The zoning ordinances, parking availability, transportation facilities and natural barriers — such as hills and bridges — also are important in considering the location of the B&B.

Possible sources for this information are chambers of commerce, trade associations, tourist offices, real estate companies, local newspapers, banks, city officials and personal observations.

Market Research

In order to answer such questions, you'll need to do market research. As you collect your data, be sure to keep this in mind and decide what factors are important for determining the best location for your bed-and-breakfast.

There are generally four steps of research in finding a location if you are starting from scratch. Depending on your particular situation, you may need to go through all four steps of research, or you may only need to do two or three.

National research. If you and your spouse are still working but talking about opening a B&B when you retire, this type of research may be useful if you haven't committed to a particular area yet. Maybe you're tired of winter and want to retire somewhere warm, or perhaps you want to move to a small mountain town. There are many tools you can use to research areas and the feasibility of opening a B&B in a new area.

Market area research. A market is a technical way of referring to a city or a metropolitan statistical area (MSA), which is a concept used when talking about census research. Once you have chosen a city in which to locate your business, you need to begin looking at the parts of the city and focus on finding one that will be good for your individual operation. If the town has a historic area, you may want to look closely at that. If you are looking at a ski area, you'll want to find the right pocket of town where the ski bunnies will be able to find you easily!

Trade area research. Trade area refers to the area from which most of your customers come. Since B&Bs (and other more traditional forms of accommodations) don't rely as much on local traffic for their business, this area probably won't be of great concern for you, but it's still worth noting.

Site research. Finally you get to look at actual sites. At this stage, you will look at a few potential sites and compare characteristics to find the best location for your inn or B&B.

Population and Demographics

Population and demographics will be factors in choosing your location. This information can be obtained from various resources; many of these sources will be used at any and all levels of your search. The United States Census Bureau (**www.census.gov**), for instance, can provide important data at the national level of your search, as well as the site level. Most businesses that rely on local people for business will use more of this information than you will, but the information on this site might help you determine how much new business the area is attracting, and this could help you determine the amount of bookings you might receive from business travelers. If the area has a high population, it is also more likely you could receive bookings from relatives and families staying in town.

Be sure to pay specific attention to statistics on the lodging industry. Even though these refer to traditional-style hotels, the information can come in handy.

Four areas on the Census Bureau's website of particular interest are: the American Community Survey, Censtats, County Business Patterns and American FactFinder.

The American Community Survey. This survey can provide you with information from the census supplemental survey. This information includes tables with demographic information by county and MSAs. As defined by the U.S. Census Bureau, an MSA is an area made up of at least one major city (over 50,000 people) and includes the county or counties located within the MSA.

The American Community Survey is a new survey that is replacing the Census Bureau's long survey. It provides economic, social, demographic and housing information for communities every year instead of every 10 years.

Censtats. This portion of the website gives you economic and demographic information that you can compare by county. The information is updated every two years. This section also includes information on residential building permits, which are updated every month.

County Business Patterns. County Business Patterns gives you economic information arranged by industry and it is updated every year. It includes data on the total number of establishments, employment and payroll for over 40,000 zip codes across the country. Metro Business Patterns provides the same data for MSAs.

American FactFinder. This website, located at **http://factfinder.census.gov**, lets you search, browse and map United States census data, including economic, population, geographical and housing statistics.

The drawback to most census information is that it is collected only every 10 years. If you are looking in an area that has changed a great deal in the last decade, you may want to supplement the information you get from the U.S. Census Bureau with information from demographic research firms. These firms typically use census data to generate information on population and demographics for areas between census years.

Other Demographic Information Websites

While the U.S. Census Bureau can provide you with a great deal of demographic information, the following websites are worth exploring as well.

FedStats. This website, at **www.fedstats.gov**, lets you track economic and population trends. The statistics are collected by more than 70 federal agencies.

Service Annual Survey. This part of the U.S. Census Bureau's website offers annual estimates of receipts for some service industries. This information can be found at **www.census.gov/services/index.html**.

Statistical Abstract of the U.S., Section 27, Domestic Trade and Services. This Web page, located at **www.census.gov/prod/2001pubs/statab/sec27.pdf**, provides information on sales, employees, payrolls and other business statistics.

Statistical Resources on the Web. This website, located at **www.lib.umich. edu/govdocs/stats.html**, is an index to statistical information available on the Internet. It lists over 200 topics.

Statistics of Income. Hosted by the Internal Revenue Service, this site contains financial information concerning businesses in the retail and service industries. You can find it by logging on to **www.irs.gov/uac/Tax-Stats-2**.

U.S. Bureau of Economic Analysis, U.S. Department of Commerce. This agency hosts a website at **www.bea.gov**, which provides publications and data on businesses by industry.

Site Research

Gordon Watkins of The Inn at 410 in Flagstaff, Arizona, stresses that you need to have a sustainable business model. Gordon says, "Ask yourself, "Where is your business going to come from?" Make sure you have the answer. There are many beautiful old homes in communities across the U.S., but would people have a solid reason to go there on an ongoing basis?"

When starting your search for the ideal bed-and-breakfast location, keep this advice in mind and use the following list to help you evaluate areas and their potential for attracting guests. Some of the best spots for a B&B are near colleges, vacation areas and cultural or historical sites.

- Downtown area
- Historical district
- Business district
- Government offices
- Colleges/universities
- Technical schools
- Religious schools
- Military bases
- Theaters/Opera/Symphony
- Hospitals
- Airport
- Train station
- Major highway
- Local transportation
- Museums
- Art galleries
- Beaches/Ocean
- Lakes
- State parks
- Sports arenas
- Casinos
- Rivers
- Mountains
- Nature preserves
- Zoo
- Caves/Caverns
- Historical/Archaeological sites
- Bed-and-breakfasts
- Flea market
- Antique stores
- Shopping

- Aquarium
- Swimming
- Hiking
- Boating

- Skiing
- Hunting
- Bird watching
- Golfing

Once you have found several locations you are interested in, you can use this score sheet to see how they each rate.

Grade each factor: "A" for excellent, "B" for good, "C" for fair and "D" for poor.

PROPERTY LOCATION:	
FACTOR	**GRADE**
1. Located in a good spot for the market	
2. Merchandise or raw materials readily available	
3. Nearby competition situation	
4. Transportation availability and rates	
5. Proximity to area attractions (hiking trails, Amish country, wine country, museums, etc.)	
6. Quality of available employees	
7. Prevailing rates of employee wages	
8. Parking facilities	
9. Adequacy of utilities (sewer, water, power, gas)	
10. Traffic flow	
11. Taxation burden	
12. Quality of police and fire protection	
13. Housing availability for employees	
14. Environmental factors (schools, cultural, community activities, enterprise of businesspeople)	
15. Physical suitability of building	
16. Type and cost of building/business	
17. Proven for future expansion	
18. Estimate of overall quality of site in 10 years	

Competition

Once you've narrowed down your location choices, you'll want to take a good, long look at the competition. Information on competition may be harder to access than demographics, but you can be creative here and you will probably learn a lot. Your best source for information on the competition may be simply to visit competitors' establishments in areas you are interested in. Other sources of information on competition include the following ideas.

Telephone book. You can at least get a count and the location of your competitors.

Chambers of commerce. These often keep a list of area businesses. Be careful using this list; it often only includes businesses that are members rather than all the businesses in the area.

Tourist offices. State tourist office websites usually list bed-and-breakfasts under their accommodations list. These lists will provide links to the individual bed-and-breakfast's website, so it's an easy way to get an overview of the competition, as well as what each competitor has to offer. A listing of state offices can be found at **www.usatourist.com/english/traveltips/state-tourist-offices.html**.

Local newspapers. You can get a sense of the competition from advertisements and job classifieds. Many papers may list a number of the bed-and-breakfasts in town with information on their prices and menus in their weekly entertainment section.

Reservation Service Agencies (RSAs). These agencies make reservations for bed-and-breakfast guests. Usually members (B&B owners) pay an annual fee and a percentage of each booking to be part of this network. While it is an added expense, it is one well worth considering, especially if you are new to your business. RSAs offer an abundance of information as well. The following two websites contain some national RSA information that might help you find information more specific to your region: The Mi Casa Su Casa Bed-and-Breakfast Reservation Service page at **www.azres.com** may prove quite helpful to you if you're interested in the Southwestern U.S. while The Bed-and-Breakfast Inn Worldwide Directory at **www.bnbboston.com/resources/worldwide-bab-directory.html** serves a significantly wider spread. You can also do a quickly online search for reservation service agencies by state.

Visiting the Competition

You'll have to play this one by ear. Many innkeepers are very forthcoming, but others may be concerned about teaching others their livelihood. You can glean information from innkeepers in various ways:

- By phone/email
- Interviews (in person or Skype)
- By staying as a guest

You may get your best, most objective results by staying as a guest. Even if B&B owners in the area you are researching may not be open to discussing their business, you can still stay at these bed-and-breakfasts to get a flavor of what works in that particular area.

You'll have to decide if you want to work undercover or be upfront. If you are upfront, you may get a lot more insider information. If owners are willing to discuss their business, not only will you get to see the premises, but you'll be able to talk about how they get their guests (through RSAs, referrals, over-bookings from area hotels, etc.) and what type of food service works best, etc.

If this approach doesn't appeal to you, check with local RSAs. They may have some suggestions for people who would be willing to talk to a prospective owner in their area.

Another option is to talk with people and stay at B&Bs outside of the competition area. While you may not get information that is specific to your chosen area, the information you do accumulate will still be extremely helpful in regards to how to successfully run a B&B in general.

Industry Research

You'll also want to investigate your industry's market research. There are many online publications you can easily access such as:

- International Bed-and-breakfast Pages (**www.bnb-international.com**)
- WorkingInnkeepers.com (**http://workinginnkeepers.com**)
- Bed & Breakfast Inns Online (**www.bbonline.com**)

There are also several national bed-and-breakfast associations that you can contact for information.

Professional Association of Innkeepers International

PO Box 90710

Santa Barbara, CA 93190

805-569-1853

www.paii.com

Select Registry

PO Box 150

Marshall, MI 49068

800-344-5244

www.selectregistry.com

American Bed & Breakfast Association

PO Box 795923

Dallas, TX 75379

www.abba.com

You should also check for state and regional bed-and-breakfast associations. To find state associations, you can go The B&B and Country Inn Marketplace website at **http://innmarketing.com**.

Some Location Considerations

Here are some other factors you'll want to consider in any location you choose.

Neighborhood. What is the immediate neighborhood like around the bed-and-breakfast you want to open? Is it like the Garden District in New Orleans with stately homes people will love to stroll by on a quiet evening, or is it in a run-down part of town with several boarded-up stores? In a location like the second one, no matter how beautiful your home is, guests may be uncomfortable staying with you. A single woman who likes to run in the evenings may think twice before booking with you, for instance. The neighborhood is an extension of the piece of real estate anyone buys, business or residential, so make sure when searching that you take your eyes off the house and take note of your surroundings.

Noise. Is the cutest Painted Lady you've ever seen located right next to a railroad track? If so, you may want to think twice before this purchase. Many guests will come to your inn for peace and relaxation. Those who don't may need to get a good night's sleep for a big sales presentation or job interview. No one will appreciate a noisy neighborhood.

ADA requirements. Approximately 57 million Americans have a physical disability. The Americans with Disabilities Act (ADA) was created to make sure public facilities, such as lodging establishments, are accessible to those with disabilities. As a public lodging establishment, you may be subject to the rules of the ADA. If you live in the B&B and don't have more than five guest rooms, you're exempt from having to meet ADA requirements. Keep in mind that not meeting ADA requirements may also keep you from potential customers in that 19 percent chunk of the American population.

In existing buildings, owners must remove architectural barriers if this is achievable. If not, owners must still provide alternate accessible accommodations (check the IRS website; you may be eligible for a tax credit for this work). New construction is regulated by the criteria in the ADA's Accessibility Guidelines; also, anything opened after Jan. 26, 1993, must be accessible.

Here are some ways to make your B&B accessible for people with disabilities:

- If you are renovating, look into widening doorways so someone in a wheelchair can get around (a minimum of 32 inches is required).
- Keep paths in hallways and rooms clear so people who are sight impaired can get around easily.
- Install grab bars in showers and bathtubs.
- Install a wheelchair ramp on the exterior steps.
- Buy smoke alarms with flashing lights for the hearing impaired.

You also can find more information at the U.S. Department of Justice's website for ADA Checklist for New Lodging Facilities at **www.ada.gov/hsurvey.htm**

Working with Contractors

Unless you're extremely handy and have a lot of free time, you will end up working with contractors for some, if not all, of your renovation work. Contractors could include an architect, a general contractor, plumbers, electricians, landscapers, roofers, painters and carpenters. If you have a large renovation project, you could work with a general contractor who will hire the appropriate subcontractors, or you could coordinate and hire all the workers yourself. Keep in mind that there will be certain tasks that will need to be completed before others begin. For example, the drywall has to be hung before you bring in the painters. If you are unfamiliar with the renovation process or don't have the time to deal with the headache of scheduling, it would be wise to find a general contractor you trust and let that person handle everything.

Your next question will be "How do I find a contractor I can trust?" You may want to consider asking other B&B owners who have had renovations done as well as other homeowners you know who have had home renovations completed. There are also online resources such as Angie's List (**www.angieslist. com**). A membership fee of $49 a year gives you access to customer satisfaction ratings on companies. Angie's List currently has chapters throughout cities in every state in the U.S. as well as Vancouver and Toronto if you're looking in Canada. Also, don't forget the Better Business Bureau (BBB) as a source of information on contractors. BBBs usually offer online and telephone reports on their members (of course, this won't help you if the contractor you are investigating isn't a member of the Better Business Bureau).

Make sure you get bids from several contractors; don't just go with the first bid you get. You'll often find there is a great difference in the prices. After you've done your research, pick three to five contractors to give you a bid and make sure you ask them for references you can check — you'll want to take a look at a project they've completed so you don't have any nasty surprises at the end of your work!

When you've made your decision on which contractor you want to hire, make sure you get a contract and ask for a delivery date — you can't start booking guests until you're certain your B&B is actually going to be opened  when promised. Keep in mind that things beyond the contractor's control can affect this date (weather, an item being out of stock, etc.), so this date may have to change, but if you get the contractor to commit to a date, you have a little control.

When signing the contract, your contractor may give you the option of doing the work for a flat fee or for "time and materials." If the contractor works on time and materials, you are paying for the supplies and then basically paying an hourly fee. With a flat fee, all of this is included in one lump-sum price. If you have a smaller job, you may actually save a little on a time-and-materials job, but it is a risk. For larger jobs, it's almost always safer to go with the flat fee.

Don't forget friends and relatives for those small jobs. Need to strip wallpaper in two of the guest rooms? Offer a couple of friends a free night at your bed-and-breakfast and you'll probably get several takers!

CHAPTER THREE

· · · · ·

Buying An Existing B&B

If you buy an existing bed-and-breakfast, you start with a leg-up because you will already have a built-in clientele. This also would require less capital at the start of your venture because, in many cases, when someone sells an existing operation, this includes all the equipment as well.

When looking at existing businesses, however, there are a number of things to keep in mind. You need to be careful if you are considering buying an existing operation; you don't want to buy one that is a failing business.

Check the financial records. You'll want to take a look at the inn's financial records from the past several years to get a good sense of its financial health. While you may be able to breathe some life back into the business, don't expect miracles.

Why are they selling? Do some sleuthing to find out why the owner is selling and what the word on the street is about the location. Be on-site for a few days and see what happens at the operation now. Lastly, make sure the location is a good one for your ideal operation.

Where to find existing bed-and-breakfasts for sale. Existing operations for sale can be found in the classified section of newspapers and in trade publications. Also look at the following websites for sale listings:

- Bed & Breakfast For Sale® – **www.bedandbreakfastforsale.com**
- About.com – **http://bandb.about.com/cs/innsforsale**
- Professional Association of International Innkeepers – **www.paii.org**
- Bed & Breakfast Inns Online – **www.bbonline.com/innkeeper/innsale.html**

Real Estate and Its Value

The real estate property of a bed-and-breakfast is often its most valuable feature. In many cases the real estate is a bigger attraction to the buyer than the business itself. "Real estate" is the land itself and any permanent improvements made on the land, such as utility connections, parking lots, buildings, etc. Real estate is a reversion asset, which means that it's expected to retain most or all of its value, regardless of whether the business operating on it is successful. If you are buying an existing B&B, the value of real estate is one of the major assets that need to be calculated when determining its value. Generally, there are three primary procedures for determining real estate value: Market Approach, Cost Approach and Income Approach.

Market Approach. The Market Approach is based on the idea of substitution. Basically, this means that the value of a property is determined by comparing it to like pieces of property in similar areas. Since these comparable properties are usually not exactly the same as the property you are trying to value, you'll need to make adjustments to place an accurate market value. The determining of these adjustments is a subjective process at best, and at worst it is impossible because owners of similar properties are extremely unlikely to tell you the details of their businesses.

Cost Approach. The Cost Approach is based on the idea of replacement. In simple terms, the property is valued on what it would cost to replace it completely. To determine this, you must add the replacement costs of all the assets in the establishment. Obtain purchase prices for new equipment and assets that exactly match the existing ones. In the case of equipment that is no longer made, add the price of what a new piece of equipment that provides the same utility would cost. Include all taxes, freight and installation in your quotes, and factor in depreciation. The Cost Approach is not widely used to estimate the value of a B&B's real estate, but is used mostly by insurance companies while processing a claim.

Income Approach. The Income Approach bases its valuation on the anticipation of future income to be derived from the property. The real estate value, then, is the present value of the estimated future net income, plus the present value of the estimated profit to be earned when the property is sold. This is the preferred approach when determining an accurate sales price for an income-producing property. This is because investors are concerned with the amount of income they can earn while using a property's assets, not with what it would cost to replace those assets.

There are other approaches to value as well. If your property was recently assessed for tax purposes, the Assessed Value may be a useful estimate to you, even if the valuation doesn't match current market conditions. The Book Value Approach is based on the initial purchase price for the property, minus accrued depreciation. This value will no doubt have very little to do with current market conditions, but it can be useful if you want to compute a low estimate of value for other reasons. The Underwriter Approach is used by lenders to determine the amount of loan proceeds an income property can support. This is determined by multiplying the DSC, or debt-service-coverage, ratio (the amount of income available for debt service, divided by the annual amount of debt-service payment demanded by the lender) by the loan constant, then dividing this sum by the annual income available for debt service.

It is often useful to use several valuation procedures to determine the most likely sales price. This is because establishments may have separate aspects of their business that can be valued separately. For instance, a bar may have its real property as well as its tavern license. The real estate may be valued through the Income Approach, and the license through the Market Approach.

The Value of Other Assets

A B&B's assets are often broken down into three categories: real estate, other reversion assets and the business. A reversion asset is one that retains its value regardless of the success or failure of the business. These are assets such as the real estate, equipment, inventories, receivables, prepaid expenses (deposits, taxes, advertising, etc.), leasehold interest, antiques, licenses, franchises and exclusive distributorships like lottery ticket sales. These assets keep their value even if a business goes under, and they can be sold at market value.

The business itself consists of everything the owner wishes to sell. Usually this means the furniture, fixtures, equipment, leasehold improvements, etc. It may also include tax credits, favorable operating expenses, customer lists and name recognition.

When a seller sets a sales price, it is not a straightforward process, and there are many other factors that need to be considered. Here are a few:

- **Profitability.** This has the most influence on sales price and salability of a B&B. The most common way to determine profitability is to examine the net operating income figure. If the inn earns an average net operating income, its most probable sales price will be equal to 50 percent of the previous 12 months' booking sales. The net income should be compared to the industry standard and the regional standard for that type of operation.

- **Track record.** Businesses need to show acceptable track records to entice buyers. This usually means the business must be at least a year old. The track record will be used to project the business's future prospects. If a business depends on the work of highly skilled employees, such as a well-known chef, this, too, can affect the price because it makes the business more difficult to expand and more expensive to operate.

- **Below-market financing.** When a B&B is sold, usually the buyer puts up a small down payment and the seller then carries back the remainder of the sales price at favorable terms. Seller financing is almost always below market, and the buyer avoids the fees associated with bank loans.

- **Personal goodwill.** If enough of a B&B's business depends on the personal relationships between staff and management who won't be staying on, then the sales price will probably be diminished.

- **Grandfather clauses.** New owners are expected to meet fire, health and safety codes that the previous owner may have been able to avoid because of being "grandfathered in" when the regulations were passed. Grandfather clauses usually expire when a business changes hands. If this is the case, the seller or buyer may need to bring the building up to code. If the buyer is responsible for this, he or she will usually ask that the expense be deducted from the sale price. If the cost is very high, this could affect the salability of the business altogether.

Strategies for Buying

Before contacting sellers, potential buyers should prepare a document that outlines for themselves their desired sales price, terms and conditions. A close examination on the buyer's part of how the seller is arriving at the sales price, terms and conditions  is also invaluable. This will give you, the buyer, considerable flexibility in negotiations and the ability to anticipate the seller and effectively counteroffer. Through careful preparation, you will be able to take your desired sales price, terms, conditions, initial investment and revenue goals from the page to a signed contract on a business that has a high probability of meeting those goals. You must determine the type of B&B that is right for you. Consider the bed-and-breakfast's investment yield, taxes and the effect the business will have on your personal life. Basically, buyers should be looking for a B&B that will meet their numbers, and ones that they are going to be happy working at 12–14 hours a day. PAII has a list of appraisers with experience in bed-and-breakfast sales. You can access this information on their website at **www.paii. com/?page=_VendorOpps**.

Buyers should prioritize their objectives and consider the trade-offs that must be made to attain them. Buyers generally want to accomplish the flowing objectives:

- **Best possible sales price.** Serious buyers and sellers compromise on the sales price, terms and conditions in order to reach a mutually satisfying end, and buyers are almost always willing to trade price for terms and conditions. Most buyers will draw the line at a sales price that exceeds the bed-and-breakfast's replacement cost.

- **Reasonable down payment.** Most serious buyers are willing to maintain a 1:1 debt-to-equity ratio. A typical down payment is, then, the amount of money that, when added to other initial investment charges, will total 50 percent of the total investment needed to acquire and run the business. Many buyers want to lower their down payments to reduce risk and unfortunately find themselves with businesses that cannot support their debt load.

- **Reasonable initial investment.** Serious buyers are willing to equally match dollars of debt with dollars of personal equity. Buyers do want most of their equity to go towards the down payment.

- **Maximum future profits.** Buyers are buying a B&B's current financial performance but are always looking for the highest *potential* revenue-generating business.

- **Reduced possibility of failure.** Only one out of five established businesses that are purchased go under. That is much better than the four-out-of-five failure rate of new businesses. The typical buyer of an existing business is an optimist with real-world experience.

- **Enhancement of borrowing power.** Most lenders prefer financing an existing, profitable operation to a new venture.

- **Minimizing tax liabilities.** Buyers need to be aware of the tax consequences of the B&B they're buying. Both buyer and seller should work at minimizing taxes. The only way to ensure that this happens is for both parties to hire accountants. Most buyers focus on deferring income-tax liabilities through asking sellers to accept a lower sales price in exchange for a higher interest rate on seller financing. The interest can then be deducted over the life of the loan.

Buyers should develop a purchase plan that lists potential sellers, analyzes their motivations for selling, analyzes bed-and-breakfasts and develops planned responses to counteroffers. Research into a seller's motivation is crucial here, and can serve the buyer in a number of ways. The following is a list of major seller motivations:

- **Owners who want to retire.** These folks usually want to move out of the area and receive a retirement income. They usually seek acceptable seller financing or an annuity arrangement.

- **Disillusioned owners.** The neophyte or absentee owner often decides to get out of the business when it starts doing poorly. Often the business is not as profitable or fun as they had thought, and they don't know what to do to remedy those problems.

- **Owners with tax problems.** Once depreciation expenses and interest expenses have evaporated, owners often sell in order to move into a larger operation and to reinstate these tax shelters.

- **Owners with other investment opportunities.** Often owners want to use the money received from the sale of their bed-and-breakfasts for investments elsewhere or, if the market is favorable, just to cash out at a very good price.

- **Owners with distressed properties.** Struggling properties often do not throw off enough profit to fund necessary remodeling or overhaul.

- **Distressed owners.** Often profitable operations are run by people having troubled relationships with their business or marital partners or their shareholders. In some cases, one of these parties has died. These can give serious cause for an owner to leave a profitable operation.

Once a buyer has responded to a sales solicitation, he or she will receive enough information to determine if the bed-and-breakfast meets or exceeds their investment requirements. The buyer should do more preliminary work to find out further specifics about whether a bed-and-breakfast is or is not a good opportunity. Experienced buyers know almost immediately from the sales brochure if the bed-and-breakfast will meet their needs. One of the ways they determine this is through the real-property lease payment. If it's less than or equals 6 percent of the bed-and-breakfast's total sales volume, most buyers know it's worth further investigation. Buyers also consider future sales volume and profit-generating capacity.

When a buyer decides to pursue more research, he or she should tour the facility; learn the lease highlights and other purchase options; and evaluate the neighborhood, the competition, the customer viewpoint, the history of ownership and the owner's reason for selling. After doing a deeper analysis, the buyer must once again determine if it meets their investment requirements. If he or she determines that it does, an earnest money deposit and offer should be delivered to the seller in return for detailed information on the bed-and-breakfast.

Terms, Conditions and Price

In most cases, sellers will determine likely sales price, terms and conditions, and then pad those somewhat to create room for negotiation and compromise. In general, unrealistic asking prices generate unrealistic offerings, or none at all. Sellers should prepare a pragmatic and well-documented solicitation and then search for buyers who will appreciate these considerations.

As much as possible, anticipating every potential problem that may arise during negotiations will put sellers in a good position to offer solutions to a buyer's objections. It is a good idea for a seller to hire an attorney, accountant or business broker when preparing a preferred sales price, terms and conditions. The savvy buyer and seller also incorporate their transaction costs — brokerage fees, lawyers, etc. — into the prices that are being asked or offered. In most cases there are higher transaction fees for the seller. It is a good practice for the seller to enumerate all the assets that are included in the sale. At the least this will garner respect from potential buyers, and it may give the seller a leg up during initial negotiations.

Terms. The terms of sale are the procedures used by the buyer to pay the seller. A buyer is usually willing to accept a proposed sales price if the seller will accept the buyer's terms. In most cases, sellers receive a minimal down payment and the remainder of the purchase price over a three- to five-year period. All-cash offers are rare, and seller financing is usually necessary to attract buyers. In most cases, it's in the seller's interest to receive a large down payment because this demonstrates the buyer's commitment to the long haul. Sellers are also more likely to grant favorable terms to a buyer making a substantial down payment because the financial risk is lessened.

Sometimes buyers will want to pay with property or corporate stock instead of cash. These can be great from a tax perspective, but stock can be problematic because it can decrease in value, and usually the stock used for this type of deal cannot be sold for a year or more, and often only in small amounts.

Seller financing is probably the most desirable aspect of the investment in a bed-and-breakfast, and most buyers want to assume favorable loans. Sellers offering favorable terms must be sure they receive adequate compensation in the form of a higher sales price. Seller financing is negotiable, but usually the marketplace suggests typical loan amounts and terms. The loan payments should not be tied into sales volume or any other performance measures because the seller doesn't want to suffer if a new owner drives the business under. The only instance where loan payments should be tied into performance measures is in an "earn-out agreement," where the premium part of the sales price is contingent on its future performance.

Conditions. There are several conditions the seller and buyer will attach to most sales contracts. Sometimes they are separate agreements, but most of the time they are part of the sales contract. The following lists conditions that are the largest concern to the seller:

- **Conclusion of sale.** Sellers want to finish the transaction as fast as possible because delays give buyers time to second-guess. Sellers want the new owners into the operation as quickly as possible.

- **Buyer access.** Sellers generally want minimal contact with the buyer while waiting for the transaction to close, and they don't want the buyer spending time with the bed-and-breakfast staff. It's good for a seller to provide the needed assistance for the ownership transition, but it should only be after the buyer has taken possession of the business.

- **Guarantees.** Sellers usually have to guarantee the condition of assets. Sometimes sellers have to guarantee that buyers can assume some of the bed-and-breakfast's current contracts. Sellers should never guarantee things they don't have total control over. Imprecise language should also be avoided here. If the seller is making guarantees, then buying the relevant insurance to back up these claims is prudent.

- **Indemnification.** Sellers will want to be compensated if a buyer backs out of the deal. Sellers should also be protected for expenses paid to fix code violations, or for legal expenses if the seller needs to sue the buyer to uphold an agreement.

- **Escrow agent.** Independent escrow agents are usually hired to supervise transactions. These agents see that all terms and conditions are met, and that after that point, ownership can be transferred. The seller should insist that the buyer agree to an independent third-party escrow agent. This ensures the many details of this transaction are handled well and legally.

- **Legal requirements.** Seller and buyer must agree to comply with all pertinent laws and statutes. Escrow agents ensure that all current creditors are notified of the bed-and-breakfast's sale, and that all legal requirements are met. This ensures that the buyer can begin with a clean slate, without any of the seller's responsibilities to creditors.

- **Buyer's credit history.** Before agreeing to seller financing, the seller must investigate the buyer's credit history. It is standard for buyers to give personal financial statements, résumés, references and permission to run a credit report. Serious buyers have no problem with this because it secures the seller's respect and encourages the revealing of confidential information.

- **Security for seller financing.** Many deals go bad because buyer and seller can't agree on financing. If a seller agrees to hold paper, the buyer must sign a promissory note and security  agreement. The note represents the buyer's promise to pay, and the security agreement is the collateral pledged to secure the loan. If the seller is the only lender, a clause should be added that requires his or her approval before the new owner can obtain additional financing. The promissory note should contain a default provision that the lender can foreclose if loan payments are not met, in addition to other specific provisions pertinent to the business. These might be that the seller can foreclose if the new owner doesn't maintain a required balance sheet, or if he or she does not produce previously agreed upon menu items.

- **Assumable loans and leases.** Buyers will want to assume any contract that calls for below-market payments. Sellers should do everything possible to ensure a favorable transition, because many deals rest on buyers being able to assume outstanding contracts.

- **Life and disability insurance.** If the seller carries the paper, the buyer should be required to purchase the appropriate insurance naming the seller as beneficiary. If the buyer refuses to purchase this, the seller should. If the new owner dies or becomes ill, without insurance, the previous owner would potentially lose his investment.

- **Collection of receivables.** It is reasonable for the owner to receive a modest fee for the collection of receivables. This can be true for business booked prior to the change of ownership.

- **Inventory sale.** This is usually handled at the close of escrow. Physical inventory of all food, beverages and supplies should be taken by an independent service and a separate bill of sale prepared for the agreed-upon price of this merchandise.

- **Non-compete clause.** This is quite common in the sale of an ongoing business, because the new owner doesn't want the seller to open up a competing business nearby. Sellers try to avoid these, but understand that they're inevitable.

- **Repurchase agreement.** Sellers often include agreements that grant them the option to buy back the bed-and-breakfast within a certain time period. This usually notes the purchase price and terms of the sale. If the bed-and-breakfast becomes incredibly valuable all of a sudden, the former owner can buy it back or sell the repurchase agreement to someone else.

- **Employment contract.** If a seller agrees to remain as an employee of the new bed-and-breakfast, a very specific contract should be drafted. Most sellers have no interest in these contracts and just want out. However, his or her offering to stay on may increase the potential for selling the bed-and-breakfast, and he or she could enjoy a good salary during this time.

- **Consulting contract.** This may be a more acceptable employment contract that gives the new owner a tax-deductible expense but doesn't burden the former owner either.

- **Conditions not met.** Often buyers cannot meet every sales condition. Sellers can use this as a way to back out of the deal. However, the seller should also reserve the right to proceed with the sale even if certain conditions are not met.

Determining Price from a Buyer's Perspective

Potential buyers must do a thorough financial analysis of the bed-and-breakfast. They should carefully study its current profitability and use this information to determine its potential capacity for generating revenue. Because there is a very close relationship between a bed-and-breakfast's current profitability and its likely sales price, the buyer should examine this income very carefully. Understandably, sellers are not particularly eager to divulge their financial records to buyers. However, if a seller is forthcoming with this information, it can signal to the buyer that he or she has nothing to hide.

It's a good idea for the buyer to hire a good accountant to assist in this financial analysis. This will help determine whether the deal meets the buyer's investment requirements. Buyers should also consider hiring other specialists to work with contracts, unemployment compensation, insurance and banking. If the buyer qualifies, Small Business Development Centers (SBDC) throughout the country offer free consulting services to businesses with fewer than 500 employees.

The buyer should also complete at least a rough market and competition survey before performing the financial evaluation. This will ensure a familiarity with the bed-and-breakfast's location and will help him or her estimate future revenues and expenses. If the buyer is unfamiliar with the area, an independent consulting service can be hired to provide a useful survey.

A seller expects a written offer with price, terms, conditions and an earnest money deposit before he or she will allow a potential buyer to review confidential financial information. It must be agreed that the buyer can withdraw if he or she is unhappy with the financial records. This is because the earnest deposit is at risk unless the right to retract the offer is in place. When reviewing the seller's financial records, buyers should expect that an independent CPA has never audited them. This is because auditing is a costly process, and most small businesses don't do it unless they absolutely have to. A lucky buyer is one who is given audited financial statements.

Buyers need to reconstruct historical financial statements to show what they could have been had the buyer been operating the business. This is usually done from only the previous year's statement. Patience is important here. This is a time-consuming process, and if errors are made, the estimate of the bed-and-breakfast's sales price may be inaccurate. Sellers will tend to overestimate customer counts and check averages and underestimate utilities and other expenses. The inexperienced buyer should be wary when evaluating these numbers and may want to hire professional counsel.

Also, it is important to be aware that sellers will usually include only the financial details they initially want to reveal. These numbers are usually pretty optimistic, but can give the buyer a good idea of whether the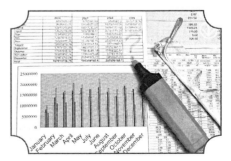

bed-and-breakfast matches his or her investment needs. The typical listing agreement contains the asking price, financing possibilities, current sales volume, current expenses, and age and size of the bed-and-breakfast. Buyers should evaluate this information carefully, with special attention to the apparent net cash flow, before spending a lot of time and money on detailed analysis.

Most lenders require a cash budget to be prepared by buyers. This will point out the operation's daily cash requirements and the times of year when short-term money must be borrowed to cover brief shortages.

Potential buyers also should analyze balance sheets and income statements carefully. Balance sheets can reveal the anxiety level of a seller, and can indicate the current management's ability. If this ability is in question, this could predict greater earnings under sound management. Income statements are used by the buyer to determine whether the bed-and-breakfast could have satisfied salary demands and provided a return on the initial investment had it been under the buyer's management for the previous 12 months. Most sellers require a pro forma income statement for the coming year as part of the loan application process. Because a buyer is basing the price on *current* income, but purchasing the operation's *future* revenue-making ability, this is one of the most critical tasks the buyer will perform.

Initial Investment

Equally as important as price, terms and conditions is the total amount of money required to begin operating. Bed-and-breakfasts require large amounts of cash when starting, and buyers must estimate as accurately as possible the total initial investment needed to get their businesses up and running the way they envision them. There are, however, a number of start-up costs even with transfer of ownership. Here are a number of items to be aware of:

- **Investigation costs.** Buyers must be willing to spend time and money to thoroughly examine the opportunities that are available. Typical buyers want to begin running their new establishment as soon as possible and don't want to be bothered with extensive analyses. By contrast, bed-and-breakfast developers or chain bed-and-breakfast companies spend great time and effort before investing in a property. Many investors falsely believe that once initial development work is complete, the start-up costs are eliminated. While they usually are reduced considerably, these costs still exist, and wise investors calculate them in their analyses.

- **Down payment.** Standard down payment is usually around a quarter of the sales price. Buyers who offer this down payment usually can expect the seller to provide below-market financing for the remainder of the sales price. The down payment can affect the sales price, and, in many cases, sellers will accept a lower sales price with a larger down payment and vice versa.

- **Transaction costs.** Escrow agents will prorate insurance, payroll, vacation pay, license renewal fees, advertising costs, etc., on the close-of-escrow date. The buyer will usually have a debit balance that the escrow agent will transfer to the seller. The fees paid to the escrow company and for the drawing of documents needed to close the transaction constitute the closing costs.

- **Working capital.** Buyers must budget necessary amounts of money to ensure sufficient supplies are on hand to run the bed-and-breakfast.

- **Deposits.** Most creditors require cash deposits as assurance they will be paid for their products and services. Utility, telephone, sales tax, payroll tax and lease deposits all must be factored in.

- **Licenses and permits.** Most B&Bs will have some permits to acquire.

- **Legal fees.** Competent legal advice is a very good idea for buyers. Escrow agents should not be counted on to draw papers correctly and to make sure that the interests of various parties have been represented. Buyers should have their own counsel looking out for their interests solely, and fees for these services should be budgeted in.

- **Renovations, furniture and equipment.** There may be building code violations to rectify or large renovations necessary to bring the B&B into a competitive position. It may also be necessary to purchase new china, beds and tables to replace worn, older ones.

- **Advertising.** Promoting an opening or reopening, rebuilding signage and offering promotional discounts or other incentives can be good ways to build patronage for a new establishment.

- **Fictitious name registration.** If the name of a bed-and-breakfast is fictitious, the name usually must be registered at the local courthouse or County Recorder's Office.

- **Loan fees.** Buyers who are not acquiring seller financing will accrue loan fees from the lending parties.

- **Equity fees.** Buyers who want to sell common stock to a few investors will incur attorney, document preparation and registration fees.

- **Insurance.** A lender will require a borrower to have appropriate life and disability insurance, and that the lender be named sole beneficiary.

- **Pre-opening labor.** This is one of the expenses that are greatly minimized by purchasing an existing operation instead of starting one from scratch. Buyers usually plan to make some personnel changes, and a portion of current staff members should be expected to leave during the change of management.

- **Accounting fees.** Fees for assistance in the evaluation of a bed-and-breakfast purchase need to be budgeted.

- **Other consulting fees.** A bed-and-breakfast owner's primary consultants are an attorney and an accountant, but several other consultants should be retained if the buyer needs specific advice. Menu consultants, labor-relations specialists and computer consultants can all be retained to support management.

- **Other prepaid expenses.** When new ownership takes over an existing business, it is not uncommon for creditors to demand a form of prepayment.

- **Sales taxes.** Property may be subject to a transfer tax, and non-food supplies are often subject to sales tax.

- **Locksmith.** Most buyers will change all the locks after the sale is concluded.

- **Security.** A typical buyer will transfer the current security service into the business. If one doesn't exist, the buyer should invest in one to protect the new business.

- **Contingency.** It may be a good idea to have a contingency fund large enough for the first six months' operating expenses.

Financing

The typical offer and acceptance agreement includes several conditions necessary for the deal's completion. Most of these are met easily, but there are two that are difficult to meet: The buyer's qualification for financing and the attainment of all necessary permits and licenses. There is little you as a buyer can do if you don't qualify for permits, unless you need to fix only simple code violations to qualify. In the financing realm, however, the seller and buyer have more control and can adjust the final sales contract to suit the buyer's needs. Buyers should be aware that there is no bigger threat to their success than inadequate or inappropriate financing. Excessive debt burden is one of the most consistent reasons bed-and-breakfasts go under.

Equity Funds

Equity is capital that is at risk. Owners invest this money without any guarantee on a return. There are several types of equity financing techniques. The following are the most common:

- **Personal equity.** These are ventures that are funded entirely with personal equity or with a combination of personal equity and lease and debt financing.

- **Partnerships.** Some B&Bs solicit funds by getting partners to invest. Typical partnership arrangements are general or limited. General partnerships usually mean both parties will be involved in the operation. In limited partnerships there is usually a general partner and one or more inactive, limited partners, with the general partner acting as manager and the limited partners as passive investors.

- **Corporation.** Corporate ownership can be a great way to raise capital. Generally it is done through a stock offering — in the case of a large corporation, to the public, and in a small company, to private investors.

- **Venture capital.** Venture capitalists normally do not fund a venture unless it has expansion potential and is well-run. Venture capitalists are interested in long-term financial gain and are less interested in the net operating profits of a new establishment. Buyers intending to purchase chain bed-and-breakfasts might be able to obtain venture capital because of the high earning potential.

SBA Financial Programs

The Small Business Administration (SBA) offers a variety of financing options for small businesses. Whether you are looking for a long-term loan for machinery and equipment, a general working capital loan, a revolving line of credit or a micro-loan, the SBA has a financing program to fit your needs. These programs are discussed in detail on the SBA's website at **www.sba.gov**.

SBA Assistance

The SBA is the largest source of long-term small-business financing in the nation. In order to determine whether you qualify or whether an SBA business loan best suits your financing needs, contact your banker, one of the active SBA-guaranteed lenders or an SBA loan officer.

The 7(a) Loan Guaranty Program

The 7(a) Loan Guaranty Program is the SBA's primary loan program. The SBA reduces risk to lenders by guaranteeing major portions of loans made to small businesses. This enables the lenders to provide financing to small businesses when funding is otherwise unavailable at reasonable terms. The eligibility requirements and credit criteria of the program are very broad in order to accommodate a wide range of financing needs.

When a small business applies to a lending institution for a loan, the lender reviews the application and decides if it merits a loan on its own or if it requires additional support in the form of an SBA guaranty. The lender then requests SBA backing on the loan. In guaranteeing the loan, the SBA assures the lender that, in the event the borrower does not repay the loan, the government will reimburse the lending institution for a portion of its loss. By providing this guaranty, the SBA is able to help tens of thousands of small businesses every year get financing they could not otherwise obtain.

To qualify for an SBA guaranty, a small business must meet the 7(a) criteria, and the lender must certify that it could not provide funding on reasonable terms except with an SBA guaranty. The SBA can then guarantee as much as 85 percent on loans of up to $150,000 and 75 percent on loans of more than $150,000. In most cases, the maximum guaranty is $1 million. Exceptions are the International Trade, DELTA and 504 loan programs, which have higher loan limits. The maximum total loan size under the 7(a) program is $2 million.

Friends and Relatives

Many entrepreneurs look to private sources such as friends and family when starting out in a business venture. Often, money is loaned interest-free or at a low interest rate, which can be quite beneficial when getting started. Though they are personal acquaintances, it's still important to have on hand statistics and well-thought out, formal plans that demonstrate your future business is a viable venture worth supporting.

Banks and Credit Unions

The most common sources of funding, banks and credit unions will provide a loan if you can show that your business proposal is sound.

Borrowing Money

It is often said that small-business owners have a difficult time borrowing money. This is not necessarily true. Banks make money by lending money. However, the inexperience of many small business owners in financial matters often prompts banks to deny loan requests.

Requesting a loan when you are not properly prepared sends a signal to your lender. That message is: High Risk!

To be successful in obtaining a loan, you must be prepared and organized. You must know exactly how much money you need, why you need it and how you will pay it back. You must be able to convince your lender that you are a good credit risk.

How to Write a Loan Proposal

Approval of your loan request depends on how well you present yourself, your business and your financial needs to a lender. Remember, lenders want to make loans, but they must make loans they know will be repaid. The best way to improve your chances of obtaining a loan is to prepare a written proposal. A well-written loan proposal contains:

General Information

✔ Business name, names of principals, Social Security number for each principal and business address.

✔ Purpose of the loan: exactly what the loan will be used for and why it is needed.

✔ Amount required: the exact amount you need to achieve your purpose.

Business Description

✔ History and nature of the business: what kind of business it is, its age, number of employees and current business assets.

✔ Ownership structure: details of your company's legal structure.

Management Profile

✔ Provide a short statement about each principal in your business: include background, education, experience, skills and accomplishments.

Market Information

- ✔ Clearly define your company's products as well as your markets.
- ✔ Identify your competition and explain how your business competes in the marketplace.
- ✔ Profile your customers and explain how your business can satisfy their needs.

Financial Information

- ✔ Financial statements: balance sheets and income statements for the past three years. If you are starting out, provide a projected balance sheet and income statement.
- ✔ Personal financial statements on yourself and other principal owners of the business.
- ✔ Collateral you are willing to pledge as security for the loan.

How Your Loan Request Will Be Reviewed

When reviewing a loan request, the lender is primarily concerned about repayment. To help determine your ability to repay, many loan officers will order a copy of your business credit report from a credit-reporting agency. Therefore, you should work with these agencies to help them present an accurate picture of your business. Using the credit report and the information you have provided, the lending officer will consider the following issues:

- ✔ Have you invested savings or personal equity in your business totaling at least 25 to 50 percent of the loan you are requesting? Remember, a lender or investor will not finance 100 percent of your business.

- ✔ Do you have a sound record of creditworthiness as indicated by your credit report, work history and letters of recommendation? This is very important.
- ✔ Do you have sufficient experience and training to operate a successful business?
- ✔ Have you prepared a loan proposal and business plan that demonstrate your understanding of and commitment to the success of the business?
- ✔ Does the business have sufficient cash flow to make the monthly payments?

Closing the Sale

Once buyer and seller have agreed on the particulars, they will commit themselves to a binding sales contract and transfer ownership. There are often lawyers, brokers, accountants, lenders, escrow agents, government officials, trade unions, family members and other people involved in this transaction. It usually takes 30–60 days to finish the ownership transfer.

The close of escrow happens when all the documents necessary to complete the sale are recorded at the County Recorder's Office. This usually happens the morning after the closing date.

The documents usually recorded include:

- Deed
- Promissory note
- Mortgage or deed of trust
- Other security agreements
- Sales contract
- Options
- Bill of sale
- Assignments
- Request for notice
- Notice of completion of work

If the new owner doesn't make payments on an assumable loan, the seller will want to be notified. If they have made the request for notification in advance — and made it part of public record — it will happen. The notice of completion of work is also included in these filings because many people will record guarantees and warranties to make sure there are no questions regarding their dates of expiration.

· · · · ·

CHAPTER FOUR

The Business Plan

Perhaps the most important task to accomplish right now is writing the formal business plan, which will be your road map for success. Every business needs to have a business, or strategic plan, in place. Having this plan will help you keep your goals in focus at all times. A business plan is basically a written statement that guides you in your business in the future. In addition, if you are searching for financing for your operation, most banks and lenders will require a business plan before offering you a loan. When you look for a bed-and-breakfast location, you can pretty much assume you'll need to get financing, especially if it involves buying a new piece of property.

Business Plan Outline

Elements of a Business Plan

I. Cover sheet

II. Statement of purpose

III. Table of contents

A. The Business

1. Description of business
2. Marketing
3. Competition
4. Operating procedures
5. Personnel
6. Business insurance
7. Financial data

B. Financial Data

1. Loan applications
2. Capital equipment and supply list
3. Balance sheet
4. Break-even analysis
5. Pro forma income projections (profit and loss statements)
   a. Three-year summary
   b. Detail by month, first year
   c. Detail by quarters, second and third years
   d. Assumptions upon which projections were based
6. Pro-forma cash flow
   a. Follow guidelines for No. 5

C. Supporting Documents

1. Tax returns of principals for last three years
2. Personal financial statement (all banks have these forms)
3. Copy of proposed lease or purchase agreement for building space
4. Copy of licenses and other legal documents
5. Copy of resumes of all principals
6. Copies of letters of intent from suppliers, etc.

The Business Plan—What it Includes

What goes in a business plan? This is an excellent question. It is one that many new and potential small business owners should ask, but oftentimes don't ask. The body of the business plan can be divided into four distinct sections: 1) the description of the business, 2) the marketing plan, 3) the management plan and 4) the financial management plan. Addenda to the business plan should include the executive summary, supporting documents and financial projections.

Description of the Business

In this section, provide a detailed description of your business. An excellent question to ask yourself is: "What business am I in?" In answering this question, include your products, market and services, as well as a thorough description of what makes your bed-and-breakfast unique. Remember, however, that as you develop your business plan, you may have to modify or revise your initial questions.

The business description section is divided into three primary sections: Section 1 actually describes your business; Section 2, the product or service you will be offering; and Section 3, the location of your business and why this location is desirable. When describing your business, generally you should explain:

1. **Legalities.** Business form: proprietorship, partnership or corporation. What licenses or permits you will need.
2. **Business type.**
3. **What your product or service is.** Perhaps the sample menu could be included.
4. **Business character**. Is it a new independent business, a takeover, an expansion?
5. **Why your business will be profitable.** What are the growth opportunities? Will franchising impact growth opportunities?
6. **When your business will be open.** What days? Hours?
7. **What you have learned about your kind of business** from outside sources (trade suppliers, bankers, publications).

A cover sheet will precede the description. It includes the name, address and telephone number of the business and the names of all principals. In the description of your business, describe the unique aspects and how or why they will appeal to consumers. Emphasize any special features that you feel will appeal to customers and explain how and why these features are appealing.

The description of your business should clearly identify goals and objectives and it should clarify why you are, or why you want to be, in business.

Product/Service

Try to best describe the benefits of your goods and services from your customers' perspective. Successful business owners know, or at least have an idea of, what their customers want or expect from them. This type of anticipation can be helpful in building customer satisfaction and loyalty. And, it certainly is a good strategy for beating the competition or retaining your competitiveness. Describe:

- What you are selling — include your menu here.
- How your product or service will benefit the customer.
- Which products/services are in demand (if there will be a steady flow of cash).
- What is unique about the product or service your business is offering.

The Location

The location of your business can play a decisive role in its success or failure. Remember the old maxim "Location, Location, Location." Your location should be built around your customers, it should be accessible and it should provide a sense of security. Consider these questions when addressing this section of your business plan:

- What are your location needs?
- What kind of space will you need?
- Why is the area desirable? Why is the building desirable?
- Is it easily accessible? Is public transportation available? Is street lighting adequate?
- Are market shifts or demographic shifts occurring?

It may be a good idea to make a checklist of questions you identify when developing your business plan. Categorize your questions and, as you answer each question, remove it from your list.

The Marketing Plan

Marketing plays a vital role in successful business ventures. How well you market you business, along with a few other considerations, will ultimately determine your degree of success or failure. The key element of a successful marketing plan is to know your customers—their likes, dislikes and expectations. By identifying these factors, you can develop a marketing strategy that will allow you to arouse and fulfill their needs.

Identify your customers by their age, sex, income/educational level and residence. At first, target only those customers who are more likely to purchase your product or service. As your customer base expands, you may need to consider modifying the marketing plan to include other customers.

Develop a marketing plan for your business by answering these questions. Your marketing plan should be included in your business plan and contain answers to the questions outlined below.

- Who are your customers? Define your target market(s).
- Are your markets growing? Steady? Declining?
- Is your market share growing? Steady? Declining?
- Are your markets large enough to expand?
- How will you attract, hold or increase your market share? How will you promote your sales?
- What pricing strategy have you devised?

Competition

Competition is a way of life. We compete for jobs, promotions, scholarships to institutes of higher learning, in sports — and in almost every aspect of our lives. Nations compete for the consumer in the global marketplace, as do individual business owners. Advances in technology can send the profit margins of a successful business into a tailspin, causing them to plummet overnight or within a few hours. When considering these and other factors, we can conclude that business is a highly competitive, volatile arena. Because of this volatility and competitiveness, it is important to know your competitors.

Questions like these can help you:

- Who are your five nearest direct competitors?
- Who are your indirect competitors?
- How are their businesses: steady? increasing? decreasing?
- What have you learned from their operations? From their advertising?
- What are their strengths and weaknesses?
- How does their service differ from yours?

Start a file on each of your competitors. Keep manila envelopes of their advertising and promotional materials and their pricing strategy techniques. Review these files periodically, determining when and how often they advertise, sponsor promotions and offer sales. Study the copy used in their advertising and promotional materials, and their sales strategy. For example, is their copy short? Descriptive? Catchy? How much do they reduce prices for sales? Using this technique can help you to better understand your competitors and how they operate their businesses.

Pricing and Sales

Your pricing strategy is another marketing technique you can use to improve your overall competitiveness. Get a feel for the pricing strategy your competitors are using. That way you can determine if your prices are in line with competitors in your market area and if they are in line with industry averages.

Some of the pricing considerations are:

- Menu cost and pricing
- Competitive position
- Pricing below competition
- Pricing above competition
- Price lining
- Multiple pricing
- Service components
- Material costs
- Labor costs
- Overhead costs

The key to success is to have a well-planned strategy, to establish your policies and constantly monitor prices and operating costs to ensure profits. It is a good policy to keep abreast of the changes in the marketplace because these changes can affect your competitiveness and profit margins.

Advertising and Public Relations

How you advertise and promote your bed-and-breakfast may make or break your business. Having a good product or service and not advertising and promoting it is like not having a business at all. Many business owners operate under the mistaken concept that the business will promote itself and channel money that should be used for advertising and promotions to other areas of the business. Advertising and promotions, however, is the lifeline of a business and should be treated as such. We have devoted a whole chapter to marketing and promoting your bed-and-breakfast.

Devise a plan that uses advertising and networking as a means to promote your business. Develop short, descriptive copy (text material) that clearly identifies your goods or services, its location and price. Use catchy phrases to arouse the interest of your readers, listeners or viewers. Remember, the more care and attention you devote to your marketing program, the more successful your business will be.

The Management Plan

Managing a business requires more than just the desire to be your own boss. It demands dedication, persistence, the ability to make decisions and the ability to manage both employees and finances. Your management plan, along with your marketing and financial management plans, sets the foundation for and facilitates the success of your business.

Like plants and equipment, people are resources — they are the most valuable assets a business has. You will soon discover that employees and staff will play an important role in the total operation of your business. Consequently, it's imperative that you know what skills you do and do not possess since you will have to hire personnel to supply the skills that you lack. Additionally, it is imperative that you know how to manage and treat your employees. Make them a part of the team. Keep them informed of changes, and get their feedback regarding said changes. Employees oftentimes have excellent ideas that can lead to new market areas, innovations to existing products or services, or new product lines or services that can improve your overall competitiveness.

Your management plan should answer questions such as:

- How does your background/business experience help you in this business?
- What are your weaknesses and how can you compensate for them?
- Who will be on the management team?
- What are their strengths/weaknesses?
- What are their duties?
- Are these duties clearly defined?
- Will this assistance be ongoing?
- What are your current personnel needs?
- What are your plans for hiring and training personnel?
- What salaries, vacations and holidays will you offer?
- What benefits, if any, can you afford at this point?

The Financial Management Plan

Sound financial management is one of the best ways for your business to remain profitable and solvent. How well you manage the finances of your business is the cornerstone of every successful business venture. Each year thousands of potentially successful businesses fail because of poor financial management. As a business owner, you will need to identify and implement policies that will lead to and ensure that you will meet your financial obligations.

To effectively manage your finances, plan a sound, realistic budget by determining the actual amount of money needed to open your business (start-up costs) and the amount needed to keep it open (operating costs). The first step to building a sound financial plan is to devise a start-up budget. Your start-up budget will usually include such one-time-only costs as major equipment, utility deposits, down payments, etc.

The start-up budget should allow for these expenses.

- Personnel (costs prior to opening)
- Legal/Professional fees
- Occupancy
- Licenses/Permits
- Equipment
- Insurance
- Supplies
- Advertising/Promotions
- Salaries/Wages
- Accounting
- Income
- Utilities
- Payroll expenses

An operating budget is prepared when you are actually ready to open for business. The operating budget will reflect your priorities in terms of how you spend your money, the expenses you will incur and how you will meet those expenses (income). Your operating budget also should include money to cover the first three to six months of operation.

The operating budget should allow for the following expenses:

- Personnel
- Insurance
- Rent
- Depreciation
- Loan payments
- Advertising/Promotions
- Legal/Accounting
- Miscellaneous expenses
- Supplies
- Payroll expenses
- Salaries/Wages
- Utilities
- Dues/Subscriptions/Fees
- Taxes
- Repairs/Maintenance

The financial section of your business plan should include any loan applications you've filed, a capital equipment and supply list, balance sheet, break-even analysis, pro forma income projections (profit and loss statement) and pro forma cash flow. The income statement and cash flow projections should include a three-year summary, detail by month for the first year, and detail by quarter for the second and third years.

The accounting and inventory-control systems that you will be using are generally addressed in this section of the business plan also. Whether you develop the accounting and inventory systems yourself or have an outside financial adviser develop the systems, you will need to acquire a thorough understanding of each segment and how it operates. Your financial adviser can assist you in developing this section of your business plan.

Other questions that you will need to consider are:

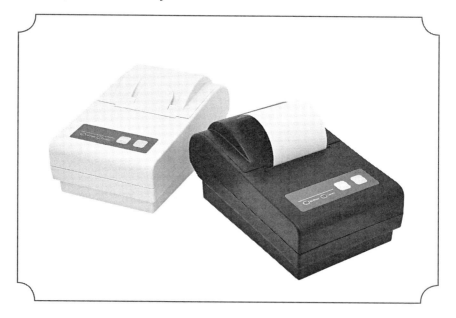

- What type of accounting system will you use? Will you use a specific program like QuickBooks or do you need an accountant to do that for you?
- What will your sales and profit goals be for the coming year?

- What financial projections will you need to include in your business plan?
- What kind of inventory-control system will you use?

Your plan should include an explanation of all projections. Unless you are thoroughly familiar with financial statements, get help in preparing your cash flow and income statements and your balance sheet. Your aim is not necessarily to become a financial wizard, but to understand the basic financial tools well enough to gain their benefits. Your accountant or financial adviser can help you accomplish this goal.

Legal Forms of Business

When organizing a new business, one of the most important decisions to be made is choosing the structure of the business. Factors influencing your decision about your business organization include:

- ✔ Legal restrictions
- ✔ Liabilities assumed
- ✔ Type of business operation
- ✔ Earnings distribution
- ✔ Capital needs
- ✔ Number of employees
- ✔ Tax advantages or disadvantages
- ✔ Length of business operation

The advantages and disadvantages of sole proprietorship, partnership, corporation and the new hybrid limited liability company are as follows:

Sole Proprietorship. This is the easiest and least costly way of starting a business. There are likely to be fees to obtain business name registration, a fictitious name certificate and other necessary licenses. Attorney fees for starting the business will be less than those of the other business forms because less preparation of documents is required and the owner has absolute authority over all business decisions.

Partnership. There are several types of partnerships. The two most common types are general and limited partnerships. A general partnership can be formed simply by an oral agreement between two or more persons, but a legal partnership agreement drawn up by an attorney is highly recommended. Legal fees for drawing up a partnership agreement are higher than those for a sole proprietorship, but may be lower than incorporating. A partnership agreement could be helpful in solving any disputes. However, partners are responsible for the other partner's business actions, as well as their own.

A partnership agreement should include the following:

- ✔ Type of business
- ✔ Amount of equity invested by each partner
- ✔ Division of profit or loss
- ✔ Partners' compensation
- ✔ Distribution of assets upon dissolution
- ✔ Duration of partnership
- ✔ Provisions for changes or dissolving the partnership
- ✔ Dispute settlement clause
- ✔ Restrictions of authority and expenditures
- ✔ Settlement in case of death or incapacitation

Corporation. A business may incorporate without an attorney, but legal advice is highly recommended. The corporate structure is usually the most complex and is more costly to organize than the other two business forms. Control depends on stock ownership. Persons with the largest stock ownership control the corporation, not the total number of shareholders. With control of stock shares or 51 percent of stock, a person or group is able to make policy decisions. Control is exercised through regular board of directors' meetings

and annual stockholders' meetings. Records must be kept to document decisions made by the board of directors. Small, closely held corporations can operate more informally, but record keeping cannot be eliminated entirely. Officers of a corporation can be liable to stockholders for improper actions. Liability is generally limited to stock ownership, except where fraud is involved. You may want to incorporate as a "C" or "S" corporation.

Limited Liability Company (LLC). An LLC is not a corporation, but it offers many of the same advantages. Many small business owners and entrepreneurs prefer LLCs because they combine the limited liability protection of a corporation with the "pass through" taxation of a sole proprietorship or partnership.

- LLCs have additional advantages over corporations.
- LLCs allow greater flexibility in management and business organization.
- LLCs do not have the ownership restrictions of "S" corporations, making them ideal business structures for foreign investors.
- LLCs accomplish these aims without the IRS's restrictions for an "S" corporation.

LLCs are now available in all 50 states and Washington, D.C. If you have other questions regarding LLCs, be sure to speak with a qualified legal and/or financial adviser.

CHAPTER FIVE

. . . . .

Governmental Laws, Regulations And Licenses

When a person starts a business, he or she needs to learn about the federal, state and local regulations affecting that business. There may be zoning laws to consider, licenses to purchase and inspections to pass. The federal government has many resources a new business owner may find helpful. The U.S. Business Advisor's website, at **http://business.usa.gov**, for example, offers resources such as:

- A business resource library.
- The Small Business Administration's start-up adviser.
- Online counseling.
- Information on financial resources.
- Links to laws that affect various industries.
- Legal and regulatory information for small businesses.

Other federal websites that have information you might find useful are:

- The Small Business Administration's website has information about laws and regulations that affect small businesses at **www.sba.gov/category/navigation-structure/ starting-managing-business/starting-business/business -law-regulations**.

- The IRS also offers information for small business owners on their website at **www.irs.gov/businesses**.

- The U.S. Department of Labor has a web page that focuses on helping small business owners comply with that department's rules at **www.dol.gov/dol/audience/aud-employers.htm**. Their elaws web page also provides employment laws assistance to small business owners (**http://webapps.dol.gov/elaws**).

Many states' Department of Development offer one-stop shopping for new entrepreneurs, such as Ohio's 1st Stop Business Connection (**http://development.ohio.gov/bs/bs_entrepreneurship.htm**). This site takes you through the steps to create a business information kit that contains all the forms and copies of the state regulations you'll need for your business enterprise for free. You can find out whether your state has a state agency such as the Ohio's 1st Stop by contacting your local economic development center, chamber of commerce or small business development center.

For any local regulations that may affect your business, you should check with your chamber of commerce and your local Equal Employment Opportunity Commission (EEOC) office for information. You can contact the U.S. EEOC for help in finding your local office. They can be reached at 800-669-4000, or log onto **www.eeoc.gov/field/index.cfm** to find the office closest to you.

State Registration

Contact the Secretary of State's office as early as possible and discuss your plans of opening a new business. All states have different regulations. This office will be able to describe all of the state's legal requirements and direct you to local and county offices for further registration. There is generally a fee required for registering a new business, most often it is less than $100. The city, county and/or state agency will most likely run a check to make certain no other businesses are currently using your particular business name. You may also be required to file and publish a fictitious name statement in a newspaper of general circulation in the area. You must renew this fictitious name periodically in order to legally protect it.

Should your state have an income tax on wages, request all pertinent information from your state's Department of Labor or Taxation. This would include all required forms, tax tables and tax guides. Also contact your state's Department of Employee Compensation for their regulations and filing procedures.

City Business License

Contact the city business department. Almost all cities and most counties require a permit to operate a business. Your application will be checked by the zoning board to make certain that the business conforms to all local regulations (purchasing an existing bed-and-breakfast will eliminate most of these clearances).

Motel/Hotel License

In some states, Ohio for example, your B&B may have to purchase a hotel/motel license. In Ohio, any B&B that has five or more bedrooms must purchase a motel license.

Sales Tax

In many states, you may also be required to obtain a vendor's license if you collect sales taxes on your food and/or lodging accommodations. These taxes may be state, county and local. Check your state's Department of Taxation website for information concerning these taxes in your state.

In Ohio, for example, bed-and-breakfast owners are required to purchase a vendor's license from the local county auditor's office. For B&Bs with four or fewer guest rooms, sales tax has to be collected only on the food. If a B&B has five or more rooms, sales tax is collected on the total.

Contact your state's Revenue or Taxation Agency concerning registry and collection procedures. Each state has its own various methods of taxation on the sale of lodging and food products. Most states that require collection on food and beverage sales also require an advance deposit or bond to be posted against future taxes to be collected. The state's Revenue Agency will often waive the deposit and accept instead a surety bond from your insurance company. The cost of this insurance is usually around 5 percent of the bond.

Sales tax is only collected on the retail price purchased by the end user. Thus, when purchasing raw food products to produce menu items, it will not be necessary to pay sales tax on the wholesale amount. However, you must present the wholesaler with your sales tax permit or number when placing orders, and sign a tax release card for their files. A thorough investigation into this area will be required for your particular state's requirements.

Health Department License

In order to serve food in your bed-and-breakfast, you may need to get a food service license. You will need to contact the local or state Department of Health for information on how to obtain a food service license.

According to the Ohio Revised Code, Ohio bed-and-breakfasts with an occupancy of five or fewer guests can serve a continental or full breakfast without a food service license. If the bed-and-breakfast houses more than five guests, however, you must obtain a license or you must limit the menu to a continental breakfast.

In Iowa, on the other hand, a bed-and-breakfast is exempt from the food sanitation code if they only serve food to their overnight guests and not the general public. And the owner of a bed-and-breakfast in Saint Paul, Minnesota, must have a food license unless there are accommodations for 10 or less people.

The health department should be contacted as early as possible. A personal visit to discuss your plans and their needs would be in order. It would be to your advantage to show cooperation and compliance from the very beginning. The health department can and will close your facility until you comply with its regulations. A bed-and-breakfast shut down by the health department will almost surely be ruined if the closure becomes public knowledge. Prior to opening, the health department will inspect the bed-and-breakfast. If the facilities pass the thorough inspection, they will issue the license enabling the bed-and-breakfast to open. The cost of the license is usually less than $50. Should they find faults in your facility, you will be required to have them corrected before they will issue a license.

Periodically during the year, the health department will make unannounced inspections of the bed-and-breakfast. An examination form will be completed outlining their findings. You must have all violations rectified before their next inspection. You can be certain that they will be back to see if you have complied.

Many health inspections are brought about by customer complaints. The health department will investigate every call they receive. Depending upon the number of calls and the similarity among the complaints, a pattern will be formulated. They will then trace the health problem to its source. Usually the problem is a result of some mishandling of a food product by a member of the staff. However, the problem can sometimes be traced to your supplier.

Although the health department can at times seem like a terrific nuisance, they really are on your side; their goals and yours are the same. Cooperation on both sides will resolve all the bed-and-breakfast's health conditions and make it a safe environment.

Many states now have laws requiring that at least the manager — and in some states, the entire staff — completes and passes an approved health and sanitation program. Check with your state's bed-and-breakfast association. The most common approved program is the ServSafe program developed by the NRA Educational Foundation. Materials may be purchased at **www.atlantic-pub. com** or by calling 800-541-1336. The ServSafe products, including instructor guides, answer sheets, instructor slides, manager training, food safety CD-ROMs and instructor tool kits are available in English and Spanish.

Fire Department Permit

A permit from the fire department, also referred to as an occupational permit, will be required prior to opening. As with the health department, contact the fire department as early as possible, preferably in person, and learn of their regulations and needs. The fire department inspectors will be interested in checking fire exits, smoke detectors, extinguisher placements and the hood and sprinkler systems. Many city fire departments do not permit the use of open-flame candles, flaming foods or flaming liquor in the building. If this was your intention, it would be best to ask in advance.

Based upon the size of the building, the local and national fire code and the number of exits, the fire inspectors will establish a "capacity number" of people permitted in the building at one time. Follow their guidelines strictly, even if this means turning away customers because you've reached capacity.

Check with your local fire department to find out the specific fire regulations that will affect your bed-and-breakfast.

Building and Construction Permit

Should you plan on doing any renovating to the bed-and-breakfast that is going to change the structural nature of the building, you may need a local building permit.

Building permits are generally issued from the local Building and Zoning Board. The fee is usually around $100, or it may be based on a percentage of the total cost of the project. You will need to approach the building inspector with your blueprints or plans to initially determine if a permit is required. Should a permit be required, he or she will inspect your plans ensuring that they meet all the local and federal ordinances and codes. Once the plans are approved, a building permit will be issued. The building inspector will make periodic inspections of your work at various stages of completion to ensure that the actual construction is conforming to the approved plans.

Most states have building codes in place that provide standards for new construction and renovations. The areas included in the codes are structural standards, plumbing and electric. Most states will require you to get a permit for any new building or renovation as well, especially if there is a change in use, such as changing a private home into a bed-and-breakfast.

Again, check with local authorities in your area to determine how local building codes will affect you.

Sign Permits

Many local city governments are beginning to institute sign ordinances and restrictions. These ordinances restrict the sign's size, type, location and lighting, and the proximity of the sign to the business. This is especially true if there is a particular neighborhood atmosphere the local government may be trying to keep intact, or if the neighborhood is designated as a historic district.

Even if there aren't any regulations, if your B&B is in a residential area, it's unlikely your neighbors would appreciate a neon sign. Keep your B&B's ambiance and your neighbors in mind when choosing signage for your business.

Zoning

Zoning laws prohibit certain activities from being conducted in particular areas. For example, a factory can't operate in areas zoned for residential use. Often mixes are allowed; one area of a county may allow mixed commercial and residential use, for example. Zoning laws also affect elements such as parking, signage, noise and appearance. In historic districts, you'll find fairly heavy restrictions on what type of signage you can use and many laws concerning the appearance of your building, including acceptable remodeling plans.

Some cities also restrict the number of particular types of businesses in a certain area; these cities may only allow three bed-and-breakfasts in an area, for instance. There may be particular commercial areas not zoned for bed-and-breakfasts, or there may be ordinances concerning permits, parking or liquor licenses that make a location unusable for you. Do a thorough check with the local zoning office BEFORE you purchase property.

Historic Buildings and Historic Districts

Many bed-and-breakfasts are in older, historic homes. Some of these may be eligible for the National Historic Register. Since 1976 there have been provisions in the federal tax code to benefit tax payers who own historic commercial buildings. These buildings are structures that are listed on the National Register of Historic Places, in national historic districts, in local historic districts, or are National Historic Landmarks. This tax credit has gone a long way in helping cities revitalize historic areas. Currently there is a 20 percent rehabilitation tax credit. For further information on this tax credit, visit the Internal Revenue Service's website at **www.irs.gov**, or write to: Federal Historic Preservation Tax Incentives, Heritage Preservation Services, National Park Service, 1849 C St. NW, Washington, D.C. 20240. They can be reached by email at hps-info@nps.gov, or by phone at 202-513-7270.

If your business is in a historic district you will be required to follow any zoning and construction regulations the local, state or federal government has in place for national historic districts. Which guidelines you will need to follow will depend on if your property is within the boundaries of a local historic district, state-defined historic district or federally recognized historic district. In general these regulations are set up to preserve the character of the properties within the boundaries of the district. Your local historic preservation office, can be very helpful in finding these rules and figuring out how to work with them. If you search on Google.com for your state historic preservation office you'll be able to find contact information. As with individual properties, if your inn is within a federal historic district, you will be able to apply for a tax credit. Check your local and state guidelines for information on local or state historic district tax credits.

State Liquor License

If you are considering serving complimentary wine or selling alcoholic beverages at your inn, you'll need to investigate state liquor laws.

A state liquor license requires extensive investigation because of its complexity. Many states do not allow the sale of liquor in hotels; others allow only beer and wine. Certain states vary the restrictions on sales of alcoholic beverages by county. A license to sell liquor in some states may cost but a few hundred dollars; in others a license can

cost upwards of $100,000. Several states are on quota systems and licenses are not even available. Certain counties in some states prohibit liquor sales entirely. A thorough investigation concerning your particular state, possibly with your lawyer, is in order.

Once you do obtain a license, it is imperative that you adhere to its laws and regulations. Most states have several thousand rules, so many in fact that they must be put into book form to contain them all. Most are just based on common sense; they all have a designated purpose. You can easily lose the license due to an infraction; obviously this would be disastrous and could spell ruin for your organization.

If you have other employees, make certain they all are thoroughly familiar with all the liquor laws. Carefully train new employees and test them if necessary. Constantly reiterate the laws. Employees will become lax if they are not often reminded of this big responsibility.

Get to know the liquor commissioner or inspector for your area. Demonstrate your wish to cooperate, and understand the responsibility of having a license.

To find out more about your state's liqour laws, visit the National Conference of State Liquor Administrators' directory at **www.ncsla.org/states.htm** and choose your state from the drop-down menu.

Internal Revenue Registration

In conjunction with the liquor license, you may also need to obtain from the Internal Revenue Service their tax stamps. Simply call the local IRS office and have them send you application Form #11. Based on the information about the bed-and-breakfast you supply on the form, the IRS will assess a fee. This application makes the IRS aware that you are engaging in the retail sale of liquor.

Federal Identification Number

All employers, partnerships and corporations must have a Federal Identification Number. For most sole proprietors, this number is usually your Social Security number. This number will be used to identify the business on all tax forms and other licenses. To obtain a Federal Identification Number (other than your Social Security number), fill out Form #55-4, obtainable from the IRS. Also at this time, request from the IRS the following publications, or you can download them via the Internet at **www.irs.gov**:

1. Publication #15, circular E "Employer's Tax Guide."
2. Several copies of Form W-4, "Employer Withholding Allowance Certificate." Each new employee must fill out one of these forms.
3. Publication #334, "Tax Guide for Small Businesses."
4. From the Occupational Safety and Health Administration, request free copies of "All About OSHA" and "OSHA Handbook for Small Businesses." Depending upon the number of employees you have, you will be subject to certain regulations from this agency. Their address is: OSHA, U.S. Department of Labor, 200 Constitutional Avenue NW, Washington, D.C. 20210 (**www.osha.gov**).
5. From the Department of Labor (**www.dol.gov**), request a free copy of "Handy Reference Guide to the Fair Labor Standards Act." The Department of Labor can be reached at: Department of Labor, Frances Perkins Building, 200 Constitutional Avenue NW, Washington, D.C. 20210.

State Tax Assistance

Many states offer tax assistance to small business owners through their Department of Revenue. With a quick Google search, you can find your specific state's site and it should be pretty simple from there.

CHAPTER SIX

· · · · ·

Before You Open

Before you swing the doors wide open for your first guest, there are a number of tasks and chores you need to take care of to ensure you're completely ready to make the B&B experience for your first guest one they will cherish forever.

The purpose of this chapter is to list and describe the activities fundamental to opening a bed-and-breakfast. Each bed-and-breakfast offers its own unique and challenging obstacles. The following chapter will make the prospective owner aware of all the pre-opening procedures which must be completed for any bed-and-breakfast. Before engaging in any business activity, seek the guidance of a lawyer. You will undoubtedly have many legal questions, and you will need legal counseling during the opening period. The services of a local accountant or C.P.A. should also be retained. The accountant will be instrumental in setting up the business and can provide you with a great deal of financial advice to inform your decision-making.

Choosing a Name

This is one of the most exciting pre-opening activities you'll do — naming your B&B! You want the image of your B&B to be inherent in its name so as soon as potential guests hear the name they will be attracted to it. Think about the image you want to create. What is the ambiance of your inn? What makes it special? Is the B&B in a gorgeous old Victorian home? Are you located in Amish country? Do you have a collection of antique spinning wheels on display? Are you located in the foothills of the Blue Ridge Mountains? All of these questions can give you clues for naming your bed-and-breakfast. For example, an inn in the foothills of the Appalachians is called Murphin Ridge Inn. One in Indiana with a distinctive type of architectural element was named Gothic Arches. Still another, Amos Shinkle Townhouse in northern Kentucky, was named after the house's builder, a prominent figure in the area in the 19th century.

After you have selected your name, you'll want to look into having it registered. After all the work and attention you've given to this detail, you don't want to have someone else come along and use the same name later on! In general, if you are going to do business in a state under a name other than your own personal name, you'll need to check with your state's Attorney General's office to see if you need to register. You can find these offices online. They often provide a good deal of information concerning how to register for a name. If you need some help finding this office, visit State and Local Government on the Net at **www.statelocalgov.net**.

You might also want to trademark your name to protect it. You can trademark on a national or statewide level. With a B&B it is wise to trademark on the national level since in many ways your competition is national. To register your bed-and-breakfast as a local trademark, contact the Secretary of State's office in your state. To register as a national trademark, you will need to contact the

United States Patent and Trademark Office (**www.uspto.gov**). They also have a search engine (Trademark Electronic Search System – TESS) that can help you determine if the name has already been trademarked.

Opening the B&B Bank Account

One of the first business-related things you should do is separate your private funds from your business funds, and opening a business checking account is a good way to start. Opening a business bank account is a great deal more important than it may appear at first. If you received your financing through a local commercial bank, it would be suggested you also use this bank for your business account, if it fills all your needs.

Whichever bank you decide to use, it is important that it can provide you with the following services:

- Night deposits
- All credit card services (if you will be using them)
- Change service (coins, small bills)
- A line of credit to certain suppliers
- Nearby location for daily transactions

It is very important that you get to know all the bank personnel on a first-name basis, particularly the manager. You will be in the bank every day. Make an effort to meet them and introduce yourself. Their assistance in obtaining future loans and gaining credit references will be invaluable. It is suggested you use a smaller bank, if it provides all your needs. Your account will mean a lot more to them than a larger bank.

Take plenty of time to shop around for the bank that will serve you the best. When you go into a prospective bank, ask to see the bank manager, tell him or her of your plans and what your needs are. All banks specialize in certain services. Look at what they charge for each transaction, and all other service charges. Compare very closely the handling charges on charge card deposits. A small percentage over thousands of dollars over a couple of years adds up to a great deal of money. Look at the whole picture very carefully. After you have selected a bank, you should order:

- Checks
- Deposit slips
- Deposit book
- Night deposit bags and keys
- Coin wrappers for all change
- Small bank envelopes

Establishing Room Rates

This is probably the most difficult pre-opening activity you'll undertake! How do you determine how much to charge for your rooms? There is no exact answer; you're going to have to do some research in order to come up with prices.

One of the first things you should do is check out your competition's prices. Call around to area bed-and-breakfasts and see if they'll give you rate information. If you identify yourself as a possible competitor, they may not be very forthcoming, but there are other ways to get this information. The easiest thing to do is get on the Internet to see if they have websites. Most of the time if a B&B has a website, room rate information will be there. You might also be able to see pictures of their guest rooms and determine if the amenities they are offering are comparable to the amenities you plan to offer. If the inns don't have websites, you can try a sneakier approach; ask family and friends to call the B&Bs as prospective guests to acquire the information for you.

You may also want to gather information on inns outside of your immediate area, but keep in mind that prices may vary by area. You probably can't command the same rate at your B&B in a small Indiana town as you could if your inn was located in a Colorado ski area, for example.

Once you have an idea of what the competition is doing, take a look at your own rooms and classify them according to size and amenities.

Here is a list of amenities to consider when pricing your rooms:

- Full breakfast
- Other included food service (evening snack or glass of wine)
- Fireplace
- Hot tub
- Telephone in room
- TV in room
- Fax service
- Computer line
- Guest refrigerator
- Private bath
- Swimming pool
- Tennis courts
- Bicycles
- Voicemail
- Snacks
- Picnic area
- Ceiling fans
- Meeting rooms
- Icemaker
- Refrigerator
- Beach passes
- Hair dryer
- Ironing board
- Laundry service
- Airport pick-up
- Turndown service
- Discounts to area attractions
- Exercise equipment

Take a look at the following list as an example.

Blue Room (double)	Green Room (single)	Rose Room (double)	Suite
Private bath	Shared bath	Shared bath	Private bath
Phone in room	Phone in room	Phone in room	Fireplace
			Desk and computer connection
			Phone in room

Think of all your rooms as modest, moderate and luxury. Keep in mind that not only are you pricing rooms in comparison to your competitors, but you are also pricing them in comparison to each other. If you use these three categories the rooms in the list probably fall out in the following way:

Modest	Moderate	Luxury
Green Room	Blue Room	Suite
Rose Room		

Now, look at your competition's prices and amenities and see what types of prices are associated with these categories. If you have no competition to look at, a baseline you can use is:

	Modest	Moderate	Luxury
Singles	$50-$135	$55-$150	$75-$250
Doubles	$60-$140	$70-$155	$85-$275

While these categories are wide, they do allow for differences in a bed-and-breakfast's location. If you are still having trouble deciding how to price your inn, check out the area's traditional hotels. While it isn't comparing apples to apples, it will still give you a foundation on which to base your price structure. If you take this approach, however, remember to think about and compensate yourself for amenities a traditional hotel won't have such as a full breakfast or afternoon tea service.

According to the PAII's *Statistics for Bed-and-Breakfasts/Country Inns for 2000*, rates can range from $30 for a shared bath to $595 average for a two-room whirlpool suite. Room rates by region are: Northeast $140, Southeast $110, Midwest $111, West $133.

Also keep in mind that you might have off and peak seasons and you might want to adjust your rates accordingly. Or, you might have a full house on the weekends and empty rooms on the weekdays. Adjusting your weekday rates to attract guests for this slow time is a good idea.

When is it time to raise your rates? Anytime you have a major renovation or upgrade in services you should increase your rates. A good rule of thumb in your first year to gauge your rates is to look at your occupancy history. If you were at 80 percent occupancy during busy season you can adjust your rates by 5 to 8 percent because you seem to be doing everything right! If you reach 90 percent occupancy, you might have your rates set too low. Remember, if you feel like business is slow and you are considering dropping your rates, you will probably attract a few more guests, but that may not have a positive effect on the bottom line.

Insurance

Properly insuring a bed-and-breakfast is similar to the coverage of any business enterprise where members of the public are in frequent attendance. Liability protection is of the utmost concern. Product liability is also desirable, as the consumption of food and beverages always presents a hazard. Described in this section are all the different types of insurance coverage applicable to bed-and-breakfasts. By no means is it recommended that you should obtain all of this insurance, for you would probably be over-insured if you did. A discussion with your agent is needed to determine under which insurance coverages you should be placed. Any policy written, however, should contain a basic business plan of Fire/Theft/Liability/Workers' Compensation.

If you currently live in the building you will be opening as a bed-and-breakfast, you should already have homeowner's insurance. However, it is very unlikely that this insurance will extend to cover your business. Check with your insurance agent to find out. There are many agencies that now specialize in B&B insurance. You can search "bed-and-breakfast insurance" online and come up with a number. It is advisable, however, to check with other B&B owners or check with professional B&B associations to make sure you get the right amount and kinds of insurance from a reputable agency. The following is a list of different types of insurance you may need to consider.

Fire. Fire insurance covers the buildings and all permanent fixtures belonging to and constituting a part of the structures. Coverage usually includes machinery used in building services, such as air-conditioning systems, boilers, elevators, etc. Personal property may also be covered.

Replacement Cost Endorsement. Provides for full reimbursement for the actual cost of repair or replacement of an insured building.

Extended Coverage Endorsement. Covers property for the same amount as the fire policy against damage caused by wind, hail, explosion, riot, aircraft, vehicles and smoke.

Vandalism. Covers loss or damage caused by vandalism or malicious mischief.

Glass Insurance. Covers replacement to show windows, glass counters, mirrors and structural interior glass broken accidentally or maliciously.

Sprinkler Damage. Insures against all direct loss to buildings or contents as a result of leakage, freezing or breaking of sprinkler installations.

Flood Insurance. Flood insurance is written in areas declared eligible by the Federal Insurance Administration. Federally subsidized flood insurance is available under the National Flood Insurance Program.

Earthquake Insurance. Covers losses caused by earthquakes.

Contents and Personal Property Damage. This insurance may cover any or all of the following:

- General property
- Replacement cost
- Improvements and better-ments
- Extended coverage
- Direct damage
- Vandalism
- Business interruption
- Consequential damage

Business Operations Insurance. Business operations insurance may cover:

- Valuable Papers
- Electrical signs
- Transportation policy
- Business interruption
- Endorsement extending period of indemnity
- General liability
- Comprehensive general liability
- Earnings insurance
- Product liability
- Contractual liability
- Rental value insurance
- Owner's protective liability
- Lease hold interest
- Personal injury
- Vehicle insurance
- Umbrella liability
- Fidelity bonds
- Crime
- License bonds
- Dishonesty, destruction and disappearance
- Liquor liability
- Business legal expense
- Fiduciary liability

- Life insurance
- Group life insurance
- Partnership
- Travel-Accident

- Key Man insurance
- Health insurance
- Major medical

Make sure to check into your state's specific liquor laws; even if you are offering liquor free rather than selling it, you will probably want some form of liquor liability insurance to cover you in case a guest was involved in an accident after consuming alcohol on your premises.

Workers' Compensation Insurance. Workers' Compensation insurance covers loss due to statutory liability as a result of personal injury or death suffered by an employee in the course of his or her employment. This insurance coverage pays all medical treatment and costs plus a percentage of the employee's salary due to missed time resulting from the injury. Workers' Compensation insurance is highly regulated by both state and federal agencies, particularly OSHA. Be certain to obtain all the information that pertains to your particular state. Workers' Compensation insurance is mandatory in most states.

Keeping Records

As with any business, good record keeping is essential to your business, and you need to do this from the very start. Naturally you'll be keeping records of all sorts once guests start checking in, but you'll want to keep track of the outflow of cash when you're getting ready to open as well. Much of this expense may be able to be written off your taxes. Not only will it help you in an IRS audit situation, but it will also help you to track which advertising is paying off and help you keep track of the profits.

Before you open be sure to have all your record-keeping systems in place so you can hit the ground running.

If you've never been good at math, you should consider taking a bookkeeping course at a local college. You may also be able to find affordable part-time help; many people working as bookkeepers do so on a freelance basis. As with hiring anyone, make sure you check references!

There are basically two types of records you should be concerned with: customer records and financial records.

Financial Records

Basically you'll need to keep records of all your business revenues and all your business expenses.

Expenses. There are three general categories for expenses: direct, capital and prorated.

- **Direct.** These expenses are spent on the business alone. These types of expenses include things such as small equipment (glassware, china, etc.), business loan interest, accountant's fees and office supplies.

- **Capital.** These expenses are larger or more expensive items, like your computer or a new stove. Because your B&B would get the benefit of the item over a period of time, the cost is also extended over a period of time in your tax documents. Different items have different depreciation rates, so you should check with the IRS or your tax consultant on these items.

- **Prorated.** These expenses usually are related to things such as mortgage interest and property tax. If you are operating the business out of your primary residence, you will be able to prorate these expenses on your taxes.

When tracking your expenses keep your receipts. This bears repeating: Keep your receipts! You should also create a monthly expense record and record each expense on this. After your record the expense on your spreadsheet, file all your receipts by month and year. At the end of the year you can store these in case you need them for a tax audit in the future. Purchase an expandable pocket folder, and file your annual receipts by month.

You can use any money software program to track your monthly expenses such as Quicken® or Microsoft's Money®. You can also just create your own Microsoft Excel spreadsheet. Here's an example of what a monthly expense sheet might look like.

The following standardized chart of accounts offered by the PAII can be used to track your revenue and expenses.

Revenue Accounts

Rooms Room rental with breakfast, excluding sales and bed taxes.	
Food - Restaurant All meals served onsite, except breakfast (when included in room rate). Includes MAP allocation for meals other than breakfast.	
Beverage - Restaurant Alcoholic beverages sold onsite.	
Telephone Guest use of telephone, fax charges.	
Gift Shop Sale of products in Gift Shop such as books and souvenirs.	
Meeting/Banquet Room Rental Room rental charges, as well as equipment charges.	
Rental of Equipment Rental fees for skis, boats, bikes, etc.	
Specialty Food and Beverage Includes services such as picnic baskets. Excludes lunch, dinner or catering revenue.	
Other Income Income from other sources not listed above (i.e., interest income, service charges, etc.).	

Expense Accounts

Payroll and Related	
Salary and Wages	
All salaries and wages for part and full-time employees.	
Employee Benefits and Taxes	
FICA, FUTA, Retirement Plan, Medicare, Insurance, etc.	
Housekeeping Services	
Amount paid to outside contracted housekeeping service.	
Country Inn (serving dinner regularly)	
Cost of Food - Restaurant	
Cost of food sold in restaurant and during banquet service.	
Cost of Beverage - Restaurant	
Cost of alcoholic beverages sold in the restaurant and during banquet service.	
Other F&B Expenses - Restaurant	
Napkins, glassware, china, silver, pans, etc., used in restaurant and during banquet service.	
Other Operating Expenses	
Advertising and Promotion	
Brochures, magazines, newspaper ads, printing, direct mail lists, Internet, mailing, etc.	
Auto Expenses	

Automobile gasoline, repair, maintenance, and lease.	
Bank Fees	
Check charges, credit card merchant fees, etc.	
Business Taxes and Fees	
Property taxes and business fees. Excludes income, sales or bed taxes.	
Commissions	
Travel agent commissions, RSA and other booking/referral fees.	
Donations	
Direct cash contributions. Excludes gift certificates and in-kind donations.	
Dues and Subscriptions	
Association dues, subscriptions to services, magazines, etc.	
Equipment Rental	
Rental of operating equipment. Excludes land or building leases.	
Food & Beverage - Breakfast	
Food, beverage and supplies for breakfast and special food service.	
Gift Shop	
Cost of goods offered for sale.	

Insurance	
Non-payroll insurance such as fire, theft, auto, liability, etc.	
Interest Expense	
Non-mortgage interest on business-related loans, credit cards, etc.	
Legal and Accounting Fees	
Fees for legal and accounting services.	
Maintenance Repairs and Fixtures	
Labor and materials including furniture, fixtures and equipment under $300.	
Miscellaneous Expenses	
Fixed or variable costs that are not included in any other expense account.	
Office Supplies	
Paper, tape, pens, letterhead, non-promotion postage, etc.	
Outside Services	
Services such as maintenance, gardening, etc. Excludes outside housekeeping services.	
Room and Housekeeping Supplies	
Items such as soap, toilet paper, light bulbs, cleaning supplies, etc.	
Telephone	

Telephone and related expenses.	
Towels and Linens	
Non-Food & Beverage towels and linens, blankets, pillows, bathrobes, etc.	
Training	
Fees and expenses for professional workshops and seminars.	
Travel and Entertainment	
Travel-related expenses and business entertainment.	
Utilities	
Trash, gas, electric, water, etc.	
Net Operating Income/Loss	
Income before mortgage, depreciation, income taxes and owner's draw.	

Entry No.	Date	Daily Expense Total	Legal Fees	Food	Telephone	Office Supplies	Interest	Utilities
101	11/2/16	$553	$400	$25		$16	$112	
102	11/2/16	$400		$32	$66			$302
103	11/6/16	$102		$102				
104	11/18/16	$84		$14		$5		$65
105	11/18/16	$22				$22		
106	11/31/16	$55		$55				

Quicken offers money management software for small businesses at affordable prices. Log on to **www.quicken.com** to find out more about their services and products.

Revenue. Your revenue paperwork should be similar to your expense paperwork. You should have a monthly summary sheet of all the income you have made and you should have a reservation slip for each room you have rented to accompany this summary. File the reservation slips as you do your receipts — by month.

An income summary sheet might look something like the following:

Entry No.	Date	Guest name	Reservation Source	No. of Nights	Room Rate	Tax	Deposit	Balance Received
101	11/2/16	Adams	Brochure	2	$85	$8.50	$30	$55
102	11/2/16	Jones	Area hotel	3	$65	$6.50	$30	$35
103	11/6/16	Anderson	Website	2	$135	$13.50	$50	$85
104	11/18/16	Coates	Website	2	$135	$13.50	$50	$85
105	11/18/16	Thompson	Website	4	$85	$8.50	$30	$55
106	11/31/16	Thiedeman	Brochure	2	$85	$8.50	$30	$55

Most of the reservation software packages on the market will generate income reports for you.

Customer Records

Calendar

One of the first items you'll want to purchase for keeping track of things is a calendar. Keep it by the phone so it's handy. When potential guests call, you'll have the information right at your fingertips and be able to tell them if a particular date is available. It is vital that the information you track on this calendar is accurate or you run the risk of double-booking.

Here's a sample of a calendar:

Sunday	Monday	Tuesday	Wednesday	Thursday	Friday	Saturday
					1 Jones (2) Blue Room	2 Jones (2) Blue Room
3 Jenkins (4) Green Room Jones (2) Blue Room	4 Jenkins (4) Green Room Taylor (1) Blue Room	5 Jenkins (4) Green Room Johnson (1) Blue Room	6 Jenkins (4) Green Room	7	8	9
10	11	12	13	14	15	16
17	18	19	20	21	22	23
24	25	26	27	28	29	30

It's very easy to misunderstand when a person is checking out so make sure you clarify this completely when making the reservation:

> *You:* All right Mrs. Jones, I have you down for arriving on the 1st and checking out on the 3rd.
>
> *Mrs. Jones:* Oh no, I meant we want to stay three nights. We want to check out on the 4th.

Clarify and double clarify when booking your rooms!

If you do accidentally overbook your rooms, what should you do? Try to fix the situation as soon as you realize it — don't wait to see what happens, hoping maybe one of the guests ends up canceling. You can make some calls to other area B&Bs to see if they have room for those dates. Try to give the guests at least three options when you call them back. Be as gracious and apologetic as possible (without groveling).

Register

Once you've booked the room, you need to have some way to register your guests when they arrive (this is a large folio book that people sign when they come to your establishment, much like the ones you see in old movies). This is a very easy way to keep track of the number of guests that stay in your inn each year, and the American Bed & Breakfast Association make it a mandatory requirement if you are a member.

It's also useful in tracking a bed-and-breakfast's sales history because the guest register can show you slow periods and busy seasons. You should feel free to make notes of your own in the register as well, commenting on snow storms, festivals that are in town and other things that might have affected your occupancy rate.

Guest Record

Along with the register, you should have a separate record for each guest similar to the following sample.

Registration Card

Date _____   Folio # _____

Name _____

Address _____

City _____ State _____ Zip _____

Phone _____ E-Mail _____ Affiliation_____

Arrival Date _____   Clerk _____
Room # _____   Departure date _____
Rate _____

Credit Card   ☐ Mastercard ☐ VISA ☐ American Express ☐ Discover

Card # ☐☐☐☐–☐☐☐☐–☐☐☐☐–☐☐☐☐   Expires ☐☐☐☐

Notes _____
_____
_____

Registration Card

Date _____   Folio # _____

Name _____

Address _____

City _____ State _____ Zip _____

Phone _____ E-Mail _____ Affiliation_____

Arrival Date _____   Clerk _____
Room # _____   Departure date _____
Rate _____

Credit Card   ☐ Mastercard ☐ VISA ☐ American Express ☐ Discover

Card # ☐☐☐☐–☐☐☐☐–☐☐☐☐–☐☐☐☐   Expires ☐☐☐☐

Notes _____
_____
_____

You can computerize these records for easy access, or you could keep them in a three-ring binder. Make sure that your guest record has information including the name, address and phone number of the guest. It should also include the arrival and departure dates, number of nights staying, the room rate, tax, how payment was made, the number of people in the party and the room they are occupying. You may also want to include any pertinent personal information on these records, such as food allergies the guest has told you about or the fact that the couple is celebrating an anniversary. Most B&Bs require a deposit, so you'll want to include this information as well.

You may also want to keep a daily transaction log for each room if you have a number of incidental charges guests might accrue, such as phone calls or laundry charges.

Daily Transaction Log

TOTAL	SUBTOTAL							Departures	SUBTOTAL						
															Folio #
															Room #
															# of Guests
															OPENING BALANCE DB (CR)
															Room
															Room Tax
															Restaurant
															Beverages
															Local Calls
															Long Distance
															Valet
															Laundry
															Misc. Charges
															Cash Disbursements
															Transfer Debit
															TOTAL DAILY CHARGES
															Cash Receipts
															Allowances
															Transfer to City Ledger
															Transfer Credit
															TOTAL CREDITS
															CLOSING BALANCE

Written Confirmation

After taking a reservation and receiving the deposit, you will want to send your guest a written confirmation of their booking. Print this on your stationery and staple it to a copy of the reservation sheet. You may also want to include directions and area attractions. If you have policies such as no pets or no smoking, you'll want to include this information on the confirmation. And definitely be sure to include your cancellation policy!

Reservation Service Agencies (RSAs)

Bed-and-breakfast owners have a decision to make when they are opening: should they join an RSA or not? If you are buying an existing B&B, you may not need the services of an RSA because you will already have a built-in customer base. If however, you are starting fresh, you might find their assistance welcome.

What is an RSA?

An RSA, is an organization that acts as a middleman to B&B owners. Typically this organization will list you as a member and book reservations for you. They will handle the initial call and reservation, the deposit and confirmation. They may also forward directions to guests and deal with cancellations, and they may handle regional and national advertising.

One of the most convenient services RSAs provide is screening guests. Whether you use an RSA or not, you'll want to screen potential guests for two reasons: 1) to make sure your bed-and-breakfast fits your potential guests' needs, and 2) to make sure the potential guests meet your needs.

To find out if your bed-and-breakfast will suit potential guests, you have to find out exactly what they are looking for in a bed-and-breakfast. Do they need a private bath? Do they want a full, hot breakfast? What type of beds do they want? Are they smokers? Do they have children or pets? These are all questions you or the RSA will need to ask to find out if your bed-and-breakfast is the type of accommodation they are looking for. You should also try to find out what brings the guest to your area — business or pleasure. Are they visiting a particular landmark or event? If your bed-and-breakfast is actually located quite a distance from this event, the guest may not want to stay with you. You should also find out how many people, are traveling and what the group's composition is. If there are two people it might be a father and daughter, husband and wife or two friends. The composition of the guest group will have a significant impact on how you will house them.

If it turns out that someone does not choose to stay with you, you or the RSA can keep a list of alternative accommodations to which you can direct them.

Inviting a stranger into your home is much different than selling a room to a stranger at a traditional hotel or motel. You are welcoming the guest into your home, not some sterile, isolated space. Therefore, you or the RSA must also determine if the guest is right for your bed-and-breakfast. For example, if you have a no-children policy and the potential guest is traveling with his or her family, that guest is probably not a good fit for your bed-and-breakfast. Similarly, if the B&B has a dog on the premises and a potential guest is allergic, this is not a good fit.

Many hosts will try to draw potential guests out on the telephone to see if they seem like a good fit. If you end up hosting an individual who is not, it's likely to be a bad experience all around, so if you can access this information upfront, you might save yourself and the guest from this.

There is also the issue of safety. As mentioned, you are inviting strangers into your home. Going through a screening process, either using an RSA or on your own, lessens the chances of having any safety issues arise. When talking with a guest, always be sure to ask where they heard about your bed-and-breakfast or inn and make sure to get a business or home address and phone number. You may even want to consider asking for a reference.

So what do you do if you take reservations over the Internet? You obviously can't talk to guests to get a sense of their needs. One of the best things you can do if you take reservations om the Internet is to have guests fill out an Information Form that contains the same information you would acquire if you were talking to them over the phone.

An Information Form might look like this:

Reservation Information Sheet

Guest Name: _____

Home Address: _____

Home Phone: _____

Business Address: _____

Business Phone: _____

Email: _____

How did you hear about us? _____

Arrival Date and Time: _____

Departure Date and Time: _____

Number in Party: _____

Names and Ages of Guests: _____

Pets? _____

Smoking/Nonsmoking? _____

Accommodations Desired:
❑ Queen Bed   ❑ Double Bed   ❑ Twin Beds   ❑ Suite

Purpose of visit _____

Have you stayed at a B&B before _____

Allergies? _____

Special dietary requirements? _____

If you become a member of an RSA, the organization will take care of this screening process for you. RSA employees have an abundance of experience at handling these types of calls, and if a particular guest does not seem like a good fit for your B&B, they will suggest another that is better suited.

Having someone else handle potential calls, as well as calls that result in actual reservations, can be a big time-saver, but as with all things there is usually a cost associated with all this help. Typically RSAs charge a membership fee and a percentage of each booking (this is usually between 20 and 25 percent). The membership fee for The National Network of Bed & Breakfast Reservation Services (TNN) is $350 annually, plus an annual $75 conference fee. This particular service has listings in Canada, Connecticut, Chicago, Illinois, Indiana, Massachusetts, Mississippi, New York, Pennsylvania, South Carolina, Texas, Vermont and Virginia. To apply for membership to TNN, you must also supply a copy of your business license, a copy of your listing in the local telephone directory, a brochure, flyer or other form of marketing material, a guest comment form, a copy of your guest registration form, a list of the nearby towns and all the bed-and-breakfasts located in these vicinities, your office policies and your website and email addresses.

Most RSAs are regional, but there are some national networks. Take some time to compare RSAs because they are not all the same. Bed & Breakfast Inns Online provides a directory of reservation service agencies in a number of states. This list can be found at **www.bbonline.com**. Bed-and-breakfast Associates Bay Colony also provides a listing of regional RSAs, including some international ones. You can find this list at **www.bnbboston.com/locations.html**.

In many instances an RSA may require you to go through an inspection before they will list your B&B. Don't think of this as something to be nervous about, however. The RSA may also provide consulting services for a small fee, providing you with advice and tips on how to make your bed-and-breakfast even more inviting to guests. The TNN, for example, has a host packet they offer to their B&B members.

Organizing Pre-Opening Activities

Opening a bed-and-breakfast or any business is a great test of anyone's organizational and managerial abilities. Keep track of the assignments that need to be completed, who the assignments are delegated to, and when they must be completed. Allow plenty of time for assignments and projects to be accomplished. Even the seemingly simplest task may uncover a web of tangles and delays. Delegate responsibilities whenever possible, but above all else, keep organized. Maintain a collective composure and deal with people and problems on a level and consistent basis, and you'll be off to a great start.

First Priority Items

Suggested items that must be completed well ahead of opening date include:

1. List the B&B's name and number in the phone book and Yellow Pages.
2. Order and install reservation software.
3. Allow shipping and lead time for:
   a. China, silverware, serving pieces
   b. Furniture and bed linens
   c. Equipment.
   d. Drop safe for office.
   e. Printing: stationery, business cards, matches, brochures, menus, etc.

4. Develop a list of all construction projects. It should include who is completing them, when they will be completed and a list of materials needed.

5. Set up a large calendar on the wall with deadlines, when deliveries will be expected, construction projects finished, equipment installed, meetings and, of course, the opening date.

6. Contact the art galleries or artists' groups in your area. They may be able to supply you with artwork to be displayed in the bed-and-breakfast on a consignment basis.

Pre-Opening Promotion

Described below are some pre-opening promotional ideas. It should be noted that there is a definite distinction between promotion and advertising. Promotion involves creating an interest in a new project usually at little or no cost.

As soon as possible, put up the new bed-and-breakfast sign or a temporary sign explaining briefly the name of the new bed-and-breakfast, type of bed-and-breakfast, hours of operation and the opening date. People by nature are most interested in what is occurring in their neighborhood; give them something to start talking about. This is perhaps the best and least expensive promotion you can do.

1. Meet with the advertising representatives for the local papers. Determine advertising costs and look into getting a small news story published describing the bed-and-breakfast.

2. Have plenty of the bed-and-breakfast's business cards on hand as soon as possible; they're a great source of publicity.

3. Join the Better Business Bureau and the local chamber of commerce. Besides lending credibility to your organization, they often can supply you with some very good free publicity.

4. Host an open house and invite people from the local paper, travel guides, the reservation service (if you are using one), the chamber of commerce, travel agencies in town, wedding planners, other more traditional area hotels, etc. All of these people have the potential for sending business your way. It's probably not a bad idea to invite the neighbors or local church group if you have the room. Keeping a friendly public image is important, and these people may have relatives or friends coming to town that could stay with you!

Initially Contacting Purveyors and Suppliers

If you are operating a larger bed-and-breakfast or inn, you will want suppliers to come to you. Approximately six to eight weeks prior to the scheduled opening date, it will be necessary to contact all the local suppliers and meet with their sales representatives. Make certain each sales representative understands that quality products are your top consideration. Competition is fierce among both sales representatives and suppliers. Let each know you are considering all companies equally. Never become locked into using one purveyor only. Shop around, so to speak, and always be willing to talk with new sales representatives.

Consider these points when choosing a purveyor:

1. Quality of products. Accept nothing but A-1.
2. Reliability.
3. Delivery days. All deliveries should arrive at a designated time.
4. Is the salesperson really interested in your business?

5. Does the salesperson seem to believe in what he or she sells?
6. Terms in billing (interest, credit, etc.).
7. Is the company local (for emergencies)?
8. From the first meeting with the sales representative you should obtain:
     a. Credit applications to be filled out and returned.
     b. Product lists or catalogs describing all the products.
     c. References. Check them out!

You should supply them with a list of the products you will be purchasing, with estimates as to the quantity of each item you will be using every week.

Emphasize to the sales representative that price is certainly an important consideration, but not your only one, when selecting a supplier. Point out to the sales representative the other concerns you have about using their company. Indicate that you do intend to compare prices among the various companies but wouldn't necessarily switch suppliers due to a one-time price undercutting. Loyalty is important to sales representatives, they need to expect that order from you each week. But at the same time let them know they must be on their toes and earn your business.

Most companies offer a discount to bed-and-breakfasts once they purchase a certain number of cases. Keep this in mind when comparing prices and suppliers. Choosing a supplier is often a difficult task, with so many variable factors to consider. Begin to analyze these problems in terms of the overall picture, and your purchasing decisions will become consistently more accurate.

If you are a very small B&B, you probably won't be able to find many suppliers willing to deliver small amounts. In this case your best bet, as far as cost goes, is to buy at a store such as Sam's Club or Costco. For a yearly membership fee you can get access to smaller quantities of bulk items including food, toilet paper, facial tissue and soap. Visit these stores' websites at **www.samsclub.com** and **www.costco.com**.

Payroll

Again, if you are operating a large bed-and-breakfast, you will have a payroll because you are likely to have people helping with cleaning, cooking or maintenance duties. You may need the assistance of personnel to assemble chairs, do odd painting, hang pictures, and do anything required so that the opening date may be achieved. Many of these temporary employees may be utilized for various jobs in the bed-and-breakfast after opening. The time clock should certainly be used during this period for better control. Overtime must be carefully monitored and, if at all possible, avoided. This will require a great deal of organization between assignments and scheduling.

Many of these jobs will be boring and tedious. Compensate these employees well for their efforts. Having a free lunch or dinner available would certainly be greatly appreciated. These small tokens on your behalf will be returned in gratitude many times over the small cost incurred.

We highly recommend the use of Quickbooks, Sage or other competing computer software for payroll processing. In addition, Quickbooks will be very useful in other parts of your business and in your business planning. Quickbooks can be located at **http://quickbooks.intuit.com**, and Sage at **www.sage.com/us/sage-50-accounting**.

Public Utilities

Notify public utility companies of your intention to be operating by a certain date. Allow plenty of lead time for completion. Don't lose valuable time because the utilities are not hooked up yet. Some of these companies may require a deposit before they will issue service. Every company and city has different policies, so be sure to investigate yours thoroughly.

Phone company. You can get by with just one phone, especially if you are operating a small B&B, but we recommend at least two phone lines, one for business and one for personal. Don't forget about data lines and a fax line. Don't lose customers because they can't get through. You should have two to three phones in the offices, one to two extensions at the entrance area and one to two extensions in the bar. The phones in the entrance area and bar may be wired so that they cannot call long distance. This prevents misuse from guests and employees. Place local emergency numbers at all phones.

Gas and Electric Companies. All major equipment need special hookups that can only be completed by trained technicians of either the gas or electric company or by authorized representatives. They should be contacted as early as possible to evaluate the amount of work required. In many cases they will need to schedule the work several weeks ahead of time.

Many gas and electric companies have service contracts that may be purchased. If available, it is highly recommended that you purchase them. Equipment that is maintained to the manufacturer's specifications will last longer and operate both more effectively and efficiently.

Set up a loose-leaf binder to contain all the information on your equipment and its maintenance schedules. Included in this binder should be warranties, receipts, brochures, equipment schematics, operating instructions, maintenance schedules, part lists, order forms, past service records, manufacturers' phone numbers, a chart showing which circuit breaker operates each piece of equipment, etc. Keep this manual up to date from the very beginning. Become aware of your equipment's needs and act accordingly. Train your employees thoroughly in the proper use of all equipment, and it will serve the bed-and-breakfast well for many years.

Water. Water is different in all parts of the country due to the type of chemical particles it contains. Water that has been subjected to a chemical treatment plant may contain a high level of chlorine. Water taken directly from the water table will contain any number of additives depending upon the geological makeup of the soil from where it came. Different types of water can give different results when used in cooking. Your state's Department of Natural Resources can give you information concerning the water's chemical makeup in the local area.

Chemical particles in the water can have a particularly bad effect in the brewing of fresh coffee. Food recipes using water and cocktails made with water will also be affected.

Several companies have filtering devices on the market which attach directly to the water lines. If prescribed, filters need only be connected to the water lines that are used for drinking/cooking water. Bathroom and dishwasher lines would not require a filter. Filtering devices are usually tube-shaped canisters which contain charcoal or a special filtering paper. Discuss your particular situation with your state's Department of Natural Resources and the sales representative for your coffee supplier.

Locksmith

A registered or certified locksmith must be contacted to change the locks as soon as you occupy the building. Keys to locked areas should be issued on a "need to have" basis. Only employees that need to have access to a locked area to perform their jobs should have a key to that lock. The locksmith can set door locks so that certain keys may open some doors, but not others. Only the owner and manager should have a master key to open every door. Each key will have its own identification number and "Do Not Duplicate" stamped on it. Should there be a security breach, you can easily see who had access to that particular area. The bed-and-breakfast should be entirely re-keyed when key-holding personnel leave or someone loses his or her keys. Safe combinations should periodically be changed by the locksmith.

You'll also need to decide on and establish a key policy for your guests. Do you want to give all of your guests keys? While it may be easier for you to do this on the one hand, it could become a large headache if you're not careful. For example, what if a guests checks out and leaves, forgetting to return his or her key? And, unfortunately, not everyone in the world is honest. You do run a security risk if you decided to give your guests front-door keys. However, leaving your front door open at all hours for guests to come and go may be a greater risk!

Fire and Intrusion Alarms

Every bed-and-breakfast should have two separate alarm systems. A system for fire, smoke and heat detection and one for intrusion and holdup.

The fire detection system consists of smoke monitors and heat sensors, strategically placed around the building. This system must be audible for evacuations and directly connected to either the fire department or a private company with 24-hour monitoring service. In newer buildings, the sensors also activate the sprinkler system. Most cities and states also require bed-and-breakfasts to install a hood system in the kitchen area. This consists of a sprinkler-type system situated above equipment with an exposed cooking surface or flame. The system may be operated either automatically or manually. When released, a chemical foam is immediately sprayed out over the area. This is particularly effective in stopping grease fires. Once activated, the system will automatically shut off the gas or electric service to the equipment. In order to regain service, the company which installed the system must reset it. As previously indicated, check with the local fire department for further recommendations. They may also direct you to a reputable fire and safety service company.

An intrusion alarm system is recommended for any bed-and-breakfast. Begin to research this subject by initially contacting the police department and advising them of your intentions. Contact several of the recommended companies and ask for a survey and proposal (usually at no charge) of the building and your needs.

The security system should contain magnetic contact switches on the main doors, windows, internal doors and other places of entry such as trapdoors and roof hatches. Don't overlook the air conditioning vents. The interior of the building should be monitored by strategically placed motion detectors that are zoned so that if one fails, the entire system will continue to function. The safe and/or area around the safe should most definitely be monitored. The locking-type holdup buttons, which may only be released with a key, are an excellent option and should be placed in the cashier area, bar and the office. Video monitors can also be provided by most alarm companies.

As previously indicated, the installation of an alarm system in the bed-and-breakfast is almost a necessity. The loss of business and profits due to burglary, vandalism or arson is not to be gambled upon. As a side note, the installation of an alarm system will increase the value of the property, and a 24-hour monitored system may make you eligible with your insurance company for a rate reduction of 5 to 10 percent on the insurance premium.

If you do install an intrusion alarm system, you will have to come up with a way to deal with guests who want to stay out late and guests arriving when you aren't home. You may want to consider giving a trustworthy neighbor the alarm information and having them meet guests in your absence, for instance. For guests who like to stay out late, you may need to include information on when the alarm system will be turned on in your confirmation materials or list of house rules.

Sanitation Service

In most counties, a private business must provide its own garbage pickup. A bed-and-breakfast of any size has a great deal of waste. In order to preserve a proper health environment, the services of a trash removal or sanitation service company will be required.

Receive quotes from all the sanitation companies in the area. Prices may vary considerably depending upon who purchases the dumpsters. You may wish to get advice from your health department for the selection. Any service contract should contain provisions for the following:

- Dumpsters with locking tops.
- Periodic steam cleaning of the dumpsters.
- Fly pesticide sprayed on the inside of the dumpster.
- Number of days for pickup.
- Extra pickups for holidays and weekends.

Some bed-and-breakfast waste may actually be used by manufacturers in the area. Soap manufacturers would be interested in purchasing all the meat and fat scraps for a few cents a pound. Pig farmers may buy all the food scraps. These companies will provide special containers to store the products. Scrap glass from empty liquor bottles may also be sold or donated to the local recycling or ecology project.

Plumber

A local plumber will be needed to handle any miscellaneous work and emergencies that may come up. The plumber must have 24-hour emergency service. Make every effort possible to retain the plumber that completed the original work on the building. He or she will be thoroughly familiar with the plumbing and know why certain procedures were performed. This can be a terrific advantage.

Clogs and backups can be major problems for a B&B. Extra-wide pipes should be fitted to the dishwasher and sink drains. Grease will collect in the elbows and fittings along the plumbing. When cold water is put through the drain, the grease will solidify, closing the inside diameter of the pipe. Food products or paper may then lodge into these areas causing a clog which will result in a backup. The plumber must have an electric snake and the necessary acids to remove the clog. A hand snake and plunger should always be on hand in the kitchen.

Electrician

As with the plumber, it would be a great advantage to retain the original electrician who worked on the building. An electrician will be needed when equipment is moved or installed. If it has not been done already, the electrician should check out and label all the circuits and breakers in the building. The electrician should also be on 24-hour emergency service.

Refrigeration Service

The most important consideration when choosing a refrigeration company is how fast they can respond to emergencies. At any given time the refrigeration systems and freezer could go out, which may result in the loss of several thousand dollars in food. Make certain any prospective company understands this crucial point. They must have 24-hour service.

In some situations, there may be no hope in getting the refrigeration units back to work in time, usually because of a broken part that must be replaced. Short of losing all the food, there are some possible solutions. You might contact the purveyors you use who have large refrigeration units. They may be able to store the food temporarily. Call tractor trailer companies in the area; they may have an empty refrigeration truck which could be rented. Simply transfer the perishables into it for storage.

A fully loaded freezer will usually stay cold enough to keep frozen foods frozen for two days if the cabinet is not opened. In a cabinet with less than half a load, food may not stay frozen for more than a day.

If normal operation cannot be resumed before the food will start to thaw, use dry ice. If dry ice is placed in the freezer soon after the power is off, 125 pounds should keep the temperature below freezing for two to three days in a 10-cubic-foot cabinet with half a load, and three to four days in a loaded cabinet.

Place dry ice on cardboard or small boards on top of the packages, and do not open the freezer again except to put in more dry ice or to remove it when normal operation is resumed. Monitor the temperature with an accurate recording device.

Exterminator

Exterminators must be licensed professionals with references from the other bed-and-breakfasts they service. You may wish to consult the health department for their recommendations. Exterminators can eliminate any pest-control problems, such as rats, cockroaches, ants, termites, flies, etc. Have several companies come in to appraise the building. They are experts and can read the "tell-tale" signs that might otherwise be missed. Take their suggestions. The company selected should be signed to a service contract as soon as possible. This is not an area to cut corners or try to do yourself — it won't pay in the long run.

Landscaping

You may desire to have the exterior areas of the bed-and-breakfast professionally designed and landscaped. An appealing exterior is at least as important as the interior. You may have little room to work with, but a landscaper can put together a design that can be very appealing. Contact local landscapers and get their opinions, designs, quotes and references.

List of Supplies

Before you open your bed-and-breakfast, there are a number of supplies you will want to have on hand. How much you stock up on some items partly depends on how busy you expect to be and partly on how much storage space you have.

Bedrooms

- Mattresses
- Mattress pads
- Mattress covers
- Bed frames
- Sheets
- Blankets
- Pillows
- Dressers
- Lamps
- Tables
- Chairs
- Easy chairs
- Luggage racks
- Hangers
- Curtains
- Night stands
- Waste baskets
- Ashtrays (if you allow smoking)
- Alarm clocks
- Boxes of facial tissue
- Blankets
- Bedspreads

Bathrooms

- Bath towels
- Hand towels
- Washcloths
- Liquid soap
- Bar soap
- Bath rugs
- Bath mats
- Hooks for robes
- Drying tack
- Soap dishes
- Facial tissue
- Cleaning supplies
- Toilet paper
- Shower curtain or door
- Shelf space
- Well-lit mirror

Common Rooms

- Games
- Books
- Facial tissue
- Literature about surrounding area

Kitchen

- Dry goods (flour, sugar, baking powder, salt, etc.)
- Breakfast foods (eggs, bacon, bread, etc.)
- Condiments and pantry items (butter, milk, jam, syrup, coffee, tea, non-sugar sweetener, mustard, etc.)
- Heavy-duty mixer
- Oven
- Microwave
- Dishwasher
- Towels
- Washcloths
- Cleaning supplies
- Pans (various sizes of saucepans, skillets and lids)
- Waffle maker
- Tea kettle
- Coffee machine

Dining room

- Dining room furniture
- Linens
- Napkins
- Tea cozy
- Silverware
- China
- Centerpieces
- Buffet pieces
- Sterno (if you are serving a hot buffet)
- Chafing dishes
- Serving pieces

How Much China and Silverware to Order

To compute your china needs, multiply the number indicated by the number of seats in the bed-and-breakfast. Keep in mind that all dishwashers and machines work at different speeds. Use this as a guide in ordering.

China				
Dinner plate	2	Sauce dish	1 ½
Bread plate	3	Dessert plate	2
Salad bowl	2	Cup/Mug	3
Soup bowl	2	Saucer	3
Glasses				
Water glass	3	Wine glass	1
Flatware				
Teaspoon	5	Salad fork	2
Soup spoon	1	Oyster fork	1
Tablespoon	½	Knife	2
Ice tea spoon	¼	Steak knife	1
Fork	3		

This chart will provide a basic outline to indicate what will be required in an average bed-and-breakfast that serves breakfast and dinner. Not maintaining enough stock will slow down service. Too much stock will cause you to store it in the bed-and-breakfast, tying up cash. Figures will need to be adjusted depending on the menu and how many uses you have for the same piece of china or silverware.

Exhaust Hood Cleaning Service

If you have a large kitchen and large inn, you'll want to get an exhaust hood cleaning service. Contact a company that specializes in the cleaning of exhaust hoods and ventilation systems. They should appraise and inspect the whole ventilation system prior to opening. Depending upon the amount and type of cooking performed, they will recommend a service which will keep the system free from grease and carbon buildup. Usually twice-a-year cleaning is required. Without this service, the exhaust hoods and vents will become saturated with grease, causing a dangerous fire hazard. All that would be necessary to ignite a fire would be a hot spark landing on the grease-saturated hood. Most of these companies also offer grease and fat (deep fryer oil) removal.

Heating and Air-Conditioning

You will need the services of a company that can respond 24 hours a day at a moment's notice. Losing the heating system in the winter or the air conditioning in the summer will force the bed-and-breakfast to close. Make certain the company is reliable with many references.

Heating and air-conditioning systems need regular service and preventative maintenance to ensure they function at maximum efficiency. Energy and money will be wasted if the system is not operating correctly. A service contract should be developed with these companies to ensure the machines are being serviced to the manufacturer's schedule. Keep the contract and all additional information in the equipment manual.

Music

Music in the background of the bed-and-breakfast sets the mood and enhances the atmosphere. Music is a very important part of any dining experience.

The most inexpensive way to provide a music system for the bed-and-breakfast is to set it up yourself. Contact a local stereo dealer. After examining the acoustics in the building, he or she will be able to suggest the system that will best meet your needs. Take care to camouflage the speakers into the surroundings. The speakers should have individual volume controls for each area. A radio station should never be used.

Live music is also a consideration for the bed-and-breakfast. Live music and entertainment is usually centered in the common area.

Live music will be rather expensive. An average band will cost upwards of a thousand dollars for three or four nights. However, if they blend in well and attract customers, the additional expense may be recouped many times over. Live entertainment can be a great source of additional publicity.

Music Licensing

If you are interested in playing recorded music in the bed-and-breakfast, you will need permission (a license) to play such music in your establishment. Although most people buy a song or album thinking it is then their property, there is a distinction in the law between owning a copy of the album and owning the songs on the album. There is also a difference between a private performance of copyrighted music and a public performance. Most people recognize that purchasing music doesn't give them the right to make copies of it to give or sell to others. The record company and music publishers retain those rights. Similarly, the music still belongs to the songwriter, composer or music publisher of the work. When you buy a CD, record, or mp3, the purchase price covers only your private listening use, similar to the "home" use of "home videos." When you play these songs or albums in your bed-and-breakfast, it becomes a public performance. Songwriters, composers and music publishers have the exclusive right of public performance of their musical works under U.S. copyright law. There are some distinctions in the law if the performance is by means of public communication of TV or radio transmissions and played by eating, drinking, retail and certain other establishments of a certain size which use a limited number of speakers or TVs. Further, the reception must not be further transmitted from the place where it is received (to another room, for example), and there must be no admission charged.

There are two licensing agencies in the United States: BMI and ASCAP. You can contact ASCAP at 1-800-95-ASCAP, **www.ascap.com**; and BMI at 212-220-3000, **www.bmi.com**. We highly recommend that you contact both BMI and ASCAP to ensure your compliance.

CHAPTER SEVEN

· · · · ·

Computers

Common questions when buying any computer include: What kind of computer should I get? How much RAM? How fast should the CPU be? Should I get Intel or AMD? What brand and what size monitor? What are the best accounting packages for the computer?

These are difficult questions, and today's answer will probably be out of date in a year or so. The best advice on what type of computer system to purchase for your bed-and-breakfast is, simply: Get the most powerful computer system within your budget. Here are some considerations:

- **CPU Speed.** The CPU is the engine of your computer. In general, the faster the engine, the greater its performance. Get a processor built for future capacity growth. Therefore, the fastest that your budget will allow is recommended.

- **RAM.** RAM is the temporary storage place for all information on your computer. The fastest RAM is the best to get, but nothing less than four Gigabytes (GB) on each computer.

- **Operating System.** There are several to choose from, including Chrome OS, Linux, and the most common two, Windows and Mac OS X.

- **Monitor.** You'll want to get a 17" or bigger (19" is preferred). You have lots of choices in brands and varieties.

- **Intel vs. AMD.** Both are world-class processors. There are die hard fans of each.

Computer Systems and the Hospitality Industry

Computers are integrated into every facet of most industries. And while you can run your bed-and-breakfast without one, it would be much easier with one! Computers can be used to book reservations, advertise, track sales and purchases, keep track of inventory, compare prices, maintain ledger and payroll and develop menus.

Let's take a closer look at how computer hardware and software will serve and benefit the hospitality industry, and glance at what options and features you might have.

Platform. This is essentially Windows vs. Macintosh. The choice is yours to make. Obviously, your hardware preference will select your software platform.

Point-of-Sale Systems

The most widely used technology in the food-service and hospitality industries is the touch-screen, or POS (point-of-sale), system. The POS system is basically an offshoot of the electronic cash register. Touch-screen POS systems were introduced to the hospitality industry in the mid-1980s. The touch screen is effortless. In fact, a child could be trained to use it in a few minutes.

A POS system comprises two parts: the hardware, or equipment, and the software, the computer program that runs the system. This system allows reservations people to key in their reservations as soon as the customers make them.

Some benefits of using a POS system:

- Increases sales and accounting information
- Custom tracking
- Reports occupancy usage
- Tracks credit card purchases
- Accurate addition on reservation checks
- Prevents incorrect dates from being input
- Reports possible theft of money and inventory
- Records employee timekeeping
- Reports sales forecasting
- Reduces time spent walking to front office from housekeeping, etc.

Many POS systems have been greatly enhanced to include comprehensive home-delivery, guest books, online reservations, frequent-diner modules and fully integrated systems with real-time inventory, integrated caller ID, accounting, labor scheduling, payroll, menu analysis, purchasing and receiving, cash management and reports. Up-and-coming enhancements and add-ons include improved functionality across the Internet, centralized functionality enabling "alerts" to be issued to managers, and voice-recognition POS technology.

Stand-Alone Software Applications

There are many software packages available to assist the bed-and-breakfast owner. This discussion will concentrate on current market leaders. It will provide some insight as to how they work, what they can do for your business, and what benefits you will realize if you include them in your bed-and-breakfast-management practices. These systems are what we refer to as "stand alone," as they are not part of a POS system:

For Reservations

Most software for hotel offices focus on helping owners/employee manage four areas:

- Reservations
- Rooms
- Guest accounts
- General management

These software packages can help make the reservation process streamlined, and help you keep track of your bookings so you don't overbook. They can track deposits, request deposits and record deposits made as well.

EasyInnkeeping at **www.gracesoft.com/easy-innkeeping** has reservation software specifically for bed-and-breakfasts, and they have a free download trial version. They have great pricing, excellent customer and support service, and Insight Magazine even chose them as the easiest product on the market for their particular kind of service.

iMagic (**www.imagicsoftware.biz**) also offers a reservation software package for inns called iMagic Lite. The software costs $249, and they offer a free trial version online.

Reports you can generate from this software include:

- Occupancy report
- Income summary
- Night audit
- Expected daily income
- Check in/check out
- Reservations by referral

- Birthday/Anniversary
- Group reservation report
- Financial report
- Housekeeping report
- Check out report
- Canceled reservations

In both this program and EasyInnkeeping, you can customize the room, rate and tax information. EasyInnkeeping seems to have more report-generating functions, however, and this might be the more informative software.

The **Guest Tracker** system by **RezOvation** is another choice in reservation software. It is based on Microsoft Windows operating system and provides inquiry tracking, reservation scheduling, occupancy management, guest billing and basic bookkeeping. You can get more information on this software at **www.rezovation.com**.

Another software program to investigate is **AutoClerk**® , reservation software program designed for medium to small hotel properties including bed-and-breakfasts.

They offer free upgrades, on-site training and training videos and Internet interface. You can get a customized price quote by logging onto **www.auto-clerk.com**.

Some other choices include the following software packages:

- Hotel Software Systems, Ltd. – **www.hssltd.com**
- KozyWare – **www.softwareinventors.com**
- The Innformed Manager – **www.innformed-manager.com**

Make sure you check out several software programs before purchasing since they all have different functionality and pricing.

Online Reservation Systems

An online reservation system can be incredibly simple or advanced and complex. Would you believe that a fully functional online reservation system can be free? It's true! All you need is an active website and a reservation form. Your site visitor fills out the form requesting a reservation. You set up an auto-responder to respond to the site visitor stating that they will be confirmed within a reasonable amount of time, say two hours. You receive the reservation request by email, confirm that you can accommodate the request and then reply back to the person by email or phone. Total cost: zero. Customer satisfaction: superior. That is the basic, no cost approach. There are dozens of reputable software packages and companies that can provide your online reservation system. A few of these enable you to do the following:

- Accept reservations anytime — day or night.
- Track guests' preferences in order to provide enhanced customer service.

- Use the power of direct marketing to build guest traffic and offer premium services to your most frequent customers.
- Check reservation status from any Internet-connected computer.
- Network all computers and reservation systems in a bed-and-breakfast group.
- Choose to manage all of your reservations or to put just a few of your rooms online.

A search through Google will yield dozens of software packages and consultants who can assist you to find the right one for your online reservation system.

Webervations is an online reservation system specifically designed for bed-and-breakfasts and inns. By adding one line of code to your existing website, you are able to allow potential guests to view real-time room availability. If someone wants to make a reservation, the service will either direct the guest to call your business, provide them with an online reservation request or secure credit card information immediately.

This service cost varies depending on how many rooms you offer in your bed-and-breakfast, starting with $14.03 a month for one to four rooms and going up to $67.59 a month for 50+ rooms. **Webervations** can be reached at **www.webervations.com** or 1-877-204-7245.

Availability Online is another online reservation service offering similar services. They offer a basic service at $95 a year, or premium service at $190. They can be found at **www.availabilityonline.com**, or 802-774-1124.

Room Management Software

These software packages maintain information on the rooms themselves, and while you don't have hundreds of rooms to track, you may still find this software helpful, especially if you have a larger inn and employees because it can help people access information much easier. This software can track whether or not a guest is registered in a room, the room's cleaning status and the room's rate.

This software can help you keep track of the charges for each guest, including phone and food charges. Many of the reservation software packages have this feature, such as GuestTracker from TCSHotel Software. The guest account features of this software include the ability to control and manage phone call charges, credit card processing and room billing. You can find more information on this software at **www.hotel-software.com/products_services**.

Back-Office Software

There are several other types of software you might find useful in your daily operations:

General ledger accounting. This software basically tracks accounts receivable and payable (what is owed to you and what you owe).

Financial reporting software. This software can help you develop a chart of accounts so you can create balance sheets and income statements

Inventory-control software. Again, this may be especially helpful if you run a larger B&B and have employees. It can help you track inventory so you can easier see when you are running low on certain items.

Many of these features also can be found in software packages we've already discussed. ASA Lodging Management Software, for instance, offers packages that will track accounts receivable, direct deposits, market analysis and occupancy rates.

QuickBooks is another good choice for back office software. QuickBooks is available at **www.quickbooks.com**. Another popular accounting package is Sage, available at **www.sage.com/us/sage-50-accounting**.

For the Kitchen

ChefTec. ChefTec is an integrated software program with recipe and menu costing, inventory control and nutritional analysis. More information on ChefTec is available at **www.cheftec.com**.

Recipe and Menu Costing: Store, scale and size an unlimited number of recipes. Write recipe procedures with culinary spell-checker. Instantly analyze recipe and menu costs by portion or yield. Update prices and change ingredients in every recipe with the touch of a button. Cost out bids for catering functions. Attach photos, diagrams and videos to bids, or add pictures of plate layouts to recipes for consistency.

Nutritional Analysis: Preloaded with USDA information. Add your own items. Calculate nutritional value for recipes and menus. Provide accurate, legal information on "low-fat," "low salt," etc. Print out "Nutrition Facts" labels. The nutritional-analysis module will get a quick and accurate analysis of nutritional values for up to 5,000 most-commonly used ingredients. Allows you to add your own specialty items. Calculate nutritional values for your recipes and menu items. See at a glance which menu items are low-fat, low-calorie, etc.

Inventory Control: Preloaded inventory list of 1,900 commonly used ingredients with unlimited capacity for adding additional ingredients. Import purchases from online vendors' ordering systems. Track fluctuating food costs. Compare vendor pricing. See impact of price increases on recipes. Automate ordering with par values. Use handheld devices for inventory. Generate custom reports. The inventory control module allows you to track rising food costs automatically. Compare vendor pricing at the touch of a button, from purchases or bids. Enter invoices quickly using the "Auto-Populate" feature. Generate customized reports on purchases, price variances, bids and credits. Takes the pain out of physical inventory, ordering and maintenance of par levels.

MenuPro. MenuPro allows you to quickly create your own professional menus at a fraction of the cost of print-shop menus. Whether you need "Daily Specials" or an elaborate dining room menu, MenuPro gives you quick, top-quality designs and artwork without the expense or hassle of using a graphic artist or desktop publisher. MenuPro is available at **https://softcafe.com**.

For Your Employees

Employee Schedule Partner. Another software program available is Employee Schedule Partner, a complete software package for employee scheduling. Point and click: make a schedule without touching the keyboard. Click a button and the software will fill your schedule with employees automatically. Click a button to replace absent employees, and a list of available employees with phone numbers will appear. The online coach will give helpful hints to new users. This software accommodates an unlimited number of employees and positions. You can manually override selections at any time and track employees' availability restrictions. Schedule employees to work multiple shifts per day. Track payroll and hourly schedule totals for easy budget management.

Schedules can begin on any day of the week. Track stations as well as positions. Specify maximum hours per day, days per week and shifts per day for each employee. Lock any employee into a scheduled shift so the program will not move them when juggling the schedule. Save old schedules for reference when needed. The software is even password protected to prevent unauthorized use.

Desktop Publishing Applications and Ideas

There are hundreds of reasons to own and utilize a computer in your bed-and-breakfast. The computer, if utilized effectively, will save you enormous amounts of time and money. Here are just a few ideas for desktop publishing:

Print your own customer and/or employee newsletters, table tents, menus, business cards, employee-of-the-month certificates, customer gift certificates, advertising posters, employee manuals, wine lists, catering and banquet menus and office stationery.

Here is a list of the most popular desktop publishing software programs for you computer. You can find out more about these programs at http://desktoppub.about.com/od/win.

- Adobe InDesign
- Greenstreet Publisher
- Microsoft Publisher
- QuarkXPress
- Ragtime Solo
- Serif PagePlus

Ragtime Solo and Greenstreet Publisher are good options for a small business owner because these programs cost less than some of the others.

What is the Future of Computers in the Hospitality Service?

The hospitality operation of the future will most likely resemble what it does today — with integrated software and hardware solutions to increase productivity, eliminate waste and increase profits!

The POS computers that will allow operators to more closely monitor inventory and costs, website reservations, marketing and e-commerce will increase the return on investment in a Web presence, bringing in more guests than ever imaginable. Ultimately, the bed-and-breakfast could be a paperless operation.

Proper Email Etiquette

Avoid flaming. A flame is a nasty, personal attack on somebody for something he or she has written, said or done. This applies also when replying in any form, such as when responding to customer reviews on platforms like Yelp or TripAdvisor.

Be unambiguous. If you are responding to a message, include only the relevant part of the original message. Make sure you clearly refer to the original message's contents. Always include a descriptive subject line for your message. If responding, your subject line should be the same as the original's, preceded by "RE:."

Write clearly and carefully. Your words may come back to haunt you. Read carefully what you receive to make sure that you are not misunderstanding the message. Read carefully what you send to make sure that your message will not be misunderstood. **Avoid cluttering your messages with excessive emphasis.** DO NOT USE ALL CAPS — this is perceived as yelling.

Common Email Mistakes:

- Typing the message in the subject line instead of in the body of the message.
- Forgetting that what you write, even if you think it's really funny or harmless, can be misinterpreted at the other end.
- Not signing off before leaving the computer (allowing others to send email from *your* email address).
- Not checking email often, thus missing something important.
- Forgetting your password.
- Sending a message to the wrong email address.

CHAPTER EIGHT

· · · · ·

Marketing And Marketing Literature

According to Malinda and John Anderson of the Maplevale Bed & Breakfast in Oxford, Ohio, knowing your market is very important. They suggest starting slow with everything: your website, printed materials and advertising. Never be afraid to try new things, they say, and always be flexible!

Logo

Once you have come up with a name for your bed-and-breakfast you'll want to come up with a logo. A logo should include your bed-and-breakfast's name and an image that represents your inn. Many innkeepers use a sketch, drawing or photo of the bed-and-breakfast itself. You'll need to consider the font or typeface for the lettering and colors. Because this will be such an integral piece of your marketing, don't scrimp. Look into hiring a professional to design your logo. You'll probably put the logo on every single piece of your marketing items, so you want this to look good!

Business Cards and Brochures

Long before you open, you will want to design and produce your business cards and brochures. These can be a fairly inexpensive and convenient way to market your new B&B. There are many good design programs out now so that you could try to design these by yourself. You do want to make sure these look professional though, so even if you do most of the work yourself, you may want to employ a graphic designer for artistic input.

Whether you use a designer only as a consultant or for the whole project, there are many sources for finding these artistic individuals. If you have an area college with an art program, you might try contacting the school to see if anyone is interested in bulking up his or her portfolio. Many of these students are entirely capable of producing professional designs even thought they haven't had much on-the-job experience.

There are many designers who also do freelance work. Contact one the professional design organizations such as the American Institute of Graphic Arts (AIGA) to see if they can provide you with a directory of freelancers. The AIGA can be contacted at by phone at 212-807-1990 or through their website, **www.aiga.org**. Also look at **www.sologig.com** for freelancers.

If you are designing your own business card or brochures, be sure to keep the following design principles in mind:

- Alignment
- Contrast
- Repetition
- Proximity

Contrast needs to be obvious or it might look like a mistake. For instance, you can bold all your heads in a brochure and keep all the other copy as regular text.

You can also unify a design and create contrast with repeating graphic elements. Think about using bullet lists, for example.

Alignment communicates connection between the elements of your design. When designing a business card or brochure (or any other promotional piece), think about the paper as a grid and place your elements on the grid, trying to balance them and create a pleasing design for the eye. Don't be too constricted by the grid, though; be bold and place some elements outside of it (angle a picture of your B&B on a brochure, for example) to create visual interest.

If you are designing a brochure, for instance, you may want to repeat elements to tie the brochure together. For example, you will want to use the same font for all your headers. If you have a line drawing of your inn on the front, you may want to consider repeating that image on the back of the brochure in a smaller size. Also remember that you don't have to fill up all the white space; leave your design a little breathing room.

Proximity creates a focus for your brochure or business card by creating relationships between elements. After you've designed a brochure, try the squint test. Hold the piece at about arm's length away. If all you see is gray, you need to work on proximity!

Try to use these elements in all your graphic designs. Also think about color. Two- and four-color jobs are more expensive to print, while a nice, clean black and white design might serve just as well.

A simple design for a brochure is a tri-fold or letter fold, or six-panel like below:

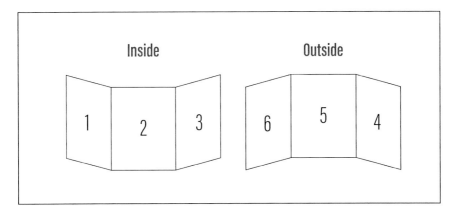

With a brochure like this, you would want to put your logo and/or a photo or line drawing of your inn on the front cover (Panel #4). Inside (Panels #1, 2 and 3) you might want to write some copy about the area or history of the house. You may also want to include photos of the rooms and a list of room amenities. On Panel #6 you could include more information on the rooms or area and on Panel #5 you could put a map with directions, your address, phone number and associations of which you are a member. You could also put this contact information on Panel #5 and save a portion Panel #6 for mailing addresses and stamps if you want to mail your brochure.

While there is less space to fill on a business card it is often more difficult to design. Because a business card is so small, you want to make sure you don't try to include too much information, and it's very important for it to be eye-catching (otherwise the person you hand your card to is just going to throw it to the back of their desk drawer with all the other business cards in there). Remember, simplicity is often best. Use an image for the focal point of your card and make sure to include pertinent information such as the B&B's name, address, phone number, website and email address. Once you get all this information on the card there is little room for anything else!

The same design principles apply to a business card for a B&B. While many people prefer the simplicity of a 1 inch by 2 inch card because it fits easily into people's card holders, others prefer a folded card because it draws people's attention and seems a little more sophisticated.

Illustrations

You will likely use a photo or original drawing of your inn for the main artwork or logo on printed materials for your business cards, brochures and other advertising pieces, but you may want to use other illustrations at times. How do you find these and what are the rules on using someone else's original material? Most prepared artwork is copyrighted and you cannot use it without permission. With art, many times you will see a copyright (©) or one of the trademark (®, ™) symbols indicating this. If you do not see one of these marks, however, it does not mean the piece is not copyrighted. You'll need to track down the person who owns the copyright and ask permission to use the piece. It's always a good idea to have this permission in writing in case of any future misunderstandings. A good place to start looking for copyright ownership is the U.S. Copyright Office at **www.copyright.gov**. The Copyright Clearance Center, Inc., (**www.copyright.com**) is also a good resource. You may be able to easily acquire permission through the service offered on this site. You can also go to the United States Patent and Trademark Office's website at **www. uspto.gov** to look for images that have been trademarked. Finally, if the image is in a published source, you can contact the publisher to inquire about permission. When acquiring permission, keep in mind that there is often a fee for usage. This fee can be as low as $10 or as high as several thousand dollars depending on the image.

There are some good free sources of images as well. Clip art are copyright-free illustrations that anyone can use. Dover Publications has a wide selection of clip art. They offer everything from books of nautical illustrations to Victorian house designs to herbs and plants. You can purchase these images at www. doverpictura.com. Other Internet sources offer free clip art as well. Check out www.clipart.com for more clip art.

A last great resource is Canva at www.canva.com. Through their site, you can design professional logos, images for social media, and basically any other visual element for your business. The best part is that Canva is completely free! (though they do offer a few copyrighted images and borders that you can buy for just a dollar and then use whatever image you can make an unlimited number of times)

If you are going to use a photo of your bed-and-breakfast, you would do well to have a professional photographer take the picture. You want the image to look professional on your literature. However, many of the new digital cameras do just as good of a job, and if you have the equipment and are inclined to try it yourself, you can get a high-quality photo just as easily.

Paper and Color

Different colors can evoke different emotions, so choose the colors for your marketing literature with careful consideration. For example, if your bed-and-breakfast is in the country, you might want to consider using a natural green for you brochure paper or business card. You could also use earth tones or reds and oranges to evoke the change of season in the country. If your house is a Painted Lady, you might want to use the color the house is painted.

There are probably thousands of choices of paper when you consider all the variables. There are colored papers, textured papers, coated papers and different paper weights. When designing a brochure or business card, you will want to use a weight heavier than regular writing paper, probably something in the 60-pound range. While coated papers are more expensive than uncoated, you might also want to consider using a coated paper because the ink does not seep into the paper when printed, and colors are much brighter and crisper since they don't bleed at the edges, as is the case with uncoated papers.

Also keep in mind that heavier paper and colored ink are more expensive than letter-weight paper and black ink. But when it comes to these key advertising pieces, you should not skimp; you want to catch potential guests' eyes and attract them to your B&B.

When it comes to printing your cards and brochures, check out local printers and compare prices. You will probably find a wide range of prices for the same service. You might find that a particular printer already has the paper or ink you want in stock from another job, so you might be able to get a discount. Even if they have a similar paper and would give you a discount, consider it; if the paper is similar enough to the one you wanted, it will not detract from the finished piece, and you could see a nice chunk of savings!

There also are many software programs you can use to design your our business cards and brochures. Here is a list of just a few and the website addresses that can give you more details about these products. Many are easy to use, professional looking, and could save you a quite a bit on printing costs!

- CAM Development – **www.camdevelopment.com**
- Avanquest Software USA – **www.avanquest.com/USA**

You can also check with your local office supply store, such as Staples or Office Depot for other software programs.

What to Do with Your Brochures and Business Cards

Now that you have all these beautiful marketing pieces, what do you do with them? Be creative when thinking about distributing your cards and brochures. Are there any local attractions that would let you drop off a stack, such as an area museum or theme park? Is there a college in the area? Check with the alumni association and office that deals with new students; they might have a way for you to get your brochures out to the public. If you're a member of the chamber of commerce or a local tourist office, try them as well. Area event planners and music venues may be other good sources.

Guidebooks

An excellent source for advertising is bed-and-breakfast guidebooks. People use these all the time when vacation planning, so it would be a big boon to your business to be listed in just one of these!

First you'll need to do some research to determine in which guidebooks you'd like to advertise your bed-and-breakfast. Here is a list of some of the national options follows:

- Bed & Breakfast and Country Inns by Deborah Edwards Sakach
- Mobil Travel Guides
- The Official Bed & Breakfast Guide and Cookbook: United States, Canada & the Caribbean (National Bed & Breakfast Association)

Check these out as well as many others by looking under "bed-and-breakfasts" on **www.amazon.com**.

As you do your research, see what types of facilities the writer includes in the guidebook. Many of these also list a website in the preface. You may be able to visit the site to get more details on their selection process. Books that are published by organizations, such as the National Bed & Breakfast Association's *The Official Bed & Breakfast Guide and Cookbook: United States, Canada & the Caribbean,* require you to be a member to be included, so look for this information in the preface or on the website as well.

For books that are written by an author for a regular press, you'll need to contact the author and show him or her why your bed-and-breakfast should be included in the book. Send the author a cover letter and your marketing literature, but remember, the authors are looking for inns that are special in some way. Do you have your own cookbook? Send a copy! Better yet, send a sample! Offer the author a free stay at your bed-and-breakfast so he or she can experience the special nature of it first hand.

Keep in mind that some authors charge inn owners a fee to be listed. Also keep in mind that it may be several months to years before the guidebook is published. The writing and publishing process can take this long.

Website

According to Joan Bradford of the Yellow Turtle Inn of New Windsor, Maryland, her best marketing tool is "the Internet, the Internet, the Internet. Did I mention the Internet?"

So, in a word, YES! You need a website!

Each day, the Internet reaches millions of people who use it for work, play and research. The Internet is the best marketing tool in the world; it allows your B&B to be visible anywhere in the world. New services, such as digital cities, RSAs, tour guidebooks and other accommodation websites will increase your website and inn visibility to levels unheard of.

A website is also important if you want to get added exposure by being a member of a bed-and-breakfast association. As a member, the association's site will provide a direct link to your site. People searching for a bed-and-breakfast often start with association sites, so this is a good way to draw new guests.

Martha of Bed-and-Breakfast at Ponder Cove was surprised by the fact that "just the right people are attracted to you through your website." She says, "Then the guests that show up fit right in and you feel you've known them forever. [It's] gratifying for you and them."

So the question begs: Do you need a website? Use the checklist of potential advantages below and see for yourself. Place a check mark next to each ability that would serve your business:

- ✔ Additional global sales and marketing tool
- ✔ Gather marketing information
- ✔ Analyze and evaluate marketing information
- ✔ Generate bookings
- ✔ Lower your phone expenses
- ✔ Improve communication
- ✔ Establish more frequent communications with customers
- ✔ Establish more meaningful communications with customers
- ✔ Reduce courier costs
- ✔ Deliver electronically encoded resources around the world

- ✔ Supplement employee training through electronic updates and bulletins
- ✔ Broadcast press releases
- ✔ Communicate to people who are not available right now
- ✔ Submit invoices and expenses more quickly
- ✔ Reduce international communications costs and improve response time
- ✔ Ease of collaboration with colleagues
- ✔ Establish contact with potential "strategic partners" worldwide
- ✔ Identify and solicit prospective employees
- ✔ Provide immediate access to your catalog
- ✔ Permit customers to place orders electronically
- ✔ Reduce costs of goods sold through reduced personnel

The Internet is everywhere. You see websites promoted in the mass media — on commercials, on billboards and in magazines. You even hear them on the radio. The Internet is the most economical way to communicate with a worldwide audience. Can you think of ANY other tool which lets you advertise or sell products to a worldwide market, 24 hours a day, for a minimal monetary investment? The possibilities are endless —t he return on investment, enormous. Here is a brief list of why you need to have a presence on the "world wide Web" (as they used to call it):

- **The World's Largest Communications Medium**
  - » The Internet provides maximum exposure and maximum potential to communicate with a worldwide audience, 24 hours a day. There are an estimated 3.2 billion people online, from nearly every country.
  - » Forty-eight percent of users use the Internet one to four times a day; thirty-nine percent use it more.
  - » One in five Internet users use their browsers more than 35 hours a week.

- **Instantaneous Access to Information**
  - » A website can be browsed at any time — day or night. Information can be downloaded, emails transmitted, supplies and services bought and sold.

- **Virtually Unlimited Potential**
  - » There are no time restraints or physical or geographical limits in cyberspace, and over 62 percent of Web users have bought something online.

- **The User Is in Control**
  - » Web users may choose where they want to "go," when they want to go there and stay for as little or as long as they choose.

- **Visual Marketing**
  - » Technology provides incredible ways to convey information about your business, products and services.

Select a Domain Name

This is a very important first step in creating a website. You should give as much thought to it as you did to naming your bed-and-breakfast. In fact, the most common and logical thing to do is name your website after your B&B. If your B&B is called Snowy Mountain B&B, your website could be **www. snowymountain.com**. Of course, you'll need to confirm that no one else is currently using this domain name. A free service that will search for domain names is **www.domainit.com**. Once you find a name that is not taken, you will need to register it. This usually involves a fee of approximately $70. This fee usually buys you rights to the name for a certain period of time (normally two years), then you will be required to pay an annual fee to keep the name registered. Make sure to take full advantage of your domain name once it is secured — put it on your letterhead, business cards and brochures.

What to Put on Your Website

Take some time to explore other B&B websites. Typically what do they contain? Most will include a picture of the outside of the inn, pictures of the rooms and rates and amenities for each room. Some may include recipes, pictures of the innkeepers or local attractions. Some, like the Myrtles Plantation in St. Francisville, Louisiana, even have pictures of their resident ghost! Make a list of what you like and don't like on these sites.

A good way to get started on what you want to put on your site is to look at your brochure. What have you included in it?

- **A picture is truly worth a thousand words.** Carefully select high-quality images and photos to truly "sell" the beauty of your inn and restaurant.

- **News, events and specials.** The opportunities are endless. Promote weekly jazz events, monthly wine dinners, holiday dining specials, or whatever events your inn may host. You may even develop web-based distribution lists from your list of customers and use email to promote the monthly and weekly events.

- **Menus.** Showcase menus with full-color photographs of each entree!

- **Directions.** Have a link to Google Maps right on your site. That way your guests can enter their address and get door-to-door directions from their home to your bed-and-breakfast.

- **Products for sale.** If you have your own cookbook or other items for sale at your bed-and-breakfast, you could sell those products over the Internet for a minimal investment and open up your sales to millions more potential customers.

- **History.** Every bed-and-breakfast has a history. Sometimes a history is truly unique — a story worth telling. Your website can do this for you. You may also choose to include a virtual walking tour through the town in which your inn is located.

- **Area attractions.** Sell your bed-and-breakfast *and* your local community to the website visitor.

The Opportunities are Endless. Be Imaginative!!

Other things to consider including on your website are:

- A layout of the house and grounds
- A room availability chart
- A neighborhood map
- Links to area attractions, such as state parks, casinos or ski resorts
- Online reservation form. Several of the reservation software programs, such as iMagic, can be linked to your website

How Do You Make an Effective Website?

The choice is entirely yours. There are thousands of website development companies throughout the world. Consider companies specializing in the hospitality industry. Gizmo Graphics Web Design of Land O' Lakes, Florida (**www.gizWebs.com**), is one of those choices. They have put together a solid, high-quality, low-cost package exclusively for bed-and-breakfasts. They offer a comprehensive cradle-to-grave cost approach, which includes all annual hosting fees, domain registrations and annual support. You should also check bed-and-breakfast association websites. They usually have a list of products and services featuring companies that specialize in work for bed-and-breakfasts.

Check out **www.blizzardinternet.com**. Blizzard Internet Marketing has tips on ways to improve your website and shows you how to put information onto your site that has the nicest overall design and functions as part of a great marketing strategy.

Some Words of Caution:

- Don't overlook the little details.

- A website can be a significant investment. Hire a professional if you want professional results.

- Keep in mind the "hidden costs." Most developers don't include website hosting, domain-name registration and renewal, support and continued development services after site completion.

- Make sure you promote your site. A site is worthless if no one knows it exists. Search engine registration is a critical part of a successful website. The favorite search engine is of course Google.com.

Web Hosting Services

Check out Web hosting services at **www.tophosts.com**. This site focuses on the top 25 hosts each month. Check with your current ISP provider to see if they will let you use some customized space (for a fee).

DIY?

Today it is possible for someone with little experience to create a website. Programs such as WordPress and DreamWeaver make it easy for non-designers and people who don't know HTML coding to create a visually pleasing W/eb page that works! Check out classes at a local community college or your local university's community classes. These courses are usually offered at reasonable rates and are often offered online. An excellent free alternative is to simply learn from the many tutorials offered by WordPress or to simply Google "how to" tutorials for whatever your specific problem and platform are.

If you do decide to create your own site, keep some basic principles in mind:

- Remember that many different people with different hardware, platforms, connection speeds and software will be accessing your site. If your main guest is a leisure traveler, you may want to limit the amount of fancy doodles on your site, such as animation, Flash and rotating images. These items take much longer to download and most of your guests will be using home computers. If you cater to a business audience, this is not as much of an issue because most business servers can handle these images. In general, you don't want load time to be longer than four seconds; otherwise the person accessing your site might get frustrated and decide not to try again.

- Keep basic design principles in mind. Keep the page simple and uncluttered. Remember to think about contrast, focus, proximity, alignment and repetition.

- Consider accessibility issues. Log on to **www.access-board.gov** for accessibility information concerning the Internet. You can also log on to **www.w3.org/wai** for a checklist of recommendations.

- There are general conventions in making a website. Make sure you follow these (such as link buttons generally run down the left side of the screen). Browse various sites on the Internet to get an idea of the unspoken conventions.

A website is an investment, not an expense. In the current marketplace, every bed-and-breakfast MUST have an Internet presence, or it is missing the boat!

Public Relations

Public relations (PR) is really the sum of its many definitions. It's the message a person, company or organization sends to the public. It's a planned effort to build positive opinions about your business through actions, and communications about those actions. In short, it's any contact your organization has with another human being, and the resulting opinion. This opinion may or may not be accurate, but it comes from everything the public reads, sees, hears and thinks about you. Effective PR has been described as becoming a positive member of your community (and getting credit for it). Basically, good PR sends a positive message to the public about your establishment.

PR should be part of your overall marketing communications program. This includes advertising, internal communications and sales promotion. Speeches, contests, promotions, personal appearances and publicity are parts of PR, but really, the results generated from all of these parts — including acquiring unpaid-for media space and time — are PR. It's who the public thinks you are and the nurturing of that opinion in a positive way.

What PR Does (and Doesn't Do) for You

If done well, PR distinguishes you from the pack in the eyes of your customers. It leaves them with a favorable impression of you and great tidbits of information to pass on to their friends about your establishment. It makes you newsworthy in a great way and can help save your reputation and standing in your community during an emergency.

Good PR improves sales by creating an environment in which people choose to spend their time and money. PR accentuates the positive and creates lasting value by highlighting what makes your establishment special. PR cannot create lasting value if none is there to begin with. What it can do is communicate existing value effectively, so it lives in your customers' minds.

Good PR can make a good story great, and a bad story less bad. But PR is not just the public's opinion of your business; it's also the physical state of your establishment. People aren't just interacting with your staff; they're interacting with your facility. If the media are reporting on something wonderful that happened at your bed-and-breakfast, but the place is in a state of disrepair, what are you communicating about your establishment?

The key to implementing an effective PR campaign is determining what your business's image is, what you want it to be and how best you can create that image in the eyes of the public. You need to clearly define your objectives and create a plan that will implement them. PR is not a way to gloss over a tarnished image or to keep the press at a safe distance; it's an organized and ongoing campaign to accentuate the positives of who you truly are.

The Marriage of PR and Marketing

Public relations is one of marketing's tools. As a result, most bed-and-break-fasts keep these two departments, or functions, close together. This is because PR is one of the crucial aspects of a successful marketing plan. In fact, in many instances, the two have been combined, and are referred to as marketing public relations, corporate public relations, relationship marketing or mega-marketing. All of these terms reflect the symbiotic relationship between PR and marketing.

On a practical level, this close relationship obtains and retains customers, which is the obvious goal of any marketing plan. When management is communicating effectively with guests, employees and community leaders, it is implementing an effective marketing plan.

Fundamentally, all marketing is integrated. Consumers don't distinguish between one message from your business and another — all the messages are yours. In that light, since it's your job to communicate as well as possible, understanding that all your marketing is integrated allows you to focus on an overall approach to building good PR.

How to Apply Your PR Plan

Once you have established the objectives of your PR campaign and integrated them into your marketing plan, it is time to execute. These questions can help you do just that:

- What's the right medium for this strategy?
- Who are the key contacts?
- How strong are the necessary personal relationships required for this plan? Do any of these relationships need to be established or reestablished?
- Is this plan thorough? Have we considered all the downside risks?
- Are we prepared to deliver a package to the media?

This delivery package is an essential part of your plan. It contains descriptions, plots, contacts, phone numbers — all the pertinent information that will inform the media and direct them to you. The press may not use one word of your materials, but there is a much greater likelihood they'll describe you the way you want them to if you've given them the resources to do just that. The following is a list of practical factors that will help you gain recognition:

- **Be honest.** The media want credible, honest material and relationships. Your message should be genuine and factual. This doesn't mean you have to reveal confidential data; it just means that your materials should be thorough and truthful.

- **Respond.** Don't lie, dodge or cover up. If you don't have every answer to a question — and you might not — don't say "no comment," or "that information is unavailable." Simply respond that you don't have that information, but will provide it as soon as possible. Then provide it as soon as possible.

- **Give the facts, and follow up.** If you supply the media with a printed handout of key facts, it greatly lessens the chances of your getting misquoted. Make a concentrated effort to follow up and go over information with the media. Again, if you don't have a requested piece of information, get it and follow up with a note and/or call to make sure the correct data reaches the media.

- **Be concise.** Usually, the media will burn you for what you say, not what you don't. Be deliberate about providing the facts without editorializing, exaggerating or pulling things out of thin air.

- **Nurture relationships.** If you follow the above steps you're on your way to building a strong and lasting relationship with the press. These relationships can sour instantly if you are reactionary, hostile, aloof, hypersensitive or argumentative in any way. No matter what you think of an interviewer, treat him or her with respect, courtesy and professionalism. Causing negative reactions from the press will deny you print space and airtime.

How you interact with the press is crucial, but it's only half the process. The content of what you communicate to them — having a clear and deliberate focus about how you are going to tell your story — is the other side of press relations. The following list will help you identify your purpose and communicate it effectively to the press:

- **Identify your purpose.** Why do you want public exposure? To what are you specifically trying to draw attention? Are you selling your inn's new lobby renovation? Then don't go on about its famous rose garden. Be sure you are conveying your purpose.

- **Identify your target.** Who are you targeting? Prospective customers? Your employees? The local business community? Civic leaders? Lay out whom you want to reach, and then determine who in the media will speak to them most effectively.

- **Think as they're thinking.** Why would this be interesting to the media? Figure out how your interests can be packaged in a way that directly matches the interests of the press. Make your story one they want to print; i.e., one that will help them sell papers, gain listeners, etc.

- **Customize your materials.** Once you have identified your purpose, who your target is and the media's angle, tailor your materials to include all three. Give the press everything they need to tell the story — photos, copy, etc. — and be sure it's in exactly the style and medium they're using.

- **Know where to send your materials.** Is your story a news story or a feature story? Do you know the difference? A news story goes to a newspaper's city desk. Feature stories go to the appropriate editor: travel, lifestyle, etc. It's a very good idea to cultivate relationships with these editors beforehand so that when the time arises, they are thinking well of you and would like to help.

- **Make their jobs easy.** Do not ask the media for the ground rules for getting press and building relationships — learn these on your own and then meet them. Spending valuable time and resources building a relationship with a reporter, only to then submit materials at the last minute or give them insufficient or inaccurate information, burns bridges quickly. Do as much of their work for them as possible; give them something that is ready to go, answers all their questions and is interesting. This is the difference between staying in the middle and rising to the top of a busy person's inbox. Also, be available immediately to answer questions. If a reporter calls and you aren't there or don't return the call immediately, your great story — prepared at considerable expense — may end up in the trash.

Building and Supporting Strong Media Relations

Media relations is one of the most important aspects of PR, because effective media relations generates publicity. Effective media relations opens the channels for your public to receive the messages you want them to receive. Media relations is how you build your relationships with the press, and this determines how they respond when you want them to report on a story.

The first goal in building strong media relations is to determine who your target media are. News media should be classified by the audiences they reach and the means they use to carry their messages. Your target media will change according to the type of message you wish to send and the type of audience you wish to reach. Your advertising agency can supply you with contact information for the newspapers, radio and television stations in your area. In addition, you may want to target national media, as well as specialized trade and business publications.

It may be a good idea to hire a part-time PR consultant, former reporter or editor who can help you present your materials to the press. If this is beyond your budgetary limits, the following is a list of essentials for building a good relationship with the press:

- **Fact sheet.** One of the most helpful items of media information, the fact sheet does most of the reporter's research for him or her. It also shortens the length of interviews by answering questions in advance. It should describe your property and what you are trying to get press for. At a glance, it tells where you are located, when you opened, your architectural style, capacity and number of employees. It should also specify the types of facilities you have and what kind of food you serve.

- **Staff biographies.** You will need to write biographies for all of your key people (which may only be you and your spouse). These list work experience, education, professional memberships, honors and awards.

- **Good photography.** Do not take chances with an amateur photographer. Space is *very* limited in the print media, and editors go through *thousands* of photographs to choose just a few. This is true even for local editors. Don't give them any reason to ignore your pictures. Have them taken by a pro. Ask for references and check them thoroughly. When the photos are done, write an explanatory caption for each picture in your collection. This gives editors an easy understanding of what they're looking at. Then, before sending photos to the media, be sure you find out how they prefer to receive photos and send them in the desired format.

- **Press kit folder.** Put all of these materials into a single folder with your property's name and logo on the cover. You might also include brochures, rate cards, package fliers, a brief on your involvement with local charities, etc. Don't overstuff it, but give the press a solid idea of what distinguishes you from the competition.

Before you begin your media campaign, you should get to know the media as much as possible. This may mean inviting them — one at a time — to have a brief tour or visit of your establishment and, perhaps, lunch. This gives them a sense of you and your business and begins to build a relationship. These visits are NOT the time to sell them on doing a story on you. It's a time for you to get to know each other and to build a relationship. If the reporters trust you, they will help you, and vice versa. They need article ideas as much as you need press, and getting to know them will give you insight into how you can help them do their job.

Once you've built this relationship, and your friends in the media trust you won't be barraging them with endless story ideas, you can begin your media campaign. It is important to remember that having a positive rapport with reporters doesn't mean they'll do a story on you. Your relationship with the reporters will help get a newsworthy story printed, but you won't get a boring story to press just because a reporter likes you. Your story needs to be newsworthy on its own. Also, reporters are always working against time. The more you can give them pertinent, accurate, concise information, the better your chances of getting their attention.

If you've built a respectful relationship with the media, reporters who get a story from an interview or news conference at your establishment will mention your place in their story. These are the "freebies" that come from developing strong relationships with the media and learning to think in their terms.

Many businesses go one step further and give their media contacts **news releases** that are written in journalistic style. A news release describes the newsworthy development in your bed-and-breakfast in a ready-to-print article. Editors can then change it or print it as is. These can be immensely valuable for getting your message out there.

If writing journalistic articles is beyond your reach or budget, **tip sheets** can be very effective in getting your story across. A tip sheet gets the message to the media by simply outlining the who, what, when, where, why and how of your story. It's basically an outline of the story the reporter will then write. Tip sheets give the spine of the story and, because they are so concise, often get more attention from busy editors.

Here are a few more tips on how to work effectively with the media:

- Earn a reputation for dealing with the facts and nothing else.
- Never ask to review a reporter's article before publication.
- Never ask after a visit or an interview if an article will appear.
- Follow up by phone to see if your fact sheet or press release has arrived, if the reporter is interested and if anything else is needed.
- Provide requested information — photos, plans, etc. — ASAP.

What's News?

Once you have identified your target media and begun your media relations program, you need to learn what makes news. To do this, pick up the paper and turn on the TV. The media is looking for the strange, volatile, controversial and unusual. It's not newsworthy that you run a nice bed-and-breakfast that provides great food at a reasonable price. It's newsworthy when a customer gets food poisoning at your bed-and-breakfast, or when a group's convention reservations get canceled. This is not the type of news you want to make, but it is news. Obviously, you want to be making great news. One of the foundations of this is taking steps to avoid negative articles — making sure your reservations system works, your staff treat guests courteously, etc.

Once you've taken these steps, you are ready to generate positive stories in the media. How? Well, what do editors find newsworthy? Here is a list of basic newsworthiness criteria:

- Is it local?
- Is it timely?
- Is it unique, unusual, strange?
- Does it involve and affect people?
- Will it provoke human emotion?

Think in terms of what it is that sets your establishment apart from the competition and what is newsworthy about those qualities. When this is done, again, target your media. When you've got a story, be smart about who would be interested in writing about it and whose audience would love to read about it. Here is a short list of possibly newsworthy ideas:

- A new manager or chef
- Visits by well-known politicians, entertainers, authors or local heroes
- Private parties, conventions or meetings of unique organizations: antique car enthusiasts, baseball card collectors, scientific organizations, etc
- Your inn's historical significance
- A new menu
- Hosting a charitable event
- Reduced rates, special menus, promotions, weekend specials
- Personal stories about the staff: the waiter who returned a doctor's medical bag, helped a patron stop choking, returned a tip that was too big, etc

PR is Different from Advertising

PR is not advertising; PR uses advertising as one of its tools. A good PR campaign is almost always coordinated with advertising, but PR is not paid-for time and space. In advertising, clients pay the media to carry a message, and the client has complete control over this message. With PR, the media receives no money. Because of this, your story about the medical dinner meeting with a noted speaker at your bed-and-breakfast may end up on the 5 o'clock news, in the paper or nowhere at all. The success of a PR story often depends on how timely it is or whether a newspaper editor feels it's worth reporting. Furthermore, only a portion of your intended message may be used. The media may not even use your inn's name. Because they are choosing to write about your topic, and you've basically given them only a potential *idea* for a story. The story could end up in a very different form than you initially presented or hoped.

Basically, with PR you have none of the control that you do with advertising in terms of the message being delivered. But when done well, PR garners positive attention for your establishment, is hugely cost-effective and is *more credible than advertising.* This is because the public is getting its information from a third party — not directly from a business. Customers assume advertising to be self-serving, but a positive message delivered by a third party to be authentic and trustworthy. Therefore, third-party messages are infinitely more persuasive than advertising.

Seeing the differences between PR and advertising, one sees differences both in guarantees of space and in the effectiveness of the different types of media. The enormous value of securing unpaid media space through your PR campaign becomes clear.

Launching a Campaign

In a small bed-and-breakfast, the owner is solely responsible for public relations.

In launching your campaign, it's important to remember that you will be competing with professionals for a very limited amount of airtime and/or editorial space. Reading newspapers and trying to determine which pieces were inspired by PR people — and what about them made editors choose them — is a good discipline. Also, many colleges offer courses in public relations. The more expertise you have, the more effective your campaign will be.

If your establishment is part of a chain, PR assistance may be available from the headquarters. If you manage an independent property, PR help may be available from your local chamber of commerce or convention/visitors' bureau. Chambers of commerce often have PR departments that will offer advice on how to launch your program.

When contacting the media, it is important to determine who will be the most useful to you. What type of customer are you seeking to attract? What's the size of your market area? Are you contacting the media who cater to those demographics? Your advertising agency can be helpful with statistical data and the interpretation of it.

Once you know who your target is, you begin building media lists. These include names of appropriate editors, reporters, news directors, assignment editors, media outlets, addresses and contact numbers. From this list, call, visit or otherwise contact the media who are crucial to your campaign. If you want to mail fact sheets, press releases, press kits, etc., you can hire a company that sells media mailing lists, and you can pay them or another firm to do your mailing for you. If that is beyond your budget, calling the editorial department of a newspaper or a newsroom will get you the contact numbers of the people you seek to reach, and you can put the mailing together yourself.

During your campaign, it's also important that you search for allies. Allies are businesses and organizations that have similar goals to yours. Your state's Tourism/Travel Promotion Office can be a great resource for this. This office is working year-round to bring business and leisure guests to your state. These, of course, are your prospective customers. Your state's travel promotion officials will be happy to give you advice on how to tie in with their advertising, PR and other promotional programs.

Most states also have a Business/Economic Development Department that will be happy to help you, since their goal is to create new business in your state. Their mailing list will keep you informed of planned promotions. When meeting with state officials, it's a good idea to volunteer to assist their promotional and PR programs. Doing this gets you "in the loop" and, often, ahead of your competition because you'll know about the programs your state is developing. Hotel and bed-and-breakfast associations can also prove to be valuable allies, since they either have PR people on staff or use national PR agencies.

There are a number of national travel industry organizations that work privately to generate travel in the United States. They couldn't be more natural allies. Locally, your chamber of commerce may organize familiarization (fam) trips to your area. These are trips for travel writers and travel agents that showcase the attributes of your area. Let the organization arranging the fam trip know that you're willing to offer free accommodations or meals to the visiting journalists and travel agents. If you are selected, make sure time is allotted for a guided tour of your property, led by your most knowledgeable manager or salesperson. Present each guest with a press kit. Also mail press kits to the agents after the tour, since most of them prefer to travel light but accumulate tons of literature and souvenirs on their trips. Making a good impression with travel agents and writers is great for you because their third-party endorsement is the best kind of advertising.

When these agents and writers do visit, make sure that your establishment is in tip-top shape. Your visitors will probably be visiting numerous other hotels and bed-and-breakfasts, and you want to stand out in every (positive) way. Only the most memorable hotels and bed-and-breakfasts will be on their "recommend" list, and you want to be one of them.

Suppliers can also be a huge ally, because the more business *you* do, the more orders you send *them* for their products or services. Airlines, tourist attractions, liquor distributors, wholesalers, etc., can all be incredible allies. They often offer attractive packages of lower room rates, food costs, car rentals, etc. Prices are usually deeply discounted to draw customers who would otherwise not use one of the packaged services. These packages are a great promotion and often garner notice from travel publications and consumer sections of newspapers eager to report a great deal. Also, airlines, car rental companies, cruise lines, etc., have PR departments that can help design and implement your PR program.

Special Events

Special events can be very effective in generating publicity and community interest. You may be opening a new property or celebrating a renovation or an anniversary. Any such occasions are opportunities to plan a special event that will support or improve your PR program. There are usually two kinds of special events: one-time and ongoing. Obviously you're not going to have a groundbreaking ceremony annually, but you might have a famous Fourth of July party every year.

The key question to ask when designing a special event is "Why?" Clearly defining your objectives before you start is crucial. Is your goal to improve community opinion of your business? To present yourself as a good employer? To show off a renovation? Once these needs have been clearly defined, a timetable and schedule of events can be made. Ample time is necessary, since contractors, inspection agencies and civil officials may be involved. If you are planning an anniversary celebration, research what events were going on in your community when you opened: Was there a huge fire? Did the President speak at the local college? Once you have this information, send it to the press. They will see your event as part of the historical landscape, as opposed to a commercial endeavor that benefits only you, and they'll appreciate your community focus.

Special events require preparation to ensure everything is ready when the spotlight of attention is turned on you. Be certain the day you have chosen does not conflict with another potentially competing event, or fall on an inappropriate holiday. With a groundbreaking or opening of a new property, you should invite the developer, architect, interior designer, civic officials — all the pertinent folks — and the media. You should prepare brief remarks and ask the architect to comment on the property. In your remarks, remind your listeners that the addition of your business does not boost school taxes or increase the need for police and fire protection; it adds new jobs and new tax revenues.

If you are celebrating an opening, tours of the property are a must and should be led by you. Refreshments should be served, and in many cases, lunch or dinner is provided. Whatever your occasion, you should provide press kits to the attending media and mail them to all media that were invited. Souvenirs are a good idea — they can be simple or elaborate, but should always be creative, fun and useful to your guests.

Communicating to Your Guests — And the Value of Loyalty

We all know first impressions last. If your guests arrive after heavy traffic or unpleasant waits, your first impression is that much more important. It's an opportunity to let them know they're welcome and that they'll be taken care of. Many bed-and-breakfasts offer a note welcoming their guests, fresh fruit or coffee — something to make them feel at home.

Obviously, how you relate to your guests affects their opinion of you. That opinion then translates into potential loyalty, and loyalty boosts your bottom line. Furthermore, it costs about five times as much to attract a new customer as it does to retain an existing one. This is another huge benefit of loyalty to your bottom line, and it comes through the overall commitment your establishment makes to its repeat customers. Focusing on your repeat customers — your most profitable clients — allows you to keep them coming back. Two things to focus on for retaining clients:

- Pay attention to your most profitable clients. Listen. Keep in touch.
- Find out what they want and need, and why they've chosen you.
- If they go to the competition, find out why.

Comment cards where guests rate your service, facilities, etc., can be a great way to find out what they think of you. You can offer discounts or promotional items for the return of these cards. If you do use a comment card, the one question that must be asked is "Would you return to stay with us again?" If you get "nos," take immediate action to determine why and then fix the situation. Another way to get feedback is to leave a guest book in each room or the common area. Ask your guests to add their comments. Most people will enjoy reading what other guests have written, and they'll enjoy adding their own feedback!

There are infinite ways for you to make your guests' stays more enjoyable and to show you appreciate them. Pamphlets describing local attractions in your community help guests plan their activities (and may entice them to extend their stay). First-aid kits, warm towels, water bottles with your logo on them — anything that makes things more convenient and enjoyable — will distinguish you from the competition. On a larger scale, whenever possible, provide upgrades; let customers know you appreciate them, inform them of services that may be useful to them and go above and beyond what they expect from you. By doing this, you not only increase the chances of their returning, you increase the chances of them telling their friends about how well they were treated. This will bring in new and, if treated well, soon-to-be-loyal customers.

Some hotels have established frequent-stay/diner plans that are similar to airline frequent flyer plans. Customers accrue "points" or "dollars" towards food, merchandise, upgrades or free rooms. Some hotels even have tie-ins with airlines that allow guests to earn frequent flyer miles through their stay. While this may not be an option for a smaller B&B, you might want to investigate it to see if it is a possibility. And while these great customer-loyalty plans may be out of reach for many smaller operations, there are many things smaller organizations can do to build loyalty. Here are a few:

- Build a database (or at least a mailing list) of your customers.
- Track purchases and behavior: food preferences, table preferences, entertainment needs, special needs.
- Constantly update your information based on interactions with your customer.
- Recognize birthdays, anniversaries and special occasions.
- Show your appreciation through holiday greetings, special discounts and other forms of recognition.
- Thank your customers for their business.
- Whenever you can, individualize your communications.
- Listen to and act on customer suggestions.
- Inform guests of new or improved services.
- Tell guests of potential inconveniences like renovations, and stress their future benefits.
- Answer every inquiry, including complaints.
- Accommodate all reasonable requests for meal substitutions, table changes, etc.
- Empower employees to solve problems.

- Talk to your customers and employees so you can let them know you're listening and find out what's going on.

This last point — the back and forth between guests and employees and you — is enormously important. Just as you need to focus on getting your message to your guests, you also need to focus on getting their messages to you. If they think their opinions are important to you, they'll think they are important to you — and they'll come back. People have more choices than ever about where to spend their money. If they know their individual needs will be met and that they'll be taken care of, their choice will be to spend it with you.

Talking to Your Community

While you could make the argument that a large portion of your business comes from out of town, it's still your local community that needs to believe in the value of your business. Bed-and-breakfasts that are not accepted by their local communities disappear. It's as simple as that. Also, you won't find a prosperous bed-and-breakfast in a depressed area. Your community and you are one and the same, and it's crucial to remember this as you design your PR program.

Bed-and-breakfasts can be considered hubs of their communities. Bed-and-breakfasts also may offer facilities for meetings, banquets, conventions and other important social/economic functions. Many decisions that affect the future of local economies take place in these facilities, so it's easy to see how and why a hotel or bed-and-breakfast can't be successful unless the local community accepts it.

So, what does that mean to the bed-and-breakfast owner? It doesn't simply mean that you should help support good causes. It means your business needs to be a leader in its community. In practice, this means building bridges between your company and your community to maintain and foster your environment in a way that benefits both you and the community. Basically, your goal is to make your immediate world a better place in which everybody can thrive. The following are a few ideas that can be part of an effective community relations program:

- Fill a community need — create something that wasn't there before.
- Remove something that causes a community problem.
- Include "have-nots" in something that usually excludes them.
- Share your space, equipment or expertise.
- Offer tutoring, or otherwise mobilize your workforce as a helping hand.
- Promote your community elsewhere.

Being a good citizen is, of course, crucial, but you also need to convince your community of the value of your business as a business. And remind your community that bed-and-breakfasts not only attract visitors from all over the country and, perhaps, the world, but most hotel income is from money earned outside your community and is spent *in* it.

These are real benefits, and they should be integrated into the message you send by being a good citizen. Designing this message is a straightforward and remarkably effective process:

- **List the things your establishment brings to the community:** jobs, taxes, well-maintained architecture, etc.
- **List what your business receives from its community:** employees, fire and police protection, trash removal, utilities, etc.
- **List your business's complaints about your community:** high taxes, air pollution, noise pollution, narrow roads, etc.

Once you have outlined these items, look for ways your business can lead the way in improving what doesn't work. As you do this, consult with your local Chamber of Commerce or Visitors' Bureau. They may be able to integrate you into existing community betterment programs aimed at your objectives.

If done well, your community relations program will create positive opinions in your community. In turn, this will cause local residents to recommend you as the place to stay when asked by tourists; will encourage people to apply for jobs; and may encourage suppliers to seek to do business with you. Also, if there is an emergency at your establishment, having a positive standing in the community will enable your property to be treated fairly.

An effective community relations program is a win-win situation because it gives you the opportunity to be a deep and abiding member of your community — improving the quality of life and opportunities around you — and, at the same time, contributes significantly to your bottom line.

Planning for the Unforeseen

Emergencies make bad news stories. Bad news stories are bad PR, and they can destroy the image you've worked so hard to build. They can wipe away years of hard-won customer relations. There are numerous kinds of emergencies — earthquakes, fires, floods, political protests, crime and more — and any of these events, if not managed properly, can destroy your public image. The law insists you have fire prevention programs and insurance, but there is no one forcing you to create a crisis–public relations program in case of emergency.

In order to meet a PR emergency, you must prepare now. If you have a strategy developed in advance, then when something bad does happen, you assure the most accurate, objective media coverage of the event. It's important that all your employees are aware of this plan and that they are reminded of it regularly. Since your employees generate a huge amount of your PR, it's crucial for them to know how to act and what to say — and not say — during a crisis. This simple detail can make all the difference in the world. Here are three basic aspects to an emergency press relations plan:

1. You should be the only spokesperson during the time of the emergency. Make sure your employees know not to talk to the press and to refer all inquiries to you. Make sure you are available at all times, day or night.

2. Know the facts of the situation before answering questions from the media.

3. Initiate contact. Once the story is out, don't wait for the media to call you. This way you will ensure that they get accurate information. Plus, the media will appreciate your forthcoming attitude, and your cooperation will reflect in their reporting.

The media will always ask the same who, what, when, where and how questions. Knowing this and being prepared to anticipate their questions, you should be able to answer accurately. If you don't know the answer to a question, don't say, "No comment." Explain why you can't comment: the police are investigating, for example, and you don't have enough information to answer now but you'll try to find the answer and get back to them. Make a point to do as promised.

In times of crisis it's crucial to put a positive slant on the news. Try to focus press attention on the diligent efforts of management to handle the emergency, or on employees whose compassion and assistance made a difference. If something happens in your establishment that is not your fault and your establishment handles it well, it's an opportunity to showcase your heart and responsiveness.

The importance of a crisis-PR plan cannot be overstated. When an employee is injured or killed in your establishment, or a guest suffers from food poisoning, the public assumes you're guilty. Whether or not you're even mildly at fault, people assume you are. Therefore, how you handle public relations during this time means the difference between a temporary loss of public support, or the permanent loss of a great deal of your business.

One always hopes that a crisis-PR plan remains unnecessary, but being prepared for the worst is the best policy. Furthermore, while the entire establishment suffers during an emergency, the owner who was caught unprepared suffers the most. Therefore, after calling the police, fire department, etc., it is the owner's job to immediately find out what happened and take corrective actions. As part of your plan, be sure to know where flashlights are in case evacuation is necessary, and you should be ready to guide guests to the nearest exits.

Next, the media must be contacted and the story disclosed, put into context and told from your side. If the media gets all the information they need from you quickly, this increases the chances of the incident appearing as one story and not showing up again. If it is difficult for reporters to gather information and they need to seek other sources, the story may be spaced out over time, which will increase people's chances of seeing it. This is obviously not what you want.

Having built strong media relations pays off during an emergency. A reporter you have a good relationship with may report an incident at a "local bed-and-breakfast," while one less acquainted with you — or downright hostile — will mention you specifically and push for the story to be on the front page. This is a crucial difference. It means that the person who will be the media liaison during an emergency should be building and nurturing good media relations now, in case anything does happen. And what have you got to lose? Strong media relations benefit you all the time.

All this is to say that if you don't guide the flow of information around your news event, somebody else will misguide it for you. With proper PR, a story that appears to the public like a bed-and-breakfast that didn't have its new computer running on time can be authentically retold to show how the bed-and-breakfast was the victim of a software glitch, that the staff heroically — and with great humor — averted what could have been a disaster. You can shift the public from viewing you as incompetent to having more faith than ever in your establishment. Public opinion depends on how effectively you manage information and how well you get your story across.

Internal Bed-and-breakfast Marketing: How to Keep Customers Coming Back

Profitability is what's going to keep you in business, obviously. How and where you focus to become and stay profitable is the key. Are you crunching numbers or are you creating an environment that leaves patrons feeling at home and eager to come back?

Customers for Life

Take care of your guests, and your sales will take care of themselves. "Customers for life" means that once guests come to your bed-and-breakfast, they'll never be satisfied with your competitors. Simple, right? It also means that the real work of building sales doesn't happen with your advertising schedule or marketing plan, but on the floor, with your customers.

Expectations

Satisfaction isn't even close to good enough. It's an improvement on dissatis-faction, of course, but in today's market, it won't keep people coming back. There is just too much competition. You need to *exceed* your guests' expecta-tions, every time. The hospitality business is built on personal connections. You serve one person at a time, and the more personal that interaction, the more you'll exceed expectations — and the happier your guests will be.

Guests expect a clean room, some kind of breakfast and a friendly, inviting atmosphere. They expect bed-and-breakfast staff to care. Do you know what your guests expect when they come through the door? Are you out to ex-ceed those expectations and give each guest a memorable and delightful stay every time?

Ways to Delight

Customers are delighted when you care — it's as simple as that. Doing things that demonstrate how much you care will make a difference. Part of the trick here, however, is that there is no trick. You've got to be sincere. People know when they're being treated with sincerity or with a mechanical technique. Sincerity works. Here is a list of practices that, when done with sincerity, can give guests a feeling of being taken care of, given real value or simply delighted. These touches may appear to guests to be extraordinary or creative — things that they never would have thought of themselves:

- **Umbrellas when it rains.** Is it possible that, given the weather pat-terns in your area, your guests could arrive without an umbrella, only to find it raining as they're leaving? Offer them umbrellas to help them get to their cars or offices. This could be a great incentive to have them come back at a later date to return the umbrella. Put your name and logo on the umbrella, and maybe it's not the worst thing if they forget to bring it back!

- **Snacks.** When someone comes to your inn, they have often traveled part, if not most, of the day. They may have spent hours in traffic or waiting for a delayed flight. They may be grumpy, hungry and tried. Having a small welcome snack prepared when guests arrive can go a long way in creating a much-needed attitude adjustment the guest will need to fully enjoy his or her stay.

- **Be available and be there when guest arrives.** People want to connect with other people when they stay at a bed-and-breakfast. They want to know who their host is and they want to be made feel welcome from the moment they arrive.

- **Books, magazines, newspapers, games, movies.** Have reading material, games and movies available in your common area.

- **Free postcards and postage.** Why not give your guests stamped postcards (depicting your bed-and-breakfast, of course) for sending their "Wish you were here" messages? It's a very low price to pay for giving your guests something they'll appreciate, and enabling them to send your advertising all over the world.

- **Email directions to guests.** Have a great, clear map on hand, and when guests ask for directions to your bed-and-breakfast, offer to email it to them. If they don't have an email, make sure you can give them clear, explicit directions over the phone. Have the directions on your website also. You don't want them frazzled when they get to you, and you certainly don't want them unable to make it at all!

- **House camera.** If guests are celebrating but forgot a camera, have an instant camera on hand, and snap a few shots for them to take home.

- **Armchairs for the elderly.** It's harder for the elderly to get in and out of their chairs. If you serve a lot of elderly customers, or even a few, have chairs with arms to make it easier for them to get in and out. Let them know you did it just for them. They will certainly appreciate it.

- **Guest book.** Make sure your guests fill in the guest book; you need a mailing list of your patrons for sending them promotional material. Try to collect birth dates and anniversaries for your database as well.

Word of Mouth

Positive word of mouth is the best advertising there is, without question, and Sherry and Darryl McKenney of Murphin Ridge Inn in Adams County, Ohio, say that if you do your job well, word will get round! Great word of mouth comes from guests having something great to talk about and sharing it effectively. Do you have a deliberate, creative and authentic plan in place to create great word of mouth? You can and should have everything to do with whether your guests have something nice to say and whether or not they're saying it.

Guests don't talk about you unless they're thinking about you. You want them thinking about you in the right way, which means you have to educate your guests on why they come to you. To do this, you must create points of difference between you and your competitors. Then people can tell their friends about why they stay at your bed-and-breakfast.

An effective word-of-mouth program has five main goals:

1. Inform and educate your patrons.
2. Make the guest a salesperson for your bed-and-breakfast.
3. Give guests reasons to return.
4. Make your service unique and personal.
5. Distinguish your business from the competition.

Tracking Your Marketing Sources

When guests call to make reservations, be sure to ask them where they heard about you. By tracking this information, you'll be able to assess the effectiveness of your marketing tools. At the end of the year you'll want to compare the cost of your advertising to the revenue you received in bookings for each source.

For example, let's say you placed an ad in a travel magazine for $300. You received reservations because of that ad for 75 rooms. Take the cost of the ad and divide by the number of bookings: $300 ÷ 75 = $4.

If you use a reservation service agency, you must remember to include the annual fee along with the percentage the agency takes for each booking.

You can track your booking sources on your reservation cards and transfer these to a spreadsheet each month. Then you will have an easy reference at year's end to look at and assess how your advertising is working. A sample spreadsheet is shown below.

	Advertisement	B&B Association	Website	Brochures at Museum Center
Jan.	0	4	10	2
Feb.	2	2	2	0
March	4	6	15	6
April	0	0	0	0
May	1	6	1	3
June	4	4	10	6
July	2	2	2	0
Aug.	4	6	15	6
Sept.	1	1	4	10
Oct.	4	8	8	1
Nov.	3	8	6	0
Dec.	2	8	7	0
TOTAL	27	55	80	34

You'll then need to track the costs of each of these. By totaling the cost compared to the number of bookings, you can determine which is your most successful and which is your cheapest form of advertising. These figures can help you decide which types of advertising are working and which ones you can fit into your budget for the coming year.

CHAPTER NINE
· · · · ·
Decorating And Renovating

Whether you've just purchased a building for your B&B or you're thinking of using your present home, it's likely you'll be doing some renovations. And you'll definitely be doing some decorating! The main selling point for bed-and-breakfast establishments is the uniqueness of the business. People who stay in B&Bs are looking for an experience other than the sterile one they receive at a hotel chain. They want something different. When you're designing your rooms, keep this in mind. Don't be afraid to have your personality showing. When getting ready to open their bed-and-breakfast in Mars Hill, North Carolina, Bed-and-Breakfast at Ponder Cove, Martha Abraham wanted their decorations to reflect their personality. "I approached the project as developing a brand and building a project," Martha said. "Everything reflects us and who we are." You also need to keep your market in mind when decorating. Bruce and Lynn Bartlett of Longwood Manor Bed & Breakfast said, "You must know your target market to decorate. Business people want less frills, more desk and task lighting; parents with children need mess-proof rooms; for example, no antiques, honeymooners need romance, etc."

Also keep your house's own character in mind as well as the character of the surrounding area. If you own a Victorian home, for example, don't furnish it in Art Deco. Take advantage of the natural features of the house. Similarly, if your bed-and-breakfast is located in an urban environment, you probably don't want to decorate it like a country inn. Brenda Guidugli's bed-and-breakfast, Christopher's Bed & Breakfast in Bellevue, Kentucky, used to be a church with stained glass windows. Brenda wanted use the colors in the stained glass in her decorating scheme, so she focused on three of them (burgundy, hunter green and beige) and incorporated these colors into her design.

Renovations

Before you begin decorating, you'll need to assess whether or not major renovations are needed to open your business. If you plan to rent a couple of rooms out of your family home, do you have enough bathroom space? You may need to consider adding a new bathroom for your guest rooms. Do the rooms have closet space? Your guests will expect some sort of space for their belongings, so you may want to consider adding a closet or two as well.

Next, and certainly before signing any contracts with contractors, check with city/town officials to make sure there aren't any regulations that could stop you from remodeling!

While you can look at the general structure of your house and say, "I think I want to add a bathroom," or "Some more lighting in that hallway would be nice," before you get too far into the aesthetics, get a professional's opinion. If you've just bought a building, you've had a whole house inspection. If you are renovating a piece of property you already own, go ahead and get a whole house inspection — they generally cost $200–$300 and are well worth it. The inspector can tell you if the electric looks up to code or if the foundation needs reinforcement — things that may not be obvious to you but are important to the safety and structure of your building.

With the inspection in hand, you can begin to make some decisions on the types of renovations you want to make. Odds are before you open, you won't be able to make all the renovations you want simply because of cost. Make a priority list based on cost, convenience and need. You probably want to get that electric updated before you start booking guests due to the safety hazard. Likewise, it would be a nightmare to refinish those hardware floors once you have furniture and guests lying about the house!

On the other hand, replacing that bathroom door can probably wait; you can just put a fresh coat of paint on it for now.

Use a list like the following to help prioritize your renovations.

Safety	Structural	Decorative
Update electric	Add third bathroom	Carpet upstairs hall
Fix broken steps	Knock wall out of kitchen to expand	Paint
Add hand railing to steps in back	Add closets to three guest rooms	Wallpaper common room
Replace furnace	Replace windows	Replace bathroom mirrors
		Re-do front flower garden

Obviously you will want to take care of any safety issues and large structural repairs or renovations before your guests start arriving, but spend some time prioritizing so you don't break the bank in the first year. Some of those renovations can wait.

Furnishing and Decorating Your Rooms

For many inn owners, this is the fun part — deciding how to decorate your inn! Customers seek out bed-and-breakfasts for their unique style. Your task is to decorate your inn in a way that lets your personality and interests show through and appeals to your clientele. According to YRB Marketing's "United States B&B/Inn Guest Study" (conducted in conjunction with PAII), 80 percent of bed-and-breakfast guests are married, 75.9 percent of them make over $50,000 per year, and 66 percent are employed in professional, administrative, executive or sales positions. In essence, the B&B guest is fairly affluent and well educated.

If you feel you need some help but don't have the funds to hire a consultant, there are some online resources that may be helpful. iVillage at **www.ivillage. ca** and About.com at **www.about.com** both have a wide variety of articles on design. About.com has advice on easy but effective DIY techniques like how to make small rooms appear larger. HGTV.com is yet another website packed with information for decorators and remodelers.

Before you get started, make sure to sketch out your plans so you don't get surprised when it's too late. Make a sketch of the room and draw in the windows, doors and furniture placement. Once you get a pretty good idea of the layout you want, get out your tape measure and make a drawing that is to scale on a piece of graph paper. Make sure you measure door openings because you'll want to make sure that armoire really can fit through the doorway! Also be sure you include symbols for electrical outlets, switches, fixtures, door swings, windows, skylights and any heating ducts or returns. These will help you figure out where to put furniture.

You may want to look into some inexpensive software to make your scaled drawing. Check online or even your local office supplies store to see what packages are available.

Decorating Styles

There are many different decorating styles, but the main ones are formal, casual, contemporary and traditional. Styles such as Colonial fall within these larger categories.

Formal (French, English). Many older, more historic homes use formal decorating styles. Formal rooms are very symmetrical, often having furniture arranged in straight lines. You will also see a lot of different patterns for fabrics and wallpapers with formal design and rich, dark woods with heavy accessories, such as brass doorknobs on wooden doors. Furniture pieces and window treatments are usually elaborate. The furniture may have carved wooden legs and windows may have tassels and multiple layers including blinds, sheers and/or valences. Formal rooms may be decorated with antiques, Oriental rugs and oil paintings.

Traditional (Colonial, Early American). Like formal rooms, rooms decorated in a traditional style are orderly. Traditional style, however, tends to be more casual than formal styles.

Traditional rooms include upholstered furniture, muted or floral fabrics and colors that tend to be dark, but not as dark and austere as those used in a formal room. The colors and general ambiance of a traditional room are understated. It is less "proper" and more homey than a formal room. Furniture tends to be arranged on a straight line and wood is used extensively, but usually darker woods are mixed with lighter woods in a traditional room.

Contemporary (Art Deco, Eclectic). The contemporary style features clean lines and bold colors. Contemporary rooms make use of less accessories than traditional or formal rooms, and colors tend to be brighter. Contemporary design often makes use of black and red as well.

Casual (Western American, American Country, French Country). Casual styles are comfortable and inviting. These rooms tend to not focus on symmetry or formal elements. They often have upholstered furniture pieces, furniture that is picked more for comfort than style, neutral colors, light wood furniture, layered window treatments without elaborate details and homey accents such as pottery, quilts and collectibles.

Once you have established a decorating style, you will want to choose furniture that fits this style. Ashley Furniture Homestore has a furniture decorating glossary on their website at **www.ashleyfurniturehomestore.com/en/ glossary**. This glossary will help you understand the differences between Art Deco and Art Nouveau, and it provides descriptions of popular furniture lines, such as Chippendale.

Creating Themes

Many bed-and-breakfasts create theme rooms centered around the owners' interest, the history of the property or simply as a way to keep track of the rooms. The Symphony Hotel located beside Music Hall in Cincinnati, Ohio, for example, named their rooms after famous composers (Beethoven, Bach, Mozart and Schubert).

If your bed-and-breakfast is located in Florida, you might want to pick a tropical theme for decorating your guest rooms. If you are in New England, perhaps you'd like to consider Early American.

Even your favorite color could be used as a decorating scheme. If you love green, you may want to use this as your dominate color for your inn's decoration.

Bedrooms

The bedrooms will be the most important rooms you furnish and decorate because this is where your guest will spend the majority of their time. A good piece of advice before decorating is to sleep in your guest rooms. Is the bed comfortable? Are there enough covers? Does the light from the bathroom stream into your eyes when you hop into bed? Is the floor cold? It's much better to find these things out and correct them prior to your guests arriving!

One of the first decisions you'll need to make in the bedrooms is choosing a color. You may choose to paint the walls or wallpaper, but you'll still need to choose a primary color and complementary colors for the room. There is no one right color for the bedroom, but different colors evoke different responses. Blue, for example, creates a calm, peaceful reaction and is often a good bedroom choice since people generally want to relax in their guest rooms. Green is also a calming color. Yellow is a cheerful color, making people think of sun and flowers, but you should be careful not to overuse it because our eyes have a difficult time taking in a great deal of yellow. Purple connotes luxury, royalty and romance. Brown and other earth tones are good decorating choices, especially if your bed-and-breakfast is in a rural area; these tones will suggest the natural colors surrounding your guests in their environment. Red is not often selected for a bedroom color; it is emotionally intense and can be rather distracting. Most decorators suggest using red as an accent color. White is a good neutral color. It suggests cleanliness and its light hue is optimistic. It can be rather troublesome, however, since it shows dirt so easily.

Try decorating with complementary colors — those opposite to each other on the color wheel, such as red and green, yellow and violet, and blue and orange. You see these schemes used everywhere; red and green are Christmas colors, and the combination of blue and yellow often calls up Mediterranean images.

Mattresses

The bed is the most important component of the bedroom, of course. Don't skimp when it comes to this area — you want to be sure to buy quality mattresses for your guest rooms.

Most people agree that a firm mattress is the best, but "firm" is a subjective term and many different people with different body types will be sleeping on your mattresses, so how do you pick a good one?

You should also pay attention to the length of mattresses. You'll want your beds to comfortably accommodate someone over 6-feet tall as well as someone who is shorter. You may run into problems with this if you are furnishing with antiques since, in general, people have gotten taller over the years and many beds from the 18th and 19th century will not accommodate someone with a 6-foot frame. When measuring for length, make sure you have at least 6 extra inches from your feet to the end of the bed and a few inches between your head and the headboard. Typical mattress sizes are 75 or 80 inches for a full-size mattress, 80 inches for queens and 80 to 84 inches for king-sized mattresses.

When you go mattress shopping, consider taking a few friends or family members to get several opinions on mattresses.

After you have bought the mattress, make sure you take care of it. While B&B mattresses will have more wear and tear than your own, a good mattress should last about 10 years. Make sure to turn it periodically (about every three months) to keep it from settling in spots, and buy mattress pads to protect them from stains.

There are over 30 brands of mattresses you can choose from, including the well-known names of Serta and Seely. Mattresses range from 9–18 inches in depth usually. If you buy something thicker, keep in mind that you will also need to buy deep-pocket sheets.

When shopping for mattresses, look for the following features:

Feature
Definition
Characteristics

Ticking
The outer layer of the mattress.
Usually a polyester or cotton-polyester blend (low-end mattresses may use vinyl; higher end may use damask).

Quilting
Attaches padding to ticking
Want uniform and unbroken stitches.
Top padding usually polyurethane foam, may have a polyester batting.

Middle padding
Located below the quilted layer.
Usually starts with foam; convoluted foam (the kind shaped like an egg carton) feels softer than straight foam.
Other padding may consist of garneted cotton (thick wads of rough batting that provide loft but compress quickly).

Insulation padding

Lies directly on the springs.

Common insulators are coco pad (the fibrous material from a coconut husk) and shoddy pad (pieces of fabric matted and glued together).

Mattresses may also contain elastic webbing, non-woven fabric or a metal grid directly on top of the springs to help keep them from destroying the pad.

Extra support

Added to specific area of a mattress, such as the edges.

Extra support is usually achieved by spacing the coils closer together, inserting thick pieces of stiff foam between the coils, using thicker wire, or inserting extra springs.

Coils

The mattress's springs.

These come in various thicknesses, or gauges. Usually the lower the gauge number, the thicker and stiffer the wire and the firmer the mattress.

Handles

Attached to the sides of mattresses so they can be moved easily.

The best handles are those that go through the sides of the mattress and are anchored to the springs. Fabric handles may be sewn vertically to the tape edging of the mattress. Most common type of handle are those inserted through the fabric and clipped to a plastic or metal strip.

Box springs

May be plain-covered wooden frame with springs, or a metal frame with springs. (A wood frame should be straight and free of cracks.) Using a wood frame may make the mattress feel firmer or harder.

When choosing a mattress, keep in mind that a firmer mattress won't prevent sagging and a thicker mattress will actually sag more because sagging occurs within the padding.

A good mattress will probably cost $450 for a twin, $660 for a full size, $800 for a queen size and $1,000 for a king size. Also, keep in mind that if you only buy the mattress (and not the mattress and box springs), you may void your warranty.

For more help on selecting a mattress, visit **www.howtobuyamattress.com**.

Bed Linens

Sheets come in all cotton and cotton-polyester blends, but the blends tend to be easier to care for. They are less prone to wrinkling and shrinking. Typical prices for sheets are $20 to $150 for blends, and $40 to $250 for all cotton (these prices are for a queen-size bed).

Thread Count. This refers to the number of lengthwise and crosswise yarns or threads in a square inch; it is seen as an indicator of quality. The higher the thread count, the tighter the weave and the better the quality. The higher thread counts also have a softer feel and are priced higher than other sheets. For a high-quality sheet, look for 180–200 threads per inch count.

Muslin has the lowest thread count at around 130, and the lowest price. It can be scratchy, however, and is not widely used. Percale is seen much more frequently. It is a cotton or cotton-poly blend with a thread count from 180 to 200. Sateen sheets (these are usually all cotton and are not related to satin sheets) start at about 230 and can climb to more than 300.

In general, a good cotton or cotton-poly blend is probably the sturdiest option, and their appearance is fine after washing (especially if you immediately take cotton sheets out of the dryer when they are done). The owner of Bed-and-Breakfast at Ponder Cove, Martha Abraham, says she started with 100 percent cotton sheets that had a 400 thread count. Tired of ironing, and seeing that this quality of sheet did not seem to matter to her guests, Martha switched to a 60/40 cotton-polyester blend and no one has said anything except how comfortable her mattresses are!

Pillows and Blankets

Pillows are almost as important as mattresses. You can find pillows that are down, synthetic or a down/feather combination. It's best to buy pillows you can see and test. Make sure to squeeze the pillows you are looking at — push the ends toward the center. If the pillow retains its shape, it's a good choice. Be sure to supply two pillows per guest. And if you opt for down or feather, keep a few synthetic ones in storage in case one of your guests has an allergy.

Many hosts, especially those in more northern climates, like to provide their guests with down coverings. Down, a natural insulator, is the coating clustered beneath the feathers of waterfowl that protect them from the elements. Most down products come from geese and ducks. Check out **www.downlite.com**, Down Lite, for down bed covering information and sales. This website provides a resource for purchasing down and feather bed coverings as well as a tutorial on down products. You may also want to look into cotton comforters (you should at least have some on hand for those guests with allergies) and quilts.

Other Furniture

While the bed is the most important piece of furniture in your guest rooms, don't forget the other pieces as well. Each room should have some sort of dresser or drawer space for guests to use for their belongings. You might want to include a nice, comfy chair and a chair and writing desk as well (especially if you get a good number of business travelers). A night table by the bed is essential and a luggage rack for suitcases is a nice touch.

Wall Coverings

Paint

Today there are many paints on the market besides the usual latexes. If you are using a traditional paint, however, you will need to decide what type of finish you want. The most popular finishes are a flat, semi-gloss or gloss. Usually gloss paints are reserved for kitchens and bathrooms, and flat paints are used in bedrooms and living areas.

There are what are called faux finishes that can give a result looking antique. You can also get different finishes by using different techniques such as sponging, rag rolling and stippling. Many hardware stores, such as Home Depot, offer free classes in painting techniques. Also check out DoItYourself.com (**www. doityourself.com**). Sherwin Williams also offers online advice on painting techniques and faux finishes at **www.sherwin-williams.com/homeowners**.

Wallpaper

Wallpaper may be particularly good if you have plaster walls that aren't in very good shape. Wallpapering can be a lot cheaper than having someone come in to beautify those walls! Check out the options at your local wallpaper distributor or hardware store. There are thousands of wallpapers from which to choose and many online distributors as well:

- Wallpaper Direct – **www.wallpaperdirect.com/us**
- Sherwin Williams Online Wallpaper Store – **www.swdecorating.com**
- American Blinds and Wallpaper – **www.americanblinds.com**

Stencils

Stenciling can give your walls a custom look. Many craft stores and hardware stores sell pre-cut stencils you can use. You can find many tutorial books to help you on Amazon.com.

Floor Coverings

There are a variety of types of floor coverings from which to choose for your bed-and-breakfast. The options for floors in general include wood, carpet and vinyl, but you will probably choose between wood and carpet. Both of these have their advantages. With wall-to-wall carpet, a smaller room can seem larger, and carpet gives a room a feeling of warmth. You can find carpet of various material and prices; they range from a low-cost synthetic to more costly wools. Durability and ease of cleaning tend to vary greatly in carpeting, so make sure to do your research!

Wood floors can be made of solid wood or a synthetic (such as Pergo). If you want wood floors but the original floors are in bad shape, you may want to consider installing a synthetic over the existing floor. This will probably be cheaper; it will definitely be less of a mess, and most people do not seem to have a problem with allergies with synthetic wood floors. If you decide to refinish your original wood, be sure to do it when you can close the inn because it is a very dusty process! Even so, if you get your floors refinished, you will be delighted with the end result!

If you have wood floors that are in so-so condition, you might decide to keep them as is and use area rugs on top. Not only do these rugs hide flaws in the floor, but they create warmth and add color to the room. Make sure that if you use area rugs, you put nonskid padding underneath to eliminate any slippage or falling problems.

If you have hard wood floors, you'll want to be sure to have area rugs at the side of all your beds. No one wants to get up on a frosty morning and hit a cold surface with their bare feet!

Window Coverings

Make sure you keep your windows in good repair, and that they all have screens in warm weather and storm windows in cold weather. You'll also want to take careful consideration of window treatments. While you might not want to block a beautiful view, you should keep in mind that some people are very uncomfortable undressing in front of an uncovered window. Some people also find it very difficult to sleep with early morning sunlight streaming into their face from an uncovered window. Try to install window coverings that give your guests a choice. If it's afternoon and they want to see the view, make the treatment easy to open, but also make sure they can shut out the world when they are craving privacy.

The Bathroom

The bathroom is the second most important room in your B&B. Make sure bathrooms are always sparkling clean and all plumbing fixtures are in good working order. If you are converting a current residence into a bed-and-breakfast, you may want to think about installing a secondary water heater. If you currently have a residential one, it probably will not produce enough hot water to be sure you, your family and all your guests have enough hot water for showers in the mornings!

Here is a list of items you should be sure your guests can find in their bathrooms:

- A mirror
- Counter space
- A place for toothbrushes
- Bath rug with a nonskid backing
- Towels (hand and bath)
- Washcloths
- Soap (liquid and/or individually wrapped bars)
- Small bottles of shampoo and lotion
- Deodorizer
- Facial tissues
- Extra bathroom tissue
- Hooks for robes and/or towels
- Wastebasket
- Grounded electrical outlet for hair dryers, etc.
- Towel racks
- Water glasses
- Fresh sponge and cleaning supplies

Also be sure your bathrooms have adequate ventilation and locks on the doors for privacy — this is especially critical if you have shared baths.

CHAPTER TEN

· · · · ·

Guest Services And Policies

There are innumerable services you could offer your guests. You'll need to take a hard look at your B&B, your competition, costs for services in the area in which you are located and your own interests to determine which ones you will offer. The extra services can be as simple as a warming rack for towels or as extravagant as in-room gas fireplaces with remote controls!

Expected Services

When people stay at a bed-and-breakfast, there are certain services they expect. These services should just be a matter of course and include:

- Comfortable bed with clean linens.
- A clean room and bathroom with adequate supplies of soap, towels, blankets, pillows, toilet tissue, facial tissue, etc.
- A breakfast to be included with the room rate.
- The ability to access the B&B owner for information and emergencies.

When considering what services to offer your guests and the prices to charge, check the local competition. If you are offering rooms with the bare minimum for $75 and your next-door neighbor is offering rooms with hot tubs for $85 a night, you need to rethink your offerings and/or your room rates!

You may want to upgrade your regular necessities, such as getting better quality towels and sheets and provide your guests with items such as small bottles of shampoo, hair dryers and ironing boards. Other simple services you could offer are clock radios in the rooms, TVs in the rooms or in the common area, a DVD player and small refrigerators.

Here is a list of just a few of the many amenities you may wish to offer:

- Snack or goodie basket in rooms
- Complimentary bottled water
- Toothbrushes
- Turndown service
- Complimentary champagne for weddings and anniversaries
- Bicycles
- Wireless Internet
- Fax service
- Tours of the area
- Hot tub/Jacuzzi
- In-room fireplaces
- Laundry service
- Reservation service (making dinner or theater reservations, etc.)
- Kitchen privileges
- Afternoon tea
- Fresh flowers
- Robes
- Warming racks for towels
- Recreational equipment such as badminton set, golf clubs, binoculars, etc.
- Literature about area restaurants and attractions
- In-room phones

Many of these items you would want to just include in the room price, such as for a hot tub or in-room phone, but others you might want to price separately.

For example, if you are going to loan out your golf clubs, you probably would want to charge guests a fee.

Breakfast in Bed

If your bed-and-breakfast caters to couples — people looking for romantic get-aways or a special place to celebrate an anniversary — breakfast in bed may be a good amenity to offer. If you offer this, be sure not to make it too elaborate or you may do yourself a disservice! Remember, while your guests are tucked in bed enjoying their meal, you'll still be serving the rest of your guests in the main dining area. Do something simple but elegant. For instance, you could serve homemade muffins, jam, coffee, juice and fresh fruit. Use a carafe for the coffee so it stays warm. And don't forget those extra touches such as doilies and a bud vase with a fresh flower.

Turndown Service

Another elegant service that won't cost much is turndown service. This service is designed to give your guests a relaxing atmosphere to return to from their adventures of the day. Basically you go into the guest room and tidy up (emptying the garbage, replacing towels, etc.) while the guests are out. You will also want to make the bed (if the guests have been staying a few days), straightening and replacing pillows and throw pillows and turn back the sheets. Finally, place a treat on the guests' pillows such as a piece of wrapped chocolate (don't choose an item that will leave crumbs in the guests' beds). If there's a fireplace and it's winter, you might want to start a fire, or a fan if it's summer, then turn the lighting to a low level.

Business Services

If many of your guests are business travelers, it's a good idea to offer them some conveniences:

Fax. You don't have to put one in every room, but have one available in the common area or your office and let them know they are welcome to use it. If the machine is in your office, it may be more convenient for you and allow you to control how much it is used as well. If you find that it becomes a major expense for you, you might to consider charging guests a fee for the use.

Internet access. If most of your business is from business travelers, you really need to investigate providing Internet service. Business people usually travel with their laptop computers, and to check their office email and access documents, they will need to be able to get online. This won't be a cheap amenity to offer, so make sure to do your research. Check into the variety of ways your can offer this service nowadays and see what option fits your needs and budget. If you're going for a more holistic, woodsy get-away kind of feel with your business, you may not have to worry about this, but you need to be 100 percent sure before making that decision since almost all hotels and B&Bs offer free Wifi.

Printer. While business people do travel with their laptops, they don't normally have a printer. Offer your guests the use of your printer. If it's for small documents, such as a letter, don't worry about charging extra. If someone needs to print a large document, however, you might want to charge a per-page rate. After all, you are supplying the ink and paper.

Shipping services. Many business travelers need to ship packages while they are on the road. Keep a supply of UPS and FedEx boxes and labels for your guests' convenience. You can also offer to call to arrange for the package pickup or offer to drop the box in the nearest drop-off location.

Ghosts

While a ghost may not exactly be considered an amenity by many, people who stay in bed-and-breakfasts want atmosphere. And what could be more atmospheric than a ghost? You can find information about bed-and-breakfasts with ghosts at About.com's website **http://bandb.about.com/od/haunted**. Here are a few B&Bs that advertise this special amenity:

- The Lizzie Borden Bed & Breakfast in Fall River, Massachusetts, advertises the fact that their B&B is the where Lizzie Borden murdered her parents with an axe in 1892.

- The Historic Cashtown Inn in Cashtown, Pennsylvania, where the ghost of a Confederate soldier has been sighted.

- The Myrtles Plantation in St. Francisville, Louisiana. The 1796 plantation advertises itself as "one of the most haunted homes in America." Guests have reported various ectoplasmic sightings over the years, and the B&B's website carries photos of the ghosts that previous guests have sent them.

Judy of the Prospect Hill B&B Inn in Mountain City, Tennessee, inherited a ghost when they opened their bed-and-breakfast. "Our ghost seems to be a 'renovator ghost.' We think the person connected was Stacy Rambo, the man who bought the inn for his wife and son in 1910. He proceeded to add electricity, plumbing and a furnace, not to mention some steel under some walls. What I have heard of him are footsteps up and down the upstairs hall and up and down the grand staircase. He mostly comes out and I hear him at night or in early morning —when we are doing renovations. One guest had a man touch him on the shoulder. The guest sat upright and turned on the lights. He was in the room Stacy's son used as his office. All in all we are pleased to have Stacy around. We define ourselves as renovators too."

Check-In/Check-Out

This is one of the most critical times for you as a host. You want to be sure to be there and to make your guests feel welcome when they arrive. This is part of the charm of staying at a B&B! One of the best ways to ensure you'll be there when guests arrive is to ask when they are making reservations. In addition, most B&Bs, like traditional hotels, have check-in and check out-times. The most common is 11 a.m. for check-out, and 3 p.m. for check-in. You may want to make this a range of time and plan your other activities that take you away from the premises around this schedule. You could, for instance, advertise check-in as between 3 p.m. and 6 p.m., and check-out by 11 a.m. Keep your cleaning and cooking schedules in mind when arranging these hours, however. If you don't have help, you don't want to be up to your elbow in toilet cleaner when a guest is trying to check out to catch a plane!

When guests arrive, be sure to greet them with a warm smile and friendly demeanor. Remember, they have been traveling, so they may not be in the best frame of mind. Try to get them through the check-in process quickly if they seem tired, and suggest that they go freshen up while you pour them a glass of wine and fix a snack for them to have by the fire in the living room. If the guest seems ready to go, see if they'd like to take a tour of the premises. While you're showing them around, you also can talk about area attractions, find out about their interests and let them know what breakfast will be the next morning.

If you can't be at the house when your guests arrive, be sure to have a plan. See if your neighbor or a relative can come over to check in the guest. If nothing else, be sure to leave a note with instructions so the guest knows what is going on. You may want to leave some cookies in their room in case they are hungry. Be sure to let them know when to expect you and check in with them when you arrive. If guests are arriving at night, leave lights on! There's nothing more uninviting than walking up to a dark, strange house.

Make sure to communicate your check-in and check-out policy to your guests when they are making reservations. You will also want to include this information on your website and advertising literature. Also be sure to make your check-in time a few hours later than your check out time so you have time to clean the rooms and get them ready for the next guests.

You'll also need to decide if you want to take care of the balance of the payment due upon check-in. Some hosts prefer not to start off their guest/host relationship with a demand for payment. And while this does set a much friendlier tone, you may not want to put off this task until someone checks out. Often guests are very hurried when checking out. They might forget they owe you money and rush off, or they may get annoyed with you for waiting until the last minute to deal with this when they are trying to catch a plane. There may be other ways to take care of collecting the balance due on a room. You could put a reminder in the room with a plate of cookies. Or as your guests are ambling back from an afternoon walk, you might ask, "Would you like to take care of the balance on the room? That way you won't need to worry about it when you check out tomorrow — I know you have to catch an early flight."

When guests arrive, you will want to do your best to make them feel at home. Be sure to be home to greet your guests when they arrive and greet them with a smile and warm attitude. Remember, this attitude is part of the reason they chose to stay in a bed-and-breakfast in the first place. Offer to help the new arrivals with their luggage and get them checked in and settled. Depending on your guest's personality and travel schedule, he or she may want to take a few minutes to freshen up — or they may want to take a few hours to nap! Whatever the case, make sure to offer them a tour and orientation whenever they are ready. While you are showing them your facilities, you can also talk about some of the amenities you offer and some of the policies or house rules. Make sure you include information on breakfast menus and times during the tour as well. As you leave them to enjoy their stay, make sure to tell your guests you'd be happy to answer any questions they have during their stay and let them know how to find you if they should need anything.

It's more difficult to be around when guests are checking out, but do try to find an opportunity to say good-bye to your guests and let them know you hope they enjoyed their stay. This opportunity might come at breakfast, or it just may be a quick thank you as they are carting off their bags. You may also need to remind guests to leave their keys if you issued any.

Safety

Your guests' safety should be one of your first priorities. States and localities have widely varying rules and regulations concerning bed-and-breakfasts; make sure you understand the rules in your particular area and you follow them to the letter. If you don't have any regulations for B&Bs in your area, it would be a smart idea to get information on the state regulations for hotels, motels and bed-and-breakfasts. You can then use these as guidelines for your own safety plan. You can find safety training materials for the hospitality industry on The Training Network's website at **www.safetytrainingnetwork.com**.

Fire

Talk with your local fire department to get their regulations and recommendations. It's wise to install fire alarms (along with carbon monoxide alarms) and to have fire extinguishers in several areas of the house. There are four types of fire extinguishers: dry chemical, halon, water and carbon dioxide. The type of extinguisher you should use depends on the class of fire. Fire extinguishers are labeled for Class A (ordinary combustibles), B (flammable liquids) and C (electrical equipment) fires. Rather than using the letters, most fire extinguishers today have graphic images displaying the classes of fire for which they should be used. Also be sure to get your fire extinguishers serviced once a year, and it's not a bad idea to receive some training on using an extinguisher. Check with your local fire department; they will often offer training sessions as a community service. Make sure you get multipurpose extinguishers.

Also be sure to have emergency numbers placed at all phone extensions and be sure to post evacuation exits on the back of each guest room door and change your fire alarm batteries once every six months. According to most states' fire codes for bed-and-breakfasts, you must have two ways to get out. For rooms on the second floor you may want to provide fire ladders. Make sure to check your state's fire codes.

Also be sure to have fireplaces inspected periodically, and you may want to consider making your B&B a nonsmoking house.

Depending on the state you live in, your bed-and-breakfast may be required to go through a fire inspection as well. In Ohio, for example, all bed-and-breakfasts with five or more bedrooms are subject to inspections by the state fire marshal's office.

You can find information on fire statistics on the National Fire Protection Association website at **www.nfpa.org**. You can also buy the section of the report "U.S. Fire Problem Overview: Leading Causes and Other Patterns and Trends" that refers to hotel and motels for $15 (free to NFPA members). This report covers cause profiles, trends and fire protection information for particular property classes.

Accidents

As we all know, accidents can happen anywhere, anytime. Do your best to protect your guests from these vacation ruiners. There are several things you can do to decrease the chance of accidents. For example, make sure you have nonskid backing on any area or bathroom rug. Be sure electrical outlets are grounded and keep walkways and hallways free of clutter. In the winter, be sure to shovel and salt walks and steps, and provide good outdoor lighting and rails around balconies and along steps. Also be sure to have good lighting inside the house. It might not be a bad idea to have night lights; many people get disoriented waking up in a strange place, and a well-placed night light may be the only thing between your guest and a bump on the head!

Security

You'll also want to make sure you have good locks on all windows and doors. You might want to consider a security system as well. Keep in mind, however, that a late-arriving guest might accidentally trip the system. Have a policy about when doors will be locked for the night or provide your guests with their own keys so you don't have to leave doors unlocked for guests who might want to stay out late. If you do give guests keys, take the extra precaution of getting the keys stamped "Do Not Duplicate." If someone did try to copy your key, it is unlikely a reputable locksmith would duplicate one with this stamp.

Children

Children create their own noise, but luckily this is something you may be able to control. If you have children, you'll want to be sure they know the rules. Kids are kids and they are going to make noise, but you may want to enforce a quiet-time policy. Be upfront when you are booking rooms as well. Some guests will love having children around while others would prefer to stay at an inn without them.

Should you accept guests who travel with children? Again, this is something you'll have to decide. Your own personality, your inn's target audience and the ambiance of your inn will help you determine if you should accept children as bed-and-breakfast guests.

If you have a lot of very expensive antiques, children may not be a good match for your house. On the other hand, you might have a lovely backyard with a swing set that children would adore.

When hosting children, make sure you have items to accommodate children such as booster seats, high chairs, cribs and baby gates for stairs. Also be sure to have toys children might enjoy, such as games, crayons and coloring books. It's also a good idea to have "kid-friendly" food in the kitchen such as cereal and toast with peanut butter for breakfast and pizza or hamburgers for the kids if you serve dinner.

Make sure you also let parents traveling with children know about quiet hours at the inn so the children don't disturb other guests when they are trying to sleep.

Pets

If your Australian Shepherd, Bongo, barks at everything, you might have a more significant problem. Perhaps some training would fix this. Be sure to take any pets you own into consideration before opening your B&B — you'll need to think about the disruptions they may cause as well as the possibilities of allergies. Again, some guests will love staying at a B&B with dogs and cats all sprawling at the fireplace. Others may not like animals or feel uncomfortable with them. Make sure guests know there are critters in the house when they call for reservations.

You'll also need to consider if you want to accept pets along with your guests. Martha Abraham of the Bed-and-Breakfast at Ponder Cove in Mars Hill, North Carolina, operates a pet-friendly bed-and-breakfast. While this isn't for everyone Martha has found her niche in the market — many B&Bs don't accept pets.

Martha will fax a "Doggy Pledge" to guests with dogs after they have made their reservations. "Originally, I had a set of strict rules on the Internet, but it sounded like 'We are pet-friendly as long as your pet is perfect.' " Says Martha, "It sounded harsh and I took it off the site. I decided to get the reservation first then hit them with some rules. Now I find myself being too lenient but afraid of losing a good client. So, I've decided to hit it in a "tongue and cheek" manner, directing the rules and regulations to the dogs themselves. Here is an example:

1. I pledge to have a strict talk with my mom and dad about what they are going to do with me when they go to the B&B.
2. I pledge not to fib anymore about not crying when they leave me behind.
3. I pledge not to tell them to ask Martha to babysit because if she is babysitting, she is not taking care of her other guests.
4. I pledge to share with them the doggy daycare suggestions Martha has furnished.
5. If I show up with fleas, I will be banished to the dungeon for the night. I think I better call that groomer myself.

I also have a $25 fee but this fee buys them the extra laundry I do to ensure cleanliness and a welcoming basket complete with treats, dog bone, pooper scooper bags and a copy of *Fido Friendly* magazine."

Other B&B owners have had less-than-positive experiences with pets. The owners of The Dickinson in Huntsville, Alabama, say that they had so many problems with people trying to sneak in pets and smoking that they now charge $200 additional if anyone brings a pet or smokes. They make this charge very clear on their confirmation letter so that there are no misunderstandings. Two things to consider if you do decide to accept pets are guests with allergies and destructive behavior by pets. You may want to implement a policy that requires guests to sign a pet policy form or put an additional deposit on the room that would be refunded once it was determined the pet caused no damage to the premises.

Here is an example of a pet policy the PAII provides on their website:

Pet Policy

I, THE UNDERSIGNED, AGREE:

1. To never leave my pet unattended in my guest room, in any common room, or anywhere on the inn's premises. (Should you need a pet sitter, please ask us.)

2. To always have my pet on a leash when on the premises of the inn and outside my guest room.

3. That my pet is well-behaved and will not disturb other guests (e.g., barking, meowing).

4. To be responsible for any and all damage caused to my guest room, including but not limited to stains and/or odors, damage to furnishings (e.g., chewing or scratching or tearing).

5. That my pet is house-broken and is spayed/neutered.

6. That my pet is at least 6 months old, no more than 3 1/2 feet tall, and no more than 50 lbs.

7. To clean up after my pet at all times (using my own towels/linens and never the inn's towels/linens to do this).

8. To never allow my pet to use the bedding for any reason at any time, and to never allow my pet to sleep on or in the bed. I agree to pay cleaning charges if necessary.

9. That my guest room will be checked prior to my departure, and that if I leave prior to a room check and there is any damage to the room, the inn is authorized to charge any and all expenses for any damage to my room or common areas to my credit card.

10. To pay a $25.00 per day charge for each pet.

I fully understand, and agree to abide by, all of the terms and conditions of the above Pet Policy.

Signature _____ Date _____

The inn reserves the right to refuse occupancy to any pet at any time with cause.

You may want to consider including some proof of health for the animals as well. Requesting vet records upfront could help you in case of a guest's pet that suddenly takes a dislike to another guest and bites the person. You could save everyone a lot of time (and possibly money if things went as far as a lawsuit) if you had a record showing the animal had its vaccines up to date.

Smoking

Most B&Bs have been way ahead of the general trend towards nonsmoking in public facilities. This is partially due to the odor smoke can leave in curtains and beddings. If you want to include smoking rooms, you may want to consider doing it like traditional hotels, making particular rooms smoking, or you may want to ask guests to only smoke in common rooms. If you are a smoker, you'll need to make sure you follow whatever policies you ask your guests to follow!

Payment and Deposit Policies

What kind of payment should you accept for your rooms and how should you handle deposits? Today almost all businesses accept one type of credit card or another. There is usually a use fee attached to being a merchant that accepts a credit card (2 to 5 percent) and there is additional paperwork if you take credit cards, but since your guests are so accustomed to using them, it would probably be in your best interest to accept them. Additionally, if you have a website and online reservation system, you would need to accept credit cards.

You'll also need to decide if you are going to accept personal checks. Some bed-and-breakfasts do accept checks for deposits, but will not accept them for final payment. This makes it easier for the guest to mail in the deposit but also protects the host from losing the entire sum if the check bounces.

Most bed-and-breakfasts require a deposit of 50 percent on a one-night deposit and require that they receive it within one week of making the reservation. To determine what bed-and-breakfasts in your area are currently requiring for deposits, you can surf some of their websites for information.

Cancellation Policy

Along with a payment and deposit policy, you will also need to have a cancellation policy in place. A cancellation policy is necessary to protect your income; you don't want to have to scramble to book a room each time a guest cancels at the last minute! Chances are you will just lose that income. Once a guest has sent in a deposit, many bed-and-breakfasts require a 14-day notice to cancel a reservation with a full refund. Often even with the 14-day notice, they still charge a small processing fee (5 to 10 percent).

If a guest cancels closer to the reservation date, you do have some options in how to structure your policy. You could decide that no refund will be given at that point, you could just have the guest be responsible for a cancellation charge, or you could still refund the full amount (minus the processing fee) if you can rebook the room.

However you decide to structure your cancellation policy, make sure it is clearly communicated to the guest, preferably in writing. When you send a confirmation of the reservation, you should include a copy of this policy. If there is no time to send a written confirmation, make sure you tell your guest and get confirmation that he or she understands.

Walk-ins and One-Night Stays

Many bed-and-breakfasts do not accept guests for one-night stays. Mildred Crane of the Queen Anne II in Lebanon, Ohio, says that she and her husband have a policy that reservations must be made 48 hours in advance. Mildred has found that people that book at the last minute or only stay one night do not tend to treat the premises very well and they are often difficult as far as scheduling breakfast or cleaning.

Many bed-and-breakfast owners require a minimum of a two-night stay because, to be honest, guests who only stay one night are a lot of work. If a guest only stays one night, you have to check in guests, check out guests, clean and do laundry each and every day for that room. However, one-nighters may be a good way for you to fill in those weeknight holes you have in your reservation schedule. Or, if you're just starting out, someone staying for one night is always better than no one for two nights!

Make careful consideration of whether or not you want to host one-nighters. You may want to consider it for the week nights, but then require a two-night stay for weekends, or you may want to accept one-night stays at certain times of the year. Remember, be flexible — if your policy doesn't work out, you can always make a change!

Phone Policies

Many people today carry cellphones, so providing phone service to your guests may not be as important as it was in the past. However, everyone does not have access to a cellphone, so you should decide what your policies are on using the bed-and-breakfast's phone and how to deal with long-distance charges. Unlike larger and more traditional hotels, most B&Bs don't have the funds to install a computer/phone system that will track each room's phone calls, but there are some options for you when it comes to providing your guests with phone services:

- Put a phone in each room. This is probably the most expensive option and it may be tricky to regulate long-distance calls. You could install a block so that only long-distance phone calls made with a calling card will go through.

- If you only have a phone in the common room, you can still use this blocking system.

- You could have a policy that guests need to use their credit card or calling card for long-distance calls rather than putting a block on the phone.

- You could work on the honor system and ask guests to tell you how long their long-distance calls were so you can add the amount to their bill.

House Rules

Every bed-and-breakfast has house rules. Some may have many and others may only have a few. You'll want to find a way to communicate these rules to your guests without sounding like they are in prison rather than on vacation! Don't try to recite all of the rules to your guests while you are showing them the bed-and-breakfast when they arrive. This can put off your guests in a major way. You may want to create written list. Put it on an attractive piece of paper and laminate the list, then place it in all the rooms somewhere the guests will see it. That way they will have it handy if they have any questions. Try to keep the tone of the list friendly rather than judgmental. The illustration gives you an example of a house rules letter.

Welcome! We're glad you're here!

To help make your stay enjoyable, we ask all our guests to please observe our house policies:

A full breakfast will be served between 7:30 and 9:30 a.m. If you need to make other arrangements or have special dietary requirements, please let us know.

Please do not smoke in the house. We have a nice covered porch on the south side of the building you are welcome to use. Ashtrays are provided.

There is a phone in the common room you are welcome to use for personal and business calls. We ask that you please stop by and let us know about any long-distance charges so we may add this amount to your final bill.

Many of our guests are traveling for business so we ask that all guests observe quiet hours starting at 11 p.m.

Please feel free to enjoy a snack and glass of wine in our common room each evening at 5 p.m. Come in to relax or chat with other guests!

We hope you enjoy your stay; please let us know if there is anything we can do to make you more comfortable.

Jack & Susan
The Blue Water Inn

. . . . .

CHAPTER ELEVEN

Food Services

An integral part of your guest services will be your food services. You'll need to decide if you are going to offer a simple continental breakfast or a full breakfast to your guests. You'll also need to decide whether or not you want to offer additional food services such as dinner, lunches, snacks and afternoon tea service. Your decision on how much food service will be determined by your facilities (if you don't have a large enough kitchen, you probably want to skip the dinner idea), the health department requirements in your state and your skill and interest in cooking.

No matter how much food service you decide to offer, you'll need to pay close attention to your kitchen and dining areas as well as the service part of the equation.

Inspecting the Dining Room

The bed-and-breakfast host is responsible for the appearance, cleanliness and order of the dining room during the service period. Before the meal service begins, make sure you check that:

- The dining room is clean and in good order.
- Window curtains, Venetian blinds and window roller-shades are adjusted to furnish satisfactory light.
- The temperature and ventilation of the dining room are properly adjusted.
- Tables are arranged properly and completely equipped.
- Serving stands and side tables are properly arranged and have adequate supplies.
- There are enough menu cards (if you use menu cards), and they are distributed properly.
- Any tables arranged for special parties are ready, and flowers, candles and other decorations provided.
- Flowers are fresh and attractively arranged. Plants should be inspected for proper care, pruning and watering.
- There is an adequate supply of tablecloths, table pads, doilies, napkins and serving towels.
- Necessary repairs have been made to furnishings and fixtures.

General Rules for Table Service

Since there are several methods of table service, each bed-and-breakfast should follow the method appropriate to its particular conditions, and each member of the waitstaff must learn to follow the serving directions exactly so that service will be uniform.

The following procedures are approved by social custom:

1. Place and remove all food from the left side of the guest.
2. Place and remove all beverages, including water, from the right of the guest.

3. Use the left hand to place and remove dishes when working at the left side of the guest, and the right hand when working at the right side of the guest. This provides free arm action for the server and avoids the danger of bumping against the guest's arm.

4. Place each dish on the table, the four fingers of your left hand under the lower edge, and your thumb on the upper edge, of the plate.

5. Never reach in front of the guest, nor across one person in order to serve another.

6. Present serving dishes from the left side, in a position so that guests can serve themselves. Place serving silver on the right side of the dish, with the handles turned toward the guest so that he or she may reach and handle them easily.

7. Do not place soiled, chipped or cracked glassware and china or bent or tarnished silverware before a guest.

8. Hold silverware by the handles when it is laid in place. Be sure it is clean and spotless.

9. Handle tumblers by their bases and goblets by their stems.

10. Do not lift water glasses from the table to fill or refill; when they cannot be reached conveniently, draw them to a more convenient position.

11. Set fruit juice and cocktail glasses, cereal dishes, soup bowls and dessert dishes on small plates before placing them in the center of the cover, between the knife and the fork.

12. When it accompanies the main course, place the salad plate at the left of the forks, about 2 inches from the edge of the table. When the salad is served as a separate course, place it directly in front of the guest.

13. Place individual serving trays or bread and rolls above and to the left of the forks. Place a tray or basket of bread for the use of several guests toward the center of the table.

14. Place the cup and saucer at the right of the spoons, about 2 inches from the edge of the table. Turn the handle of the cup to the right,

either parallel to the edge of the table or at a slight angle toward the guest.

15. Set tea and coffee pots on small plates and place above and slightly to the right of the beverage cup. Set iced beverage glasses on coasters or small plates to protect tabletops and linen.

16. Place individual creamers, syrup pitchers and small lemon plates above and a little to the right of the cup and saucer.

17. Place a milk glass at the right of and below the water glass.

18. Serve butter, cheese and cut lemon with a fork. Serve relishes, pickles and olives with a fork or spoon, not with the fingers.

Clearing the Table

The following are standard procedures for clearing the table:

1. After any course, dishes should be removed from the left side, except the beverage service, which should be removed from the right.

2. Platters and other serving dishes should be removed first when clearing the table, or they may be removed as soon as empty.

3. The main-course plate should be removed first, the salad plate next, followed by the bread-and-butter plate.

4. The empty milk or beverage glass is removed from the right side after the main course.

5. The table should be crumbed by using a small plate and a clean, folded napkin. This is especially important when hard rolls or crusty breads are served.

6. Hot tea and coffee service should be left on the table until the completion of the dessert course.

7. The water glass should remain on the table and be kept refilled as long as the guest is seated.

8. Replace soiled ashtrays with clean ones as often as necessary through-out the meal.

9. When a guest is seated at a table and it is necessary to change a soiled tablecloth, turn the soiled cloth halfway back, lay the clean cloth half open in front of the guest, and transfer the tableware to the clean cloth. The soiled cloth may then be drawn from the table and the clean one pulled smoothly into place. If this exchange of linen is accomplished skillfully, the guest need not be disturbed unduly during the procedure. Soiled linen should be properly disposed of immediately after it is removed from the table.

Breakfast

What type of breakfast you are going to offer will affect how you price your rooms; an inn offering a full breakfast can charge higher room rates than one that offers a continental breakfast.

First, ask yourself, "Do I like to cook, or would I like to learn?" This question may go a long way in helping you decide what type of breakfast to offer. Now, ask yourself what kind or regulations or permits you are under. Depending on your state and the type of license you have, you may not be able to offer a full-service breakfast. If this is the case and you want to do this in the future, look into what you would need for kitchen renovations in order to be in compliance in your state for serving a hot breakfast.

In general you can offer:

- **Continental breakfast.** This phrase often has a bad connotation, evoking images of traditional hotels with their offerings of day-old doughnuts and stale coffee. You can offer a nice continental break-fast, however. Make sure you use fresh items. Rather than offering doughnuts, have muffins, breakfast breads and scones. Set out local jams and real butter to accompany these. And offer fresh-squeezed orange juice, yogurt, homemade granola and a selection of fresh fruit.

- **Full breakfast.** Full breakfasts can be served as buffet or sit-down, and include anything from pancakes and French toast to omelets, bacon, sour cream coffee cake and broiled grapefruit. Full breakfast usually means some hot items will be served.

Depending on the size of your bed-and-breakfast (and the size of your dining room), you might consider one big table or several smaller tables. A sideboard is also a good idea. You can use this surface for coffee, rolls or buffet breakfasts.

When you set the table, think about table linens and napkins. Most likely you'll want to use linen napkins. You might decide tablecloths, runners or placemats work best for you and for your décor.

If you are offering a seated breakfast rather than a buffet, the china and silverware should be on the table.

Good breakfast service is important because many customers are in a hurry; some have little appetite, and others are "out of sorts" until they have had their coffee. A cheerful attitude on the part of the waitstaff and prompt and efficient service, therefore, may help customers start the day right.

Foods served for breakfast are most palatable when they are freshly prepared and when they are served at the correct temperature. The waitperson, therefore, should serve breakfast in courses unless the customer especially requests that the whole order be served at once. Cooked foods and hot beverages should be brought to the customer directly from the serving station and under no circumstances be allowed to remain on the serving stand to cool while the customer finishes a preceding course.

Order of Service for Breakfast:

1. When fresh fruit or fruit juice is ordered, it is desirable to serve it first, and then to remove the soiled dishes before placing the toast and coffee.

2. When customers order a combination of cooked fruit, toast and coffee, they may ask to have the whole order served at once. Place the fruit dish in the center of the cover, the plate of toast at the left of the forks and the coffee at the right of the teaspoons.

3. When the breakfast order includes a cereal and a hot dish, the service procedure may be as follows:

    a. Place the fruit course in the center of the cover.

    b. Remove the fruit service.

    c. Place the cereal bowl in the center of the cover. Cut individual boxes of cereal partway through the side near the top so the guest may open them easily.

    d. Remove the cereal service.

    e. Place the breakfast plate of eggs, meat or other hot food in the center of the cover. Place the plate of toast at the left of the forks. Place the coffee service at the right of the spoons.

    f. Remove the breakfast plate and the bread plate.

    g. Place the finger bowl, filled one-third full of warm water. At times the finger bowl is placed after the fruit course when fruits that may soil the fingers have been served.

    h. Place the sales check, face down, at the right of the cover or present it on a clean change tray.

Coffee

No matter which type of breakfast service you offer, you'll find that coffee is one of the most important aspects of your breakfast menu. You're going to want to offer good coffee, and your guests are going to expect it. There is also a certain ritual associated with coffee. It includes everything from relaxing with coffee and dessert after dinner to people in the workplace socializing during their coffee break. There are many different coffee blends available. Coffee is an extremely important part of any dining experience: get the finest and most popular blend available. Have the bed-and-breakfast employees try the different blends under consideration in a blind tasting.

In general, there are two kinds of coffee: specialty and commercial. The most obvious difference between the two is packaging: commercial coffee is ground and comes in tins or a plastic-encased brick, and specialty coffees are sold by the bean in bags. While commercial coffees may be cheaper, you'd be doing yourself a favor by investigating serving specialty coffees. Most specialty coffees are identified by region and/or roast. For example, you might have a French Espresso Roast of a Kenyan coffee or a medium roasted bean. While coffees from various locales have different flavors, the most important characteristic of coffee beans is probably the roast. The longer the beans are roasted, the darker the bean and the more intense the flavor.

Light roasts are generally used for the more inexpensive, commercial grades of coffee and are not recommended for service in your B&B. The tastes can often be sour or grainy. Medium roasts are commonly referred to as medium American roasts. These coffees are what we think of as traditional American coffee. The flavor is fully developed. Darker roasts may be called Viennese roasts or French espresso. In these coffees, a bittersweet taste is present. You can also find blends of coffees that mix the roasts. Many of the better coffee distributors often offer their own special blend.

Your first coffee decision will be where to buy your beans. Fresh-roasted coffee is best the day it comes out of the roaster, but for most of us, this just isn't a feasible option. If you keep whole beans in an airtight container (a solid glass jar with a rubber gasket to seal the lid), however, it will last seven to 10 days. You can make it last longer by putting the whole beans in the freezer. If you are going to freeze it, seal the coffee bag in a freezer bag and put it in the back of the freezer where it will remain at a more constant temperature. Remove only the beans you intend to use that day and thaw them before grinding. Coffee beans lose their freshness because roasted beans slowly emit carbon dioxide which helps keep their freshness. As the beans slowly release this gas, oxygen begins to permeate them and they begin to stale. Also remember that once you grind the coffee, it goes stale in a few hours.

Make sure you find a good purveyor for coffee. You can look around in your hometown, you might find some small roasters or you can buy from a large company such as Starbucks. There are several great coffee resources online such as Starbucks at **www.starbucks.com**, Peets (**www.peets.com**) or **http://buckscountycoffee.com**.

Coffee Equipment

Obviously we would suggest fresh grinding your coffee each morning. So one thing you will need is a grinder. Some coffee pots come with grinders (**www. william-sonoma.com**), or you can find an easily affordable grinder such as the ones manufactured by Braun. You'll also need to choose a coffee maker:

- **Automatic drip.** This is probably the most popular coffee maker used today. These come in many styles. You can find one that will automatically start the coffee for the time for which you set it. Some of these pour the coffee into a glass container, others use insulated carafes. Once the water runs through the system, the coffee maker keeps the coffee warm. There are some that pour the water through a paper filter into the holding container. These are good because of their convenience, but you want to be careful about how long you serve the coffee after it has been brewed. If you have the type of automatic drip machine that has a "hot plate" for the carafe to sit on, the coffee can become quite undrinkable rather quickly. You should also make a full pot of coffee rather than one or two cups at a time with these makers because they make better coffee when you use them at capacity.

- **Cones.** These are ceramic or plastic cones you can put on top of a mug or pitcher, put in a filter, add your grounds then pour hot water over the grounds. One of the nice aspects of this type of coffee maker is that you can stir the water and grounds as they steep, a step that many coffee nuts say you simply cannot skip. Of course, the down side of these makers is the inconvenience and the fact that you usually can't brew more than a few cups at a time. You can find ceramic cones and pots at Melitta's website at www.melitta.com.

- **French press.** The French press, or plunger pot, has been growing in popularity in the United States. You can find these in plastic, glass or stainless steel. Essentially, they are tall coffee pots with a plunger apparatus attached to a lid. The lid is attached to a post that has a fine mesh screen on the other end. You put the medium-ground beans in the pot, add hot water, stir and let steep for 4 minutes. Once the coffee has steeped, you push the plunger down and pour the coffee. This type of coffee maker is very elegant looking and not messy. While they don't make more than a few cups at a time, you could invest in a few of these and put them on the dining room tables.

If you do decide to go with a more commercial grade of coffee, you might consider using a major coffee distributor. They will provide all the equipment necessary for coffee service including: brewing machines, filters, pots, and maintenance and installation of all equipment. All that is required from you is to sign a contract stating that you will buy their coffee exclusively. The price of all the equipment and maintenance is included in the price of the coffee.

You could buy all your own equipment and pay to have someone install and maintain it. This would enable you to purchase coffee from any company at reduced prices. However, a large capital outlay would be necessary. Since there is no great advantage to doing this, it is recommended that most bed-and-breakfasts use the coffee distributor contract method.

When negotiating with the coffee salesperson, inform him or her that you want brand-new equipment. They are competing for your business, but once you sign the contract, you will be locked into it. Use this leverage now while you have it.

Various specialty teas may be purchased from these distributors as well. Sugar packets and sugar substitute packages may also be purchased from these companies. For an additional charge, your B&B's name and logo can be imprinted on the outside of each packet.

Brewing Tips

There are several things you can do to ensure a better cup of coffee:

- Grind the coffee appropriately for your coffeemaker. In general, grind it as fine as you can unless you are using a French press; for a French press, coffee beans should be a medium grind.

- Don't be afraid to use enough coffee. For every 8 ounces (most coffee mugs are 8 ounces rather than 6 ounces) use 2 1/2 to 3 level tablespoons for every mug of water.

- Keep your coffee maker clean, and rinse it with hot water before brewing.

- Use fresh water free of impurities. If your water doesn't taste good, your coffee isn't going to either. If your water has a bad taste, consider using a filter or bottled water. If you have hard water in your area or water treated with a softener, you might want to consider this as well since these two conditions will create bad cups of coffee.

- Brew with hot water, not boiling water (a temperature of 200 F is ideal).

Flavored Coffees and Decaf

While many people want regular, strong coffee in the morning, others will prefer decaf. You can find as many varieties and roasts of decaf as you can of regular coffee. And while flavored coffees aren't popular at breakfast, it might be nice to stock some of these for guests who'd like a cup in the afternoon or evening. Hazelnut seems to be the most popular flavor right now, but you can find everything from chocolate to pumpkin spice. You might also want to consider stocking up on flavored syrups. There are some brands that have a variety of flavors and a line of sugar-free syrups as well.

Espresso

Espresso has also enjoyed rising popularity in the United States, and depending on your clientele and location, you may want to consider investing in an espresso machine. You can find these anywhere from $200 to $5,000. You might want to check out used restaurant equipment stores for this purchase. If you make espresso, make sure to use one of the darker espresso roasts and grind it finely.

Sustainable Coffee

While typically more expensive, organic, Fair Trade and sustainable coffees may be an option to look into. Organically grown coffees are certified by a third party to ensure the beans are grown, processed, transported and stored without chemicals, pesticides or herbicides.

Fair Trade coffees are those that have been produced by cooperatives that have been guaranteed a fair price for their coffee based on an internationally determined price. To find out more about Fair Trade coffee, visit Global Exchange's website at **www.globalexchange.org/campaigns/fairtrade/coffee**.

Sustainable coffee growers are those who meet a variety of environmental criteria such as nonpolluting and economic practices that benefit the welfare of workers and farmers. To find out more about sustainable coffee, visit Coffeeresearch.org's website at **www.coffeeresearch.org/politics/sustainability.htm**.

While these coffees generally carry a higher price tag, you may be able to advertise that you use such products and attract a particular type of guest interested in such issues who would otherwise not select your B&B.

Tea

While most of us think of coffee as the only breakfast beverage, many people prefer tea. Along with your pot of Joe, be sure to provide a selection of teas, both caffeinated and decaf.

As with coffee, there are some things you can do to make a better cup of tea. First, make sure you use fresh water. Don't just turn the burner on under the kettle that has water in it from yesterday's breakfast. Always start with fresh, cold water.

If you are serving just cups of tea, you might invest in a handsome wooden box to display the various teas you have to offer. If you are serving pots of tea, you might want to use prepackage tea or loose tea leaves. Either way, make sure to buy a tea cozy to keep the pot warm while it sits on your guests' breakfast table.

The Menu

Even if you feel like you're all thumbs in the kitchen, there are easy ways to provide a memorable breakfast to your guests — even without offering a full, hot breakfast.

- **Use fresh items**. Even if you don't bake your muffins fresh each morning, make sure you offer the freshest muffins you can. Find the best bakery in town and get your baked goods there rather than prepackaged at the grocery store. Also buy fresh fruit to set out for breakfast.

- **Use local items**. Whenever possible, use local ingredients or items. Many cities have local farmers' markets offering everything from fresh-made mustard to pies, cookies, jams and syrups. Advertise that you are using local items.

- **Make it pretty**. Instead of putting a stick of butter on the table for the morning rolls, make butter curls, or, you can buy candy molds at a candy supply store. Let your butter soften, press it into the molds, chill, then pop out beautifully shaped pats of butter!

If you do want to try your hand at cooking from scratch, there are several bed-and-breakfast cookbooks on the market such as *The Bed & Breakfast Cookbook* by Martha Watson Murphy and *The American Country Inn and Bed & Breakfast Cookbook* by Kitty and Lucian Maynard. You can also look at any of the B&B organizations online; they offer links to recipes inn owners have submitted.

If you're going to cook from scratch, you'll want to keep a list of staples on hand so that you will be able to put breakfast together without a trip to the store because there will be days when your plans don't work and you'll never get to the store that day to purchase your breakfast items.

Here's a list of what should be in your pantry at all times:

- Eggs
- Milk (whole and 2 percent)
- Flour
- Sugar
- Baking powder
- Baking soda
- Maple syrup
- Coffee
- Tea
- Spices
- Butter
- Bread
- Fresh fruit
- Jams
- Cold and hot cereals (assorted)
- Onions
- Potatoes
- Cheese
- Herbs (fresh and/or dried)
- Breakfast meats (bacon and sausage)
- Non-sugar sweetener

Breakfast Recipes

Below you will find some breakfast recipes from bed-and-breakfasts around the United States. Hopefully this sampling will help you get started on creating and finding delicious recipes for your bed-and-breakfast!

. . . .

Welsh Cakes

PLÂS CADNANT B&B

"I bake Welsh Cakes on the griddle as part of my breakfast. Everyone loves them!"

1 1/2 cups of all-purpose flour
2 teaspoons baking powder
3 tablespoons sugar
1/4 cup currants
1 stick butter or margarine
1 egg, plus 1 tablespoon milk

In mixing bowl, sift together flour and baking powder. Add one stick of butter, cut into small pieces and mix until it resembles fine breadcrumbs. Stir in sugar, currants and add one beaten egg plus milk to make dough. Form into a ball and place on floured board. Roll to 1/4-inch thickness and cut into rounds with a 2-inch cookie cutter. Heat griddle to 375 F and spray with vegetable oil or brush with melted butter. Cook the cakes about 3–4 minutes per side until golden brown in color. Keep checking them; they cook quickly. Serve hot, just as they are or with more butter.

Yield: 18–20 cakes.

From Siân & Jon Stow

. . . .

. . . .

Dutch Apple Pancake

PROSPECT HILL B&B INN, MOUNTAIN CITY, TENNESSEE

4 tablespoons unsalted butter
1 medium apple, cored, cut into 1/2-inch thick slices
1/2 teaspoon ground cinnamon
1 tablespoon sugar
2 eggs, at room temperature
1/2 cup milk
1/2 cup all-purpose flour
1/2 teaspoon salt
Confectioner's sugar for dusting

Preheat oven to 400 F and grease two 6-inch oven-proof bowls (we use cereal bowls, Pyrex flower pots [about 5 inches] or French onion soup bowls).

In a frying pan over medium heat, melt 2 tablespoons of the butter. Add apple slices, cinnamon and sugar and sauté, stirring occasionally until apples begin to soften and brown, 5–6 minutes. Set aside and cover to keep warm.

In a bowl, beat eggs with a whisk, add milk and beat mixture until blended. Sift flour and salt into egg mixture and beat just until blended. Melt remaining 2 tablespoons butter, add to flour-egg mix and beat until smooth. Pour batter into prepared pan. Bake until pancake is puffed up and light brown, about 20–25 minutes.

Pastry easily comes out of the bowl. Place on a serving plate, fill with cinnamon/sugar-apple mixture. Dust with confectioner's sugar and serve immediately.

Serve with a side of bacon and a small serving of herbed scrambled eggs.

Serves 2.

From Judy and Robert Hotchkiss

. . . .

. . . .

Ponder Cove's Morning Apple Pudding

BED-AND-BREAKFAST AT PONDER COVE

1 stick butter
3/4 cup brown sugar
3 Granny Smith apples
8 ounces cream cheese
1 loaf French bread
8 eggs
2 cups milk
2 tablespoons vanilla
Cinnamon
Maple syrup

Melt butter in the bottom of a 9-inch by 13-inch pan. Add brown sugar apples. Put them in the microwave to break down the apples, about 3 minutes. Take 8 ounces cream cheese and tear into thumb-size pieces and drop all over apples.

Slice French bread in 1" slices and remove crust. Cut in half. Lay on top of cream cheese and apples. Fill in cracks. Beat 8 eggs, 2 cups milk and 2 tablespoons vanilla together and pour over mixture. Saturate all bread. Sprinkle with cinnamon to taste. Cook in 375 F oven for 1 hour. Cut in squares and serve with lots of warm maple syrup.

From Martha Abraham

. . . .

. . . .

Cream Biscuits (For Those Who Hate to Cut in Butter)

MURPHIN RIDGE INN, ADAMS COUNTY, OHIO

2 cups all-purpose flour
1 tablespoon baking powder
1 teaspoon sugar
1 teaspoon salt
1 cup heavy cream

Sift dry ingredients, add 1 cup heavy cream. Mix and knead 10 times. Roll out on floured board to 1/2-inch thick. Cut with biscuit cutter. Bake at 450 F until golden. Delicious with homemade cherry or raspberry jam.

From Sherry and Darryl McKenney

. . . .

. . . .

Longwood Muffins

LONGWOOD MANOR BED & BREAKFAST IN BROOKEVILLE, MARYLAND

FOR THE MOST MOIST MUFFINS:

1 orange, peeled
1 orange, with skin
1/2 cup orange juice
1/4 pound butter
1/2 cup chopped dates
Place all the above in the food processor and process until combined (will look like curdled liquid).
In another bowl mix:
1 1/2 cup flour
3/4 cup sugar
1 teaspoon baking powder
1 teaspoon baking soda
1 teaspoon salt

Add liquid ingredients to dry and stir only until moistened. Put in greased muffin pans and bake at 350 F until done, about 25–30 minutes.

From Bruce and Lynn Bartlett

. . . .

. . . .

Breakfast Egg & Bacon Puff

CHRISTOPHER'S BED & BREAKFAST, BELLEVUE, KENTUCKY

INGREDIENTS:

1 package fully cooked bacon
6 eggs
2 cups milk
1 cup Bisquick
1 8-ounce package shredded Colby or cheddar cheese

Preheat oven to 350 F. Grease a two-quart casserole dish.

In bowl, combine eggs, milk and Bisquick. Dice bacon slices into small pieces and stir into egg mixture. Pour into greased casserole dish.

Bake at 350 F for approximately 1 hour. Check consistency after 40–45 minutes.

From Brenda Guidugli

. . . .

. . . .

Breakfast Corned Beef Hash Casserole

CHRISTOPHER'S BED & BREAKFAST, BELLEVUE, KENTUCKY

INGREDIENTS:

2 cans corned beef hash
6 eggs
Tabasco sauce
1 8-ounce package shredded Colby or cheddar cheese

Preheat oven to 350 F. Lightly grease a one-quart casserole dish.

Spread two cans of corned beef hash in lightly greased casserole dish. Make six indentations in corned beef hash with spoon. Break open egg and place raw eggs in each of the indentations.

Sprinkle Tabasco sauce over entire mixture and evenly cover with shredded cheese.

Bake at 350 F for approximately 35–40 minutes until egg yolks are fully cooked.

From Brenda Guidugli

. . . .

. . . .

Orange Juice Spritzer

MAPLEVALE FARM, OXFORD, OHIO

6 ounces frozen orange juice concentrate, thawed
1 cup cold water
1 tablespoon lemon juice
1 1/2 cups bitter lemon or bitter orange (carbonated soft drink)
1 orange, sliced
1 lime, sliced

In a large pitcher, combine the orange juice concentrate with the water and lemon juice.

Just before serving, slowly add the bitter lemon/orange drink.

Pour into ice-filled, tall glasses and garnish each with a slice of orange and lime.

From John and Malinda Anderson

. . . .

· ·

Hash Brown Pie

THE INN AT 410, FLAGSTAFF, ARIZONA

"The hash brown 'crust' is unique and delicious. The key is to press as much moisture out of the potatoes as possible. I was surprised to find frozen hash browns with no fat and reasonable amounts of sodium. It's worth it to read package labels while shopping!"

9-inch pie plate
1 12-ounce package frozen hash brown potatoes, thawed (half of a 24-ounce package)
1/4 cup margarine, melted
1 10-ounce package frozen spinach, thawed
1 tablespoon margarine
1 small onion, chopped
1/2 teaspoon nutmeg

1/4 teaspoon ground black pepper
3/4 cup shredded low-fat cheddar cheese
3/4 cup shredded low-fat Monterey Jack cheese
1 cup skim milk
4 large eggs
1/2 teaspoon Beau Monde seasoning
Cherry tomatoes and parsley for garnishing

THE NIGHT BEFORE:

Preheat oven to 425 F. Spray 9" pie plate with nonstick cooking spray.

Press thawed potatoes between paper towels to absorb moisture. Make a crust of potatoes by pressing them firmly along bottom and sides of pie plate. Use pastry brush to brush with the 1/4-cup melted margarine. Bake 20 minutes.

Meanwhile, using clean hands, squeeze excess moisture from thawed spinach. In small skillet over medium heat, melt 1 tablespoon of margarine. Saute chopped onion until translucent, about 5 minutes. Crumble "dry" spinach into pan and stir in nutmeg. Remove from heat and cool to room temperature.

Spread spinach mixture evenly over the potato crust. Mix shredded cheeses together, then spread cheeses evenly over the spinach. Cover with foil and refrigerate overnight.

THE NEXT MORNING:

Preheat oven to 350 F.

In blender or electric mixer, beat the milk, eggs, Beau Monde and pepper together until thoroughly mixed. Pour over the cheese. Bake 30–45 minutes or until puffed and cooked through.

Remove pie from oven and let sit for 5 minutes to firm up. Serve hot with garnish of cherry tomatoes and parsley.

Serves six

From Gordon Watkins

· ·

Presentation

Plate presentation is an important element of any menu item. Food that is presented well is perceived to have more value by the customer, and your prices for well-plated food can be on the higher side of the price continuum.

Three elements comprise plate presentation:

- Dish type and size
- Portion size
- Garnish

You must provide the appropriate plate sizes for menu items, or kitchen staff may be prone to over-portioning. If a salad that should be plated on a salad dish is put on a dinner plate, the pantry person is likely to add more salad so the item is not swallowed up by the dish. You should include plate size information on your standardized recipe.

Portion size should also be included on your standardized recipe. Consistent portioning is important to customer satisfaction. Your customers may order the same dish many times. It's important that each time it comes out of the kitchen it looks and tastes the same.

Garnish is often overlooked in recipes and in presentation. For minimal cost, garnish can add to the appearance of your plates. Garnish can be anything from simple chopped parsley to sauces drizzled across the plate in a decorative manner. It's the slice of lemon on top of your salmon or the cheese croutons in the soup.

Along with the actual garnish ingredients, think about how you want the food to be arranged on the plate. Factors to consider when arranging a plate are:

- Layout
- Balance
- Line
- Dimension/Height
- Serviceability

Think about where you want your guest to focus. Most times you want the guest to focus on the most expensive item on the plate (this will enhance the perceived value of the meal).

You must also take the balance of the plate into consideration. By balance we are referring to the weight of the items on the plate.

Line is also important because a strong line has eye appeal. A strong line helps to draw the guest's eye to the plate.

Dimension or height also adds to a plate's appeal. Use molds to mound potatoes or rice and lean meat up against these mounds to create height and a three-dimensional plate. Do not overdo the height factor, however. You do not want to overwhelm the taste of the food itself by the presentation. Do not over stack, or over-portion, a plate.

Finally, keep in mind that your guest is eventually going to eat the masterpiece you have just created. Don't make it difficult to reach around garnishes or to cut into food.

As an example: rather than just putting the sliced roast pork beside the mashed potatoes and the green beans, tie the pieces together. Place the mound of potatoes in the center of the plate and fan the slices of pork around it, leaning against the mound. Tie the green beans into a bundle with a steamed chive and angle them on the other side of the potatoes. Think of the plate as a canvas and see what you can create.

Color is also important in plate presentation. Try to get maximum eye appeal. Perhaps top your salmon with some red pepper curls or chopped chives.

Healthy Trends and Special Diets

Since healthy eating is a current food trend in the industry, it wouldn't hurt to go over a few nutritional basics so you can determine if you should include such items on your menu.

There are six basic categories of nutrients: proteins, fats, carbohydrates, minerals, vitamins and water. In general, for menu planning, the main categories you need to focus on are carbohydrates and fats.

Carbohydrates are starches, sugars and fiber. These make up the bulk of a healthy diet and are an important energy source for the body. Examples of carbohydrates are sugar, potatoes, bread, rice, pasta and fruit. Vegetables also contain carbohydrates, but in much lesser amounts.

Fats are a concentrated energy source and provide approximately twice the amount of calories as proteins or carbohydrates. There are saturated fats and unsaturated fats. The difference relates to the fats' chemical structure. Saturated fats are more solid than unsaturated. From a health standpoint, unsaturated fats are healthier. Saturated fats include shortening and butter. Unsaturated fats include olive and canola oils.

Many people in the U.S. suffer from heart disease or other chronic illnesses, such as diabetes. These people are likely part of your customer base. If they are a significant portion of your customer base, you'd be wise to familiarize yourself with the various diets they have to follow and include menu items that they can eat.

Diabetics, for instance, must monitor the amount of fats, carbohydrates and proteins they eat daily. If you offer one or two menu selections that are low-fat and low-protein, they will have an easier time selecting an item and staying on their prescribed diet.

If you do not currently offer healthy menu alternatives and would like to do so, there are several ways to do this.

Search the Web. There are many sites that provide healthy recipes, such as the American Institute of Cancer Research at **www.aicr.org**, the American Heart Association at **www.heart.org/HEARTORG**, and the American Diabetes Association at **www.diabetes.org**.

There are also many good healthy cookbooks in print nowadays. The following is a list of a few:

- *Vegetarian Cooking for Everyone* by Deborah Madison
- *The Joslin Diabetes Gourmet Cookbook* by Bonnie Sanders Polin, PhD, and Frances Towner Giedt
- *The French Culinary Institute's Salute to Healthy Cooking* by Alain Sailhac, Jacques Pepin, Andre Soltner, Jacques Torres and the Faculty at the French Culinary Institute
- *Healthy Latin Cooking* by Steve Raichlen
- *Good Food Gourmet* by Jane Brody
- *Heart Healthy Cooking for All Seasons* by Marvin Moser, M.D., Larry Forgione, Jimmy Schmidt and Julie Rubenstein
- *Moosewood Restaurant Low-Fat Favorites* by the Moosewood Collective
- *Canyon Ranch Cooking* by Jeanne Jones

If you do not want to spend the time developing new recipes to include healthy alternatives, you can probably change some of your existing recipes. Try incorporating the following suggestions into your current menu program:

- Offer at least one vegetarian option.

- Offer at least one option without a butter or cream sauce.

- Replace the cream or whole milk in a recipe with skim milk.

- Replace butter on vegetables with lemon and herb.

- Replace sour cream with yogurt.

- Make your own stock or pick a canned stock that is low in sodium.

- Offer reduced-fat/reduced-calorie salad dressings.

- Substitute chicken broth for milk in mashed potatoes.

- Use olive or canola oil instead of butter or shortening.

- Offer whole grain breads as part of a bread basket.

- Offer low-fat mayonnaise as a sandwich condiment.

- Offer sorbet as a dessert option.

- Offer a simple fruit dessert, such as baked pears, that is low in sugar and fat.

- Offer smaller portion sizes for some of your dishes.

Food Allergies

A food allergy can be very serious and even life threatening. Symptoms can include hives, nausea, vomiting, shortness of breath and anaphylaxis, a severe respiratory reaction.

Some of the most common allergies are to nuts, eggs, shellfish, peanuts and wheat. When designing your menu, make sure ingredient information is available. If you do not list it on the menu, be certain your servers can accurately communicate this information to your customers.

To find out more about food allergies, contact the International Food Information Council at 202-296-6540, or visit their website at **www.foodinsight.org**.

Table Decorations

Just as you want your food to look appetizing, you want your dining table to look attractive. You don't need expensive china and linens to do this — a simple vase of fresh-cut flowers may be just the trick! Think about the overall ambiance and style of your bed-and-breakfast. Is it simple or elegant? What are the prominent colors in your dining room?

Dinner Service

If you offer dinner service at your inn, you'll find that the pace will be very different from breakfast. Because dinner guests are seldom in a hurry, their waitperson is able to give them a more fastidious and leisurely type of service than is possible at breakfast or lunch. Although guests should be allowed plenty of time to complete each course, long waits between courses should be avoided. The waitperson should watchfully observe guests during the meal in order to serve the next course promptly and to comply with any requests made by guests for special service.

Order of Service for Dinner:

1. From the left, place the appetizer or hors d'oeuvres service in the center of the cover. A tray of canapés and hors d'oeuvres is often offered to the guest. In this case, an empty plate should first be placed before the guest and the tray of hors d'oeuvres is then offered.

2. Remove the first-course dishes.

3. Place the soup service in the center of the cover.

4. Remove the soup service.

5. When the entree is served on a platter, place it directly above the cover. Lay the serving silver at the right of the platter. Place the warm dinner plate in the center of the cover.

6. When plate, or "Russian," service is used, place the dinner plate in the center of the cover.

7. Place salad at the left of the forks when it is served with the main course.

8. Place beverages to the right of teaspoons.

9. Offer rolls or place them to the left of the salad plate.

10. Remove the main-course dishes when the guest has finished.

11. When salad is served as a separate course following the main course, place the salad fork at the left and the salad plate in the center of the cover.

12. Remove the salad service.

13. Crumb the table if necessary.

14. Place silver for the dessert course.

15. Place the dessert service in the center of the cover.

16. Serve hot coffee or place the demitasse.

Special Details to Observe When Serving:

1. Serve hot food hot, on heated dishes.

2. Serve cold food chilled, on cold dishes.

3. Inquire how food is to be cooked:

    a. Eggs: fried or boiled, how many minutes.

    b. Steak: rare, medium or well done.

    c. Toast: buttered or dry.

4. Refill water glasses whenever necessary during the meal.

5. Serve extra butter when needed.

6. Refill coffee on request and according to management policies. Bring more cream if necessary.

7. Serve granulated sugar with fresh fruit and unsweetened iced drinks.

8. Place silver necessary for a course just prior to serving.
    a. Soup spoons on extreme right of teaspoons.
    b. Cocktail fork to right of soup spoon.

9. Offer crackers, Melba toast and other accompaniments or relishes with appetizer and soup courses, according to policies of management.

10. Provide iced teaspoons for ice drinks and place parfait spoons when a parfait is served. Place soda spoons and straws with malted milks, milkshakes and ice cream sodas.

How to Establish Your Own Menu

Thinking of serving dinner at your inn? Here are just a few ideas for entrees to get your creative juices flowing.

- Cedar Planked Salmon
- Grilled Ribeyes with Balsamic Glaze
- Brined Pork Chops with Apple Chutney
- Coq au Vin
- Pan-Fried Chicken with Buttermilk Gravy
- Pork Tenderloin with Roasted Root Vegetables
- Homemade Pumpkin Ravioli with Sage Butter Sauce
- Lemon-Roasted Chicken

Whether you only serve breakfast or you serve three meals at your inn, your menu should not just be a list of the dishes you offer, it should positively affect the revenue and operational efficiency of your bed-and-breakfast. Start by selecting dishes that reflect your customers' preferences and emphasize what your staff does well. Attempting to cater to everyone generally has you doing nothing particularly well and doesn't distinguish your bed-and-breakfast. Your menu should be a major communicator of the concept and personality of your bed-and-breakfast, as well as an important cost control.

A well-designed menu creates an accurate image of the bed-and-breakfast in customers' mind, even before they've been inside. It also directs their attention to certain selections and increases the chances of them being ordered. Your menu also determines, depending upon its complexity and sophistication, how detailed your cost-control system needs to be.

An effective menu does five key things:

1. Emphasizes what customers want and what you do best.
2. Is an effective communication, merchandising and cost control tool.
3. Obtains the necessary check average for sales and profits.
4. Uses staff and equipment efficiently.
5. Makes forecasting sales more consistent and accurate for purchasing, preparation and scheduling.

The design of your menu will directly affect whether it achieves these goals. Don't leave this to chance. Plan to have a menu that works for you. Certain practices can influence the choices your guests make. Instead of randomly placing items on the menu, single out and emphasize the items you want to sell. These will generally be dishes with low food cost and high profits that are easy to prepare. Once you have chosen these dishes, use design — print style, paper color and graphic design — to direct the reader's attention to these items. In general, a customer's eye will fall to the middle of the page first. This is an important factor. However, design elements used to draw a reader's eye to another part of the menu can be effective as well. Also, customers remember the first and last things they read more than anything else, so when you draw their eyes to specific items is also important.

Lunch and Dinner Pricing

If you just offer breakfast, the price of the meal will be included in the room, but how do you come up with an appropriate price? In addition, if you are offering other food service, how do you price those? Pricing is an important aspect of your revenues and customer counts. Prices that are too high will drive customers away, and prices that are too low will kill your profits. But pricing is not the simple matter of an appropriate markup over cost; it combines other factors as well.

Price can either be market-driven or demand-driven. **Market-driven** prices must be responsive to your competitors' prices. Common dishes that both you and the place down the road sell need to be priced competitively. This is also true when you're introducing new items for which a demand has not been developed. Opposite to these are **demand-driven** items, which customers ask for and where demand exceeds your supply. You have a short-term monopoly on these items, and, therefore, price is driven up until demand slows or competitors begin to sell similar items.

However you determine your price, the actual marking up of items is an interesting process. A combination of methods is a good idea, since each menu item is usually different. Two basic theories are: 1) charge as much as you can, and 2) charge as little as you can. Each has its pluses and minuses. Obviously, if you charge as much as you can, you increase the chance of greater profits. You do, however, run the risk of needing to offer a product that customers feel is worth the price; otherwise you will lose them because they won't think you're a good value. Charging the lowest price you can gives customers a great sense of value but lowers your profit margin per item.

Prices are generally determined by competition and demand. Your prices must be in line with the category customers put you in. Burrito joints don't price like a five-star bed-and-breakfast, and vice versa. Both would lose their customer base if they did. While this is an exaggeration, the point is still the same. You want your customers to know your image and your prices to fit into that picture.

Here are four ways to determine prices:

1. **Competitive Pricing.** Simply based on meeting or beating your competitions' prices. This is an ineffective method, since it assumes diners are making their choice on price alone, and not food quality, ambiance, service, etc.

2. **Intuitive Pricing.** This means you don't want to take the time to find out what your competition is charging, so you are charging based on what you feel guests are willing to pay. If your sense of the value of your product is good, then it works. Otherwise, it can be problematic.

3. **Psychological Pricing.** Price is more of a factor to lower-income customers who go to lower-priced bed-and-breakfasts. If they don't know an item is good, they assume it is if it's expensive. If you change your prices, the order in which buyers see them also affects their per-ceptions. If an item was initially more expensive, it will be viewed as a bargain, and vice versa.

4. **Trial-and-Error Pricing.** This is based on customer reactions to prices. It is not practical in terms of determining your overall prices, but can be effective with individual items to bring them closer to the price a customer is willing to pay, or to distinguish them from similar menu items with a higher or lower food cost.

There are still other factors that help determine prices. Whether customers view you as a leader or a follower can make a big difference on how they view your prices. If people think of you as the best seafood bed-and-breakfast in the area, they'll be willing to pay a little more to eat with you. Service also determines people's sense of value. This is even truer when the difference in actual food quality between you and the competition is negligible. If your customers order at a counter and bus their own tables, this lack of service cost needs to be reflected in your prices. Also, in a competitive market, providing great service can be a factor that puts you in a leadership position and allows you to charge a higher price. Your location, ambiance, customer base, product presentation and desired check average all factor into what you feel you can charge and what you need to charge in order to make a profit.

If you are serving lunches or dinners that you will be charging extra for, you'll need to analyze your sales mix to determine the impact each item has on sales, costs and profits. Classifying your menu items is necessary for making those decisions. Here are some suggested classifications:

- **Primes.** These are popular items that are low in food cost and high in profit. Have them stand out on your menu.

- **Standards.** Items with high food costs and high profit margins. You can possibly raise the price on these items and push them as signatures.

- **Sleepers.** Slow-selling, low food-cost items with low profit margins. Work to increase the likelihood that these will be seen and ordered through more prominent menu display, featuring on menu boards, lowered prices, etc.

- **Problems.** High in food cost and low in profits. If you can, raise the price and lower production cost. If you can't, hide them on the menu. If sales don't pick up, get rid of them altogether.

Menu Style

Menu style describes how much or how little variety the menu offers. Do you serve a limited or expansive menu? The things that may influence whether or not you offer a limited menu include kitchen size and labor cost control. Menus with more options, however, do have a broader appeal. Limited-limited menus are generally offered by fast-food operations. These menus allow them to keep production simple and maintain a tight rein on food and labor costs.

Bed-and-breakfasts that serve three meals a day may offer extensive-limited menus. While they offer more items, they limit the number of ways these items are prepared. Smaller bed-and-breakfasts have limited-extensive menus. By preparing and combining the same ingredients in different ways, these establishments are able to offer many more choices but still control inventory and costs. Large bed-and-breakfasts may choose to offer extensive-extensive menus. These establishments offer a great variety of choices of items prepared and methods of preparation.

There are advantages to both the limited and extensive menu styles:

Limited

- You need less equipment and less kitchen space.
- Food prep is simplified and can be speedy.
- You need fewer and less skilled kitchen employees.
- Purchasing your inventory is easier and less time-consuming.
- Space needed for inventory is lessened.

- Cost and quality controls are simpler.
- Operating costs are lower.
- Table turnover can be increased because transaction time is quicker.

Extensive

- You can appeal to a broader customer base.
- New customers will be intrigued.
- Regulars will return more often because they have a greater number of options from which to choose.
- The menu can be more responsive to customer taste.
- The menu is more flexible.
- You can charge higher prices for specialty items.

Formatting Your Menu

After you have defined the style of your menu, you must decide what items will go on your menu. This can be done in a four-step process:

1. You must decide what menu groups you will offer.
2. Decide what categories to offer within these groups. For entree choices, for example, you could offer the following categories: beef, poultry, seafood, pork, lamb, veal and vegetarian. Decide how many dishes you will offer in each category. You may have four beef dishes, three seafood entrees, two poultry and two vegetarian, for example.
3. After deciding the groups and categories that will go on your menu, you need to decide on the specifics of the dish. Will you be serving ground, cubed, solid or roast? Baked, grilled, broiled or fried?
4. Finally, you must decide on the dish itself. If you are offering three beef entrees, you may choose to serve two solid beef dishes and one

ground. Your actual menu items may be a strip steak, a filet mignon and a hamburger.

While this may sound like an onerous task, by keeping these four steps in mind, you will be able to maintain variety in your menu and control cost factors.

Developing the Menu Selections

All menu items selected must fit into the physical workings of the bed-and-breakfast. Thus, the menu should be finalized prior to designing, selecting equipment for and laying out the kitchen. This is necessary for maximum efficiency of time, labor and equipment. The design and layout of the kitchen and work areas must meet the needs of the menu. If it doesn't, the entire operation will become slow, disorganized and inefficient. Inefficiency can only result in a drop in employee morale and in the bed-and-breakfast's profit margin.

Just as the kitchen must meet the demands of the menu, the personnel employed to prepare the menu items must be selected to fit into the design of the kitchen. Careful consideration must be given to the number and type of employees needed. Is the menu simple enough for inexperienced workers to prepare, or are the skills of a professional, more experienced chef needed? Will the food be prepared ahead of time, or upon receipt of the order? When will these employees be needed, and for how long? Will there be enough room in the kitchen for everyone to work at the same time? Who will supervise them?

Planning the bed-and-breakfast menu involves a lot more than merely selecting menu items that are enjoyed and demanded by the bed-and-breakfast's clientele. Menu planning includes arranging equipment, personnel and food products into an efficient unit that will be affordable and in demand by the public.

Major Points to Consider When Selecting Menu Items:

1. The menu item must be of superior quality.
2. The raw materials used in preparing the item must be readily available year-round at a relatively stable price.
3. The menu item must be affordable and demanded by your clientele.
4. The menu item must be acceptable to the preparation and cooking staff system you use.
5. The raw materials used in preparing the menu item must be easily portioned by weight.
6. All menu items must have consistent cooking results.
7. All menu items must have a long shelf life. Food items prepared ahead of time and not utilized may not be sold for as long as 36 hours.
8. All menu items must have similar cooking times (approximately 8–15 minutes), as any entree requiring a longer cooking time will not be completed when the other orders are ready to serve.
9. The storage facilities must accommodate the raw materials used in preparing the menu items.
10. Menu items should be creative and not readily available in other bed-and-breakfasts.

Limiting the Menu

Begin to develop the menu by compiling those recipes and ideas which meet the requirements set forth in the previous section. Consider only the items which are compatible with the bed-and-breakfast's atmosphere, decor and anticipated clientele. Based upon these guidelines, you should have little trouble compiling a considerable list of acceptable choices. The trick is to limit the menu to only those items for which the kitchen is equipped and organized and that the staff can easily execute — while still allowing for an interesting menu with plenty of varied selections.

All too often, a new bed-and-breakfast will list numerous menu selections simply to round out the menu or offer token items that are on almost every menu. New bed-and-breakfasts should move toward specializing and serving only those menu items that they can prepare better than the other establishments in the area. It is simply not justifiable to create a diversified menu for the sole sake of offering a multitude of items. Specialization in the bed-and-breakfast business is the key to building a solid reputation. Develop the menu with only those items for which you have the trained staff and equipment to properly prepare and serve. A successful menu is one that is honed to build a reputation for excellence.

Limiting the menu in the manner described will create many advantages for the entire bed-and-breakfast. The kitchen staff will become more experienced and skilled at preparing each item, as there will be a smaller selection for customers to choose from. The waitstaff can then concentrate on promoting and recommending those items in which the bed-and-breakfast specializes. From an administrative standpoint, a smaller menu will be easier to control. Purchasing will center around only a few major food products; thus the buyer may utilize this large purchasing power to obtain price breaks, discounts and above-average service.

Side dishes and desserts must meet all of the same qualifications as the entrees. The number and kinds of side dishes and desserts should be limited only to those items that are exceptional and slightly out of the ordinary, so they may be promoted as house specialties as well.

Always try to include some menu selections which are produced in the local area. Maine lobster, Cajun cooking, Texas beef, Gulf shrimp, key lime pie and San Francisco sourdough bread are some examples. The tourist trade is an important source of revenue for most bed-and-breakfasts. In fact, many establishments depend on it. With a little promotion, this could be an important new avenue for sales.

Once the menu is finalized, it will be necessary for management to become thoroughly familiar with every aspect of each menu item. Extensive experimentation in the kitchen will be needed to discover the precise recipe ingredients, amounts and preparation procedures. Take the time to find out everything there is to know about the menu items. Determine where the raw products come from, what the best type or brand to purchase is and how the kitchen staff can best handle and store the products. How do other bed-and-breakfasts in the area serve similar dishes?

The rule for developing a portion size is to use the largest portion feasible but charge accordingly. It is far better to serve too much food than too little. The crucial element, which must be constantly reinforced, is that every menu item — entrees, side dishes and some desserts — must be a specific weight and size. Portion control is the basis for the bed-and-breakfast's entire cost-control program. Its importance cannot be overstated.

Portion-controlling all food items is an effective way to control food costs, but it also serves another important function: It maintains consistency in the final product.

Portions may have a variance of up to, but not exceeding, half an ounce. Thus, if the set portion size for a steak is 12 1/2 ounces, the steak may range from 12 to 13 ounces. Any amount over 13 ounces must be trimmed. A light steak should be utilized for something else. Although a ½-ounce variance may seem like a small amount, in actually it will add up very quickly.

Since portion-controlling is such a vital kitchen function, purchase the best scales you can. A good digital ounce scale will cost upwards of $200. However, this investment will be recouped many times over from the food-cost savings it will provide. Maintain these scales per the manufacturers' instructions; clean them periodically and oil when necessary, and they will provide years of service. To ensure the accuracy of the scales, test them periodically with an item of known weight. Most good scales come with a calibration kit.

For practical reasons, some food items, such as dressings, sauces and butter, are portioned by weight. However, they should still be portion-controlled by using proper-size spoons and ladles. Soups and condiments must be placed in proper-size serving containers.

At each work area of the kitchen, place a chart listing the portion sizes and other portion-control practices. All employees must use the measuring cups and spoons and the recipe manual when following recipes. Remember that the basis for the food-cost program you are developing is based upon the knowledge that every item has a precise portion size. Management has the responsibility to ensure that these standards are being practiced and adhered to.

Truth and Accuracy in the Menu

Careful consideration must be taken when writing the final menu to ensure its complete accuracy. Few bed-and-breakfast owners would purposely deceive their customers, as the bed-and-breakfast would only suffer in the long run. However, you must become aware of the unintentional inaccuracies you may have in the menu and the governmental regulations regarding this.

All states have one or more laws which basically say that any organization selling a product must not misrepresent the product in any manner with intent to deceive. Many states have specific "truth in menu" legislation.

Every statement made, whether it be oral or written in the menu description, must be completely accurate. For example, "real maple syrup" must be 100 percent–real maple syrup. "Imported spring lamb" must *be* imported spring lamb. Words and descriptions to watch are: fresh, real, imported, baby, 100 percent, barbecue, pure, natural, homemade, etc. The description printed on the menu must be exactly the product you are serving.

You may be wondering how you can possibly write an enticing menu (that will not read like a grocery list) and yet still remain within the boundaries of the law. The trick is to be creative in writing the descriptions. State precisely what the product is, but modify the sentences to make the product sound enticing. Creative printing and the use of artwork will boost the appeal of the menu.

Menu Size and Cover

The menu cover should reflect your bed-and-breakfast's image as well as its identity. It can include graphics (the bed-and-breakfast's logo) and copy. If your bed-and-breakfast is in a historic building, for instance, you may want to include a drawing or photo of the building on your cover. If you are operating a family bed-and-breakfast that has been in existence for generations, you may want to put a paragraph or two of copy about your family's history or food philosophy. Remember, the cover is the first step in the menu's role as a communication tool, and it's the first place on paper you can communicate your identity to the customer. The menu is the only item that customers are guaranteed to pay attention to when they walk into your establishment.

According to the National Restaurant Association, the ideal menu dimensions are 9 inches wide by 12 inches tall. Of course, other sizes can work as well, and the number of items on the menu will partially determine the menu size. Keep in mind that the menu size should be manageable for the customer.

Remember that they are often maneuvering in a limited space that includes water and wine glasses, candles, table tents and flowers.

The cover should be of some durable material; part of its function is to protect interior pages. It can be leather, vinyl, laminated paper or plastic. Your establishment's identity will help you choose the appropriate cover material. A fine-dining bed-and-breakfast would not use plastic sleeves, but for a mid-price family bed-and-breakfast, plastic-sleeve menu covers would be appropriate. The cover's color should also be chosen with care. The color should tie into the theme and decor of your bed-and-breakfast, but remember, color does have a psychological impact, so you will want colors that will evoke pleasant images and feelings. Bear in mind that the more colors you use for your menu, the more expensive the printing process becomes.

You may also want to include general information on the cover, such as your hours of operation, address, telephone number, the forms of payment you accept and any special services you provide. While your regular customers may not need this information, new customers will appreciate it, and it will make it easier for them to return if they know when you are open and how to find you again.

Menu Design Software

With the advent of the personal computer, there have been a few menu-design software programs developed in recent years. The software is generally very easy to use, having built-in templates, artwork, etc. Your finalized menu can be printed out on a laser printer. Color, artwork and graphics may be added.

Tables tents and other promotional devices can also be utilized. The initial cost of the software will be easily recouped as you save in design and printing costs. In addition, you will have complete control over the design process.

Changes can be made instantly. Daily menus can be made, which is a great way to accommodate special purchases that might have been made. The ability to generate new menus easily allows for instant price changes to reflect market conditions. One such software program is Menu Pro™. This software can be found at **https://softcafe.com**.

Printing the Menu

As indicated in the previous section, creatively printing the menu will have a marked effect upon the marketing of your offerings. The menus in bed-and-breakfasts across the country are probably more diverse than the food itself. Menus range from freehand writing on a white piece of 8 ½ x 11 paper to menus printed on boards, tables, walls and bottles to menus spoken verbally. As you can see, the menu can be easily turned into a promotional vehicle for your bed-and-breakfast; it's a crucial internal marketing tool. It is the way you communicate to your customers your objectives and identity. Your menu design will directly impact guest-check averages, so it can help you achieve your profit goals. A well-designed menu can attract a customer's attention to specific items and increase the chances that the customer will purchase those items. For instance, if you put an item in a box on the menu, the customer's eye will be drawn to this area of the menu.

Regardless of how creatively the menu is utilized, it should be typeset and either printed by a professional or with the professional menu software previously mentioned. Simply using an unusual type style will dress up any menu. Discuss the possibilities with your local printer or graphic artist, or contact a company specializing in menu production.

Artwork should be used if at all possible; use the bed-and-breakfast's logo if nothing else. Your local printer may have an artist on staff or know of some freelancers in the area who can help.

Projecting the Actual Average Cost per Customer

Once set up and operating, it will be relatively easy to compute the actual average cost per customer. The actual average cost per customer should be projected once every month. This ensures that the estimates used in computing the menu costs are accurate.

Keep a list of all the food items you do not charge for during a specific test period and their prices. You can develop this list from the invoices which detail daily purchases. Add into this figure the dollar amount of food you have on hand at the beginning of the test period. This pertains only to the food that you are not directly charging for. At the end of the test period, subtract the amount on hand from the total. Divide the total cost by the number of customers served during that period. This figure is the average actual cost per customer. Use it in projecting menu costs in place of your estimates.

Projecting Menu Prices

Projecting menu prices is a complex procedure because of the number of factors that must be considered. In order to operate profitably, most bed-and-breakfasts must achieve and maintain their food cost of sales at 35–45 percent. The food-cost percentage is the total food cost divided by the total food sales for a given period. For example: if the total food sales for a given period was $100,000 and the total food cost was $40,000 for that same period, the kitchen would be operating at a 40 percent food cost of sales. One percentage point in this example would be worth $1,000.

Computing what you must charge for each entree item is relatively easy. You will need the estimated total portion costs from the preceding section. The total portion cost (food cost) divided by the menu price (food sales) must equal a food-cost percentage of between .35 (35 percent) and .40 (40 percent).

Portion Costs ÷ Menu Price x 100 = 35%–45%

Simply plug different menu prices into the formula until you reach the desired food cost percentage.

The complications result when you've determined the price you must charge in order to make the desired profit. Some of the prices you'd need to charge would be simply too high. No one would ever purchase the item at that price. What you must do in these cases is balance out the menu with high and low food-cost items. The average cost of the menu must then be in the food-cost-percentage range desired. Poultry and seafood entrees will usually have a lower food-cost percentage than meat entrees. Try to promote these lower food cost items to offset the higher ones.

Your clientele will dictate what the market will bear. The bed-and-breakfast manager must set the menu prices based on what customers will spend and what must be charged in order to make the desired profit margin.

Appetizers, side orders, beverages and desserts can be priced at a very low food-cost percentage. These items will contribute to a large percentage of your food sales and will lower your overall food-cost percentage. Some bed-and-breakfast managers, realizing this important point, have set up promotional contests awarding prizes or money to the waiter or waitress who sells the largest percentage of side orders. This can be very effective if the waitstaff do not "hard sell" the items, but rather suggest the accompaniments to their customers.

Maintaining the food-cost percentage is critical to maintaining your profit level. However, the food-cost percentage does not tell the entire story. You must also be interested in getting the largest guest checks possible, to bring the largest percentage of gross profit to your bottom line. For example, which would you rather sell:

a) an item that sells for $5 and has a food cost of 35 percent (a gross profit of $3.25), or

b) an item that sells for $10 and has a food cost of 50 percent (a gross profit of $5.00)?

Here is an example of a higher-food-cost-percentage item actually bringing a higher gross profit. Consider this important point when pricing out the menu.

A baked haddock dinner has a total food cost of $8.18. If you were to charge $17.95, you would have a food-cost percentage of 45.6 percent. Should the percentage be too high or the retail price too high, you can reduce the portion size and the retail price. Some establishments might charge separately for the salad bar or side item. Should the retail price be lower than current market conditions or competing bed-and-breakfasts, you can match the higher price and run a lower food cost on this entree to balance out higher food-cost entree items, such as a prime rib dinner.

If you are not reaching your food-cost goals or are not getting as high a check average as you'd like, it may be because of your menu design. Not all items on your menu can be low cost and high profit. Your menu is likely a mix. Your menu design may be emphasizing high food-cost or low-profit items. Fixing this will help decrease food cost and increase profits. Remember, if you sell too many high-cost items, your food cost will go up, because many of these (such as beef and seafood) have a high cost as well. On the other hand, if you sell too many low-cost items, your check averages and gross profits will decline. Keep this in mind when designing your menu; you want to have a sales mix of both these types of items.

Inventory Levels

The first step in computing what item and how much of it to order is to determine the inventory level, or the amount needed on hand at all times. To determine the amount you need to order, you must first know the amount you have in inventory. Walk through the storage areas with your inventory sheet and mark in the "On Hand" column the amounts that are there. To determine the "Build To Amount," you will need to know when regularly scheduled deliveries arrive for that item and the amount used in the period between deliveries. Add on about 25 percent to the average amount used; this will cover unexpected usage, a late delivery or a backorder at the vendor. The amount you need to order is the difference between the "Build To Amount" and the amount "On Hand." Experience and food demand will reveal the amount an average order should contain. By purchasing too little, the bed-and-breakfast may run out of supplies before the next delivery. Ordering too much will result in tying up money, putting a drain on the bed-and-breakfast's cash flow. Buying items in large amounts can save money, but you must consider the cash-flow costs.

A buying schedule should be set up and adhered to. This would consist of a calendar showing:

- Which day's orders need to be placed
- When deliveries will be arriving
- When items will be arriving from which company
- Phone numbers of sales representatives to contact for each company
- The price the sales representative quoted

Post the buying schedule on the office wall. When a delivery doesn't arrive as scheduled, the buyer should place a phone call to the salesperson or company immediately. Don't wait until the end of the day when offices are closed.

A **Want Sheet** may be placed on a clipboard in the kitchen. This sheet is made available for employees to write in any items they may need to do their jobs more efficiently. This is a very effective form of communication; employees should be encouraged to use it. A request might be as simple as a commercial-grade carrot peeler. If, for example, the last one broke and the preparation staff has been using the back of a knife instead, the small investment could save you from an increase in labor and food costs.

Cooperative Purchasing

If bed-and-breakfasts formed cooperative purchasing groups, they could increase their purchasing power. By cooperatively joining together to place large orders, bed-and-breakfasts can usually get substantial price reductions.

Receiving and Storing

Most deliveries will be arriving at the bed-and-breakfast during the day. Deliveries should only be received during the prescribed time periods: before and after the lunch period.

Receiving and storing each product is a critical responsibility. Costly mistakes can come about from a staff member who was not properly trained in the correct procedures. Listed below are some policies and procedures for receiving and storing all deliveries. A slight inaccuracy in an invoice or improper storing of a perishable item could cost the bed-and-breakfast hundreds of dollars.

All products delivered to the bed-and-breakfast must:

- Be checked against the actual order sheet
- Be the exact specification ordered (weight, size, quantity)
- Be checked against the invoice
- Be accompanied by an invoice containing: current price, totals, date, company name and receiver's signature
- Have their individual weights verified on the pound scale
- Be dated, rotated and put in the proper storage area immediately. (For resources on stocking supplies, visit www.daymarksafety.com, or call 1-866-517-0490.)
- Be locked in their storage areas securely

Credit slips must be issued or prices subtracted from the invoice when an error occurs. The delivery person must sign above the correction.

Keep an invoice box (a small mail box) in the kitchen to store all invoices and packing slips received during the day. Mount the box on the wall, away from work areas. Prior to leaving for the day, the receiver must bring the invoices to the manager's office and place them in a designated spot. Extreme care must be taken to ensure that all invoices are handled correctly. A missing invoice will throw off the bookkeeping and financial records and statements.

Rotation Procedures

1. New items go to the back and on the bottom
2. Older items move to the front and to the left
3. In any part of the bed-and-breakfast: the first item used should always be the oldest
4. Date and label everything

CHAPTER TWELVE

· · · · ·

Houskeeping, Sanitation And Kitchen Safety

Cleaning

Cleaning is a very important aspect of all B&Bs. While you want that homey atmosphere, homey does not mean cluttered or dirty. Guests expect cleanliness. First, you must decide if you are going to do the cleaning or if you are going to hire an outside service to do this cleaning.

Whether you do all the cleaning or you have help, this checklist might come in handy.

Full-Service Hotel Checklist

ROOM: _____ INSPECTED BY: _____

DATE: _____ ROOM ATTENDANT: _____

Clean = C Dirty = D
Needs Repair = R Missing = M

ENTRY

Outside/inside door
❑ C ❑ D ❑ R ❑ M

Locks
❑ C ❑ D ❑ R ❑ M

Chain
❑ C ❑ D ❑ R ❑ M

Doorstop
❑ C ❑ D ❑ R ❑ M

"Do Not Disturb" sign
❑ C ❑ D ❑ R ❑ M

Emergency/evacuation chart
❑ C ❑ D ❑ R ❑ M

Fire pamphlets
❑ C ❑ D ❑ R ❑ M

Smoke detectors
❑ C ❑ D ❑ R ❑ M

Thermostat
❑ C ❑ D ❑ R ❑ M

IN CLOSET

Shelves/rods
❑ C ❑ D ❑ R ❑ M

Hangers – men's (6)
❑ C ❑ D ❑ R ❑ M

Hangers – women's (6)
❑ C ❑ D ❑ R ❑ M

Laundry/dry cleaning price lists
❑ C ❑ D ❑ R ❑ M

Luggage racks (2)
❑ C ❑ D ❑ R ❑ M

Telephone book
❑ C ❑ D ❑ R ❑ M

BEDROOM

Carpet
❑ C ❑ D ❑ R ❑ M

Under the beds
❑ C ❑ D ❑ R ❑ M

Walls/ceiling
❑ C ❑ D ❑ R ❑ M

Drapes/curtains
❑ C ❑ D ❑ R ❑ M

Windows
❑ C ❑ D ❑ R ❑ M

Windowsills/frames
❑ C ❑ D ❑ R ❑ M

TV/travel host
❑ C ❑ D ❑ R ❑ M

Remote control
❑ C ❑ D ❑ R ❑ M

Bed frames
❑ C ❑ D ❑ R ❑ M

Headboards (straight)
❑ C ❑ D ❑ R ❑ M

Pictures (straight)
❑ C ❑ D ❑ R ❑ M

ON NIGHTSTAND

Telephone
❑ C ❑ D ❑ R ❑ M

Memo pad/pen
❑ C ❑ D ❑ R ❑ M

Guest services directory
❑ C ❑ D ❑ R ❑ M

Alarm clock/radio
❑ C ❑ D ❑ R ❑ M

Room service menu
❑ C ❑ D ❑ R ❑ M

IN NIGHTSTAND

Bible
❑ C ❑ D ❑ R ❑ M

Guest book
❑ C ❑ D ❑ R ❑ M

LIGHTING

Bulbs
❑ C ❑ D ❑ R ❑ M

Fixtures
❑ C ❑ D ❑ R ❑ M

Lamps/shades
❑ C ❑ D ❑ R ❑ M

ON DESK/DRESSER

Folder containing:

Stationery (5)
❑ C ❑ D ❑ R ❑ M

Envelopes (3)
❑ C ❑ D ❑ R ❑ M

Directory
❑ C ❑ D ❑ R ❑ M

Pen
❑ C ❑ D ❑ R ❑ M

Postcards
❑ C ❑ D ❑ R ❑ M

Brochure
❑ C ❑ D ❑ R ❑ M

Ice bucket
❑ C ❑ D ❑ R ❑ M

Tray
❑ C ❑ D ❑ R ❑ M

Glasses w/ caps (2)
❑ C ❑ D ❑ R ❑ M

Janitorial and Maintenance Service

Depending upon the size and operating hours of the bed-and-breakfast, you may wish to use the services of a professional cleaning company. They will clean and maintain the areas previously agreed upon in the service contract. Their work is guaranteed.

The maintenance service company selected must have impeccable references. The company should be insured against liability and employee pilferage, and employees should be bonded. You will probably need to give the owner or manager of the company their own keys to the entrance, maintenance closets, security system and possibly the office for cleaning.

Some important factors to consider when choosing a maintenance company:

- Can they assist with cleaning prior to opening?
- Bids for the job. They vary widely: look at the contracts and proposals closely
- The hours they will be in the bed-and-breakfast
- Cleaning supplies. Who buys the soaps, chemicals, etc.?
- Equipment. Who buys vacuums, brooms, etc.?
- Have a trial period written into the contract
- Have your lawyer examine the contract before signing
- How will you communicate to discuss problems?
- References from other bed-and-breakfasts
- Make them aware that no toxic chemicals are allowed in the kitchen
- Inexperienced companies can cause damage to items cleaned incorrectly. Use a company with a pristine track record.

- Garbage emptied from the offices should be kept in dated plastic garbage bags and saved for one week. They may contain important information or papers accidentally thrown away.

Listed below are some basic maintenance functions any service contract should contain. This is just a basic outline; the actual contract must contain specific items that must be cleaned and when. Both your and the maintenance company's supervisor should have a checklist of everything that must be completed each night. The morning following the service, walk through the bed-and-breakfast, spot-checking from the checklist that all items have been completed as prescribed. Notify the supervisor immediately of any unsatisfactory work. At first, it may take a great deal of communication to get the desired results. Once operating a few months, however, it will run smoothly.

Items to be cleaned daily:

1. All floors washed and treated
2. Vacuum entire bed-and-breakfast
3. Dust: windowsills, woodwork, pictures, chairs, tables, etc.
4. Outside area: sweep and clean; patrol parking lot for trash
5. Bathrooms: clean, sanitize and deodorize; replace supplies; i.e., toilet paper, soap, napkins, tampons, etc.
6. Trash containers: empty, sterilize
7. All sinks and floor drains cleaned
8. Maintenance room: clean and organize

Weekly services:

1. All windows cleaned inside and out
2. Polish all chairs and woodwork
3. Strip, wax and polish decorative floors

Annually:

1. Steam clean all carpets

As previously indicated, these examples describe a generalized outline of some of the major points a service contract should contain. All of these areas, plus the ones that pertain to your bed-and-breakfast, need to be expanded to detail precisely how, when and what needs to be done.

Some manufacturers include in their equipment detailed instructions for the cleaning of their product. Special cleaners must be used on some equipment. Improperly cleaning a piece of equipment can ruin it forever. Keep all of this information in a loose-leaf binder in the office. The cleaning supervisor should have access to this manual and must be thoroughly familiar with its contents.

DIY

If you do the cleaning yourself, a good deal of it will happen when you are at your busiest — between check-in and check-out time. It's very important to establish a cleaning order or schedule to get this work done most efficiently so new guests are not arriving to dirty rooms or a dining room full of used breakfast dishes.

First, clean up the dining room and any other common area the guests are going to see first. If you are running behind schedule on the rooms, at least your guests can relax in the tidy sitting room while they wait for their rooms to be finished. Make sure to dust, sweep, remove dirty dishes and replace any fresh flowers.

Clean the bedrooms next. When cleaning the bedrooms, be sure to check for finger marks, stains, residual odors and dust. Here is a list for daily bedroom cleaning:

- Change all bed linens
- Replace water glasses
- Dust all surfaces
- Use a furniture cleaner on all wood furniture
- Clean windows and mirrors
- Empty wastebaskets
- Replenish facial tissue
- Vacuum

Clean the bathrooms next. If the room has a private bath, you'll be doing this the same time you clean the room. Here is a cleaning checklist for bathrooms:

- Replace all towels, washcloths, mats, etc.
- Clean shower, checking for soap scum and mildew
- Clean mirror and shower doors (if applicable)
- Clean toilet with a brush and cleanser
- Clean all surfaces
- Mop floor
- Empty wastebasket
- Replenish toilet tissue, facial tissue and soap

Be sure to clean hallways as you move onto the kitchen. In the kitchen you'll need to clean up all the dishes from breakfast. While bed-and-breakfasts may not be under the same strict regulations restaurants are in your state, your guests will still be concerned with the cleanliness of your kitchen.

Here is a checklist to use for your kitchen breakfast cleanup:

- ❏ 1. Turn off all equipment and pilots
- ❏ 2. Take all pots, pans and utensils to the dishwasher
- ❏ 3. Wrap, date and rotate all leftover food
- ❏ 4. Clean out the refrigerator units
- ❏ 5. Clean all shelves
- ❏ 6. Wipe down all walls
- ❏ 7. Spot clean the exhaust hoods
- ❏ 8. Clean and polish all stainless steel in your area
- ❏ 9. Clean out all sinks
- ❏ 10. Take out all trash and break down boxes to conserve space in dumpster
- ❏ 11. Sweep the floor in your area
- ❏ 12. Replace all clean pots, pans and utensils

Sanitation and Food Safety

Even if you are only serving cold breakfasts, it is crucial that you know about food safety and sanitation.

You are responsible for protecting your customers by serving safe and whole-some food. To accomplish this, you have to educate your employees and motivate them to put into practice at every step what they've learned about food safety. To do this, you need a systematic process for identifying potential hazards, putting safety procedures in place and monitoring the success of your safety system on an ongoing basis. Hazard Analysis Critical Control Points (HACCP) helps you do all of these things.

Using HACCP, you can identify potentially hazardous foods and places in the food-preparation process where bacterial contamination, survival and growth can occur. Then you can take action to minimize the danger.

HACCP is based on this principle: If the raw ingredients are safe, and the process is safe, then the finished product is safe.

Implementing HACCP involves seven key steps. As you proceed through these steps, you will:

1. Assess the hazards
2. Identify "critical control points"
3. Establish "critical limits"
4. Monitor the "critical control points"
5. Take corrective action as needed
6. Develop a record-keeping system
7. Verify your system's effectiveness

Step 1: Assess the Hazards

To assess the hazards present at each stage of the preparation process, track each food from purchasing and receiving through serving and reheating.

To begin, review your menus. Identify all potentially hazardous foods, as well as those foods that may become contaminated during the process.

At this point, you may even want to reduce risks by removing highly hazardous food items from your menu. For example, if you prepare picnic basket lunches for your guests to take on hikes, you may want to avoid egg salad sandwiches.

Once you have surveyed the foods on your menu, evaluate general preparation and cooking procedures to isolate any points where contamination might occur. Next, rank these hazards in terms of severity (how serious are the consequences) and probability (how likely are they to occur).

Step 2: Identify "Critical Control Points"

Identify the points in the process where hazards can be controlled or prevented. Develop a flowchart, or list the steps involved in preparing each potentially hazardous food. Then, identify procedures to prevent, reduce and eliminate recontamination hazards at each step you have listed.

In general, food service workers can reduce the risk of food-borne illness by:

1. Practicing good personal hygiene.
2. Avoiding cross-contamination.
3. Using proper cooking and cooling procedures.
4. Reducing the number of steps involved in preparing and serving.

Step 3: Establish "Critical Limits"

In order to be sure a food passes safely through a critical control point, you need to establish critical limits that must be met. These critical limits should be standards that are observable and measurable. They should include precise time, temperature and sensory requirements.

Specify exactly what should be done to meet each particular standard. For example, instead of saying that a "food must be thoroughly cooked," the standard might say "heat rapidly to an internal temperature of 165 F within two hours."

In addition: Make sure employees have calibrated, metal-stemmed or digital thermometers and that they use them routinely.

Make sure recipes state: 1) end-cooking, reheating and hot-holding temperatures, and 2) handling leftovers, specific times for thawing, cooking and cooling foods. Schedule sufficient staff in peak hours to prepare and serve foods safely.

Step 4: Monitor the "Critical Control Points"

Using your flowcharts or lists, follow potentially hazardous foods through every step in the process. Compare your operation's performance with the requirements you have set. Identify any areas of deficiency.

Step 5: Take Corrective Action

Take corrective action as needed. For example, if products' temperatures are unacceptable when received, reject the shipment. Also:

- If food is contaminated by hands or equipment, rewash or discard it.
- If food temperature is not high enough after cooking, continue cooking to the required temperature.
- If food temperature exceeds 55 F during cold prep or serving, discard it.

Step 6: Develop a Record-Keeping System

Develop a record-keeping system to document the HACCP process and monitor your results. This may be any simple, quick system, such as a log, in which employees can record their compliance with standards at critical control points. These records are crucial and may provide proof that a food-borne illness did not originate at your establishment.

Step 7: Verify Your System's Effectiveness

Verify that the HACCP process in your facility works. You can do this in a number of ways.

For starters, be alert to how often you need to take corrective actions. If you need to take corrective actions frequently, this may indicate a need to change, or at least fine-tune, your system.

In addition, think of tests you can do, like measuring the strength of your sanitizing solution. Also, examine your records and make sure employees are entering actual, valid data.

An inspection by the Board of Health can provide a good assessment of whether or not your process is working.

HACCP'S Eight Key Steps of the Food Service Process

In order, we'll look at:

1. Purchasing
2. Receiving
3. Storing
4. Preparing
5. Cooking
6. Serving and holding
7. Cooling
8. Reheating

There are multiple hazards at, and specific preventative measures for, each step. Depending on the size of your bed-and-breakfast or inn, all these steps may not be applicable to your situation. Safe food preparation, however, is applicable to everyone!

HACCP Step 1: Purchasing

The goal of purchasing is to obtain wholesome, safe foods to meet your menu requirements. Safety at this step is primarily the responsibility of your vendors. It's your job to choose your vendors wisely. Suppliers must meet federal and state health standards. They should use the HACCP system in their operations and train their employees in sanitation. Delivery trucks should have adequate refrigeration and freezer units, and foods should be packaged in protective, leak-proof, durable packaging. Let vendors know upfront what you expect from them. Put food-safety standards in your purchase specification agreements. Ask to see their most recent Board of Health Sanitation Reports, and tell them you will be inspecting trucks on a quarterly basis.

Good vendors will cooperate with your inspections and should adjust their delivery schedules to avoid your busy periods so that incoming foods can be received and inspected properly.

HACCP Step 2: Receiving

The goals of receiving are: 1) to make sure foods are fresh and safe when they enter your facility, and 2) to transfer them to proper storage as quickly as possible.

Let's look more closely at two important parts of receiving:

1. Getting ready to receive food.
2. Inspecting the food when the delivery truck arrives.

There are several important guidelines to keep in mind and tasks to complete as you get ready to receive food:

- Make sure your receiving area is equipped with sanitary carts for transporting goods.
- Plan ahead for deliveries to ensure sufficient refrigerator and freezer space.
- Mark all items for storage with the date of arrival or the "use by" date.
- Keep the receiving area well-lit and clean to discourage pests.
- Immediately remove empty containers and packing materials to a separate trash area.
- Keep all flooring clean of food particles and debris.

When the delivery truck arrives, make sure it looks and smells clean and is equipped with the proper food storage equipment. Then inspect foods immediately:

- Check expiration dates of milk, eggs and other perishable goods.
- Make sure shelf-life dates have not expired.
- Make sure frozen foods are in airtight, moisture-proof wrappings.
- Reject foods that have been thawed and refrozen. Look for signs of thawing and refreezing such as large crystals, solid areas of ice or excessive ice in containers.
- Reject cans that have any of the following: swollen sides or ends, flawed seals or seams, dents or rust. Also reject any cans whose contents are foamy or bad-smelling.
- Check temperature of refrigerated and frozen foods, especially eggs and dairy products, fresh meat, fish and poultry products.
- Look for content damage and insect infestations.
- Reject dairy, bakery and other foods delivered in flats or crates that are dirty.

HACCP Step 3: Storing

In general, there are four possible ways to store food:

1. In dry storage, for longer holding of less perishable items
2. In refrigeration, for short-term storage of perishable items
3. In specially designed deep-chilling units for short periods
4. In a freezer, for longer-term storage of perishable foods

Each type of storage has its own sanitation and safety requirements.

Dry Storage

There are many items that can be safely held in a sanitary storeroom. These include, for example: canned goods, baking supplies (such as salt and sugar), grain products (such as rice and cereals) and other dry items. In addition, some fruits (such as bananas, avocados and pears) ripen best at room temperature. Some vegetables, such as onions, potatoes and tomatoes, also store best in dry storage. A dry-storage room should be clean and orderly, with good ventilation to control temperature and humidity and retard the growth of bacteria and mold. Keep in mind the following:

- For maximum shelf life, dry foods should be held at 50 F, but 60–70 F is adequate for most products.
- Use a wall thermometer to check the temperature of your dry-storage facility regularly.
- To ensure freshness, store opened items in tightly covered containers. Use the "first in, first out" (FIFO) rotation method, dating packages and placing incoming supplies in the back so that older supplies will be used first.
- To avoid pest infestation and cross-contamination, clean up all spills immediately and do not store trash or garbage cans in food storage areas.
- Do not place any items — including paper products — on the floor. Make sure the bottom shelf of the dry-storage room is at least 6 inches above the ground.
- To avoid chemical contamination, never use or store cleaning materials or other chemicals where they might contaminate foods. Store them, labeled, in their own section in the storeroom away from all food supplies.

Refrigerated Storage

Keep fresh meat, poultry, seafood, dairy products, most fresh fruit and vegetables and hot leftovers in the refrigerator at internal temperatures of below 40 F.

Although no food can last forever, refrigeration increases the shelf life of most products. Most importantly, because refrigeration slows bacterial growth, the colder a food is, the safer it is.

Your refrigeration unit should contain open, slotted shelving to allow cold air to circulate around food. Do not line shelves with foil or paper. Also do not overload the refrigerator, and be sure to leave space between items to further improve air circulation.

All refrigerated foods should be dated and properly sealed. In addition:

1. Use clean, nonabsorbent, covered containers that are approved for food storage.
2. Store dairy products separately from foods with strong odors like onions, cabbage and seafood.
3. To avoid cross-contamination, store raw or uncooked food away from and below prepared or ready-to-eat food.
4. Never allow fluids from raw poultry, fish or meat to come into contact with other foods.
5. Keeping perishable items at the proper temperature is a key factor in preventing food-borne illness. Check the temperature of your refrigeration unit regularly to make sure it stays below 40 F. Keep in mind that opening and closing the refrigerator door too often can affect temperature.

Many commercial refrigerators are equipped with externally mounted or built-in thermometers. These are convenient when they work, but it is important to have a backup.

It's a good idea to have several thermometers in different parts of the refrigerator to ensure consistent temperature and accuracy of instruments. Record the temperature of each refrigerator on a chart, preferably once a day.

Deep Chilling

Deep or super chilling — that is, storing foods at temperatures between 26 F and 32 F — has been found to decrease bacterial growth. This method can be used to increase the shelf life of fresh foods, such as poultry, meat, seafood and other protein items, without compromising their quality by freezing. You can deep-chill foods in specially designed units or in a refrigerator set to deep-chilling temperature.

Frozen Storage

Frozen meats, poultry, seafood, fruits and vegetables and some dairy products, such as ice cream, should be stored in a freezer at 0 F to keep them fresh and safe for an extended period of time.

As a rule, you should use your freezer primarily to store foods that are frozen when you receive them. Freezing refrigerated foods can damage the quality of perishable items. It's important to store frozen foods immediately. It's also important to remember that storing foods in the freezer for too long increases the likelihood of contamination and spoilage. Like your refrigeration unit, the freezer should allow cold air to circulate around foods easily.

Be sure to:

- Store frozen foods in moisture-proof material or containers to minimize loss of flavor, as well as discoloration, dehydration and odor absorption.

- Monitor temperature regularly, using several thermometers to ensure accuracy and consistent temperatures. Record the temperature of each freezer on a chart.

- Remember that frequently opening and closing the freezer's door can raise the temperature, as can placing warm foods in the freezer.

- To minimize heat gain, open freezer doors only when necessary and remove as many items at one time as possible. You can also use a freezer "cold curtain" to help guard against heat gain.

HACCP Step 4: Preparing

Thawing and Marinating

Freezing food keeps most bacteria from multiplying, but it does not kill them. Bacteria that are present when food is removed from the freezer may multiply rapidly if thawed at room temperature.

Thus, it is critical to thaw foods *out of* the "temperature danger zone." Never thaw foods on a counter or in any other non-refrigerated area!

Some foods, such as frozen vegetables and pre-formed hamburger patties and chicken nuggets, can be cooked from the frozen state. It is important to note, however, that this method depends on the size of the item. For example, cooking from a frozen state is not recommended for large foods like a 20-pound turkey.

The two best methods for thawing foods are:

1. In refrigeration at a temperature below 40 F, placed in a pan on the lowest shelf so juices cannot drip on other foods.
2. Under clean, drinkable running water at a temperature of 70 F or less for no more than two hours, or just until the product is thawed.

Always marinate meat, fish and poultry in the refrigerator — never at room temperature. Never save and reuse marinade. With all methods, be careful not to cross-contaminate!

Cautions for Cold Foods

When you are preparing cold foods, you are at one of the most hazardous points in the food-preparation process. There are two key reasons for this:

1. Cold food preparation usually takes place at room temperature.
2. Cold food is one of the most common points of contamination and cross-contamination.

Chicken salad, tuna salad, potato salad with eggs and other protein-rich salads are common sources of food-borne illness. Sandwiches prepared in advance and held unrefrigerated are also dangerous.

Because cold foods such as these receive no further cooking, it is essential that all ingredients used in them are properly cleaned, prepared and, where applicable, cooked. It is a good idea to chill meats and other ingredients and combine them while chilled.

Here are several other important precautions to keep in mind:

- Prepare foods no further in advance than necessary.
- Prepare foods in small batches and place in cold storage immediately. This will prevent holding food too long in the "temperature danger zone."
- Always hold prepared cold foods below 40 F.
- Wash fresh fruits and vegetables with plain water to remove surface pesticide residues and other impurities, such as soil particles.
- Use a brush to scrub thick-skinned produce, if desired.

- Beware of **cross-contamination**! It's crucial to:
    - » Keep raw products separate from ready-to-serve foods.
    - » Sanitize cutting boards, knives and other food contact surfaces after each contact with a potentially hazardous food.
    - » Discard any leftover batter, breading or marinade after it has been used with potentially hazardous foods.

HACCP Step 5: Cooking

Even when potentially hazardous foods are properly thawed, bacteria and other contaminants may still be present. Cooking foods to the proper internal temperature will kill any existing bacteria and make food safe.

It's important to remember, however, that conventional cooking procedures cannot destroy bacterial spores nor deactivate their toxins.

Keep in mind the following safe cooking tips:

- Stir foods cooked in deep pots frequently to ensure thorough cooking.
- When deep-frying potentially hazardous foods, make sure fryers are not overloaded, and make sure the oil temperature returns to the required level before adding the next batch. Use a hot-oil thermometer designed for this special application.
- Regulate size and thickness of each portion to make cooking time predictable and uniform.
- Allow cooking equipment to heat up between batches.
- Never interrupt the cooking process. Partially cooking poultry or meat, for example, may produce conditions that encourage bacterial growth.

Monitor the accuracy of heating equipment with each use by using thermometers. In addition, always use a thermometer to ensure food reaches the proper temperature during cooking. Use a sanitized, metal-stemmed, numerically scaled thermometer (accurate to plus or minus 2 F) or a digital thermometer. Check food temperature in several places, especially in the thickest parts, to make sure the food is thoroughly cooked. To avoid getting a false reading, be careful not to touch the pan or bone with the thermometer.

HACCP Step 6: Serving and Holding

Food that has been cooked isn't necessarily safe. In fact, many outbreaks occur because improper procedures were used following cooking. Although it may be tempting to hold food at temperatures just hot enough to serve, it is essential to keep prepared foods *out of* the "temperature danger zone." This means, specifically:

- Always keep hot foods in hot-holding equipment above 140 F.
- Always keep cold foods in a refrigeration unit or surrounded by ice below 40 F.

For safer serving and holding:

- Use hot-holding equipment, such as steam tables and hot-food carts, during service but never for reheating.
- Stir foods at reasonable intervals to ensure even heating.
- Check temperatures with a food thermometer every 30 minutes.
- Sanitize the thermometer before each use, or use a digital infrared thermometer that never touches the food.
- Cover hot-holding equipment to retain heat and to guard against contamination.

- Monitor the temperature of hot-holding equipment with each use.
- Discard any food held in the "temperature danger zone" for more than four hours.

To avoid contamination, never add fresh food to a serving pan containing foods that have already been out for serving!

Some key points:

1. Always wash hands with soap and warm water for at least 20 seconds before serving food.
2. Use cleaned and sanitized long-handled ladles and spoons so bare hands do not touch food.
3. Never touch the parts of glasses, cups, plates or tableware that will come into contact with food.
4. Never touch the parts of dishes that will come into contact with the customer's mouth.
5. Wear gloves if serving food by hand.
6. Cover cuts or infections with bandages, and if on hands, cover with gloves.
7. Discard gloves whenever they touch an unsanitary surface.
8. Use tongs or wear gloves to dispense rolls and bread.
9. Clean and sanitize equipment and utensils thoroughly after each use.
10. Use lids and sneeze guards to protect prepared food from contamination.

To avoid contamination, always wash hands, utensils and other food-contact surfaces *after* contact with raw meat or poultry and *before* contact with cooked meat or poultry. For example, do not reuse a serving pan used to hold raw chicken to serve the same chicken after it's cooked, unless the pan has been thoroughly cleaned and sanitized.

Sanitary Self-Service

Like workers, customers can also act as a source of contamination. Unlike workers, customers — especially children — are generally not educated about food sanitation and may do the following unsanitary things:

- Use the same plate twice
- Touch food with their hands
- Touch the edges of serving dishes
- Sneeze or cough into food
- Pick up foods, such as rolls or carrot sticks, with their fingers
- Eat while in the food line
- Dip their fingers into foods to taste them
- Return food items to avoid waste
- Put their heads under sneeze guards to reach items in the back

Be sure to observe customer behavior and remove any foods that may have been contaminated. Also, as a precautionary measure, serve sealed packages of crackers, breadsticks and condiments, and pre-wrap, date and label sandwiches if possible.

HACCP Step 7: Cooling

Here, as at other critical points, every move you make can mean the difference between the safe and the unsafe.

It is often necessary to prepare foods in advance or use leftover foods. Unfortunately, this can easily lead to problems, unless proper precautions are taken. In fact, problems at this stage are the No. 1 cause of food-borne illness. The two key precautions for preventing food-borne illness at this point in the process are rapid cooling and protection from contamination.

Chilling It Quickly

All potentially hazardous, cooked leftovers should be chilled to an internal temperature of below 40 F.

Quick-chill any leftovers larger than half a gallon or 2 pounds.

Quick chilling involves five simple steps:

1. Reduce food mass. Smaller amounts of food will chill more quickly than larger amounts, so cut large items into pieces or divide food among several containers or shallow pans.

   Use shallow, pre-chilled pans (no more than 4 inches deep). Use stainless-steel containers when possible; stainless steel transfers heat better and cools faster than plastic.

2. Chill. Ideally, place food in an ice-water bath or quick-chill unit (26–32 F) rather than a refrigerator. These options are best for two reasons:

    a. Water is a much better heat conductor than air. As a result, foods can cool much more quickly in an ice bath than they can in a refrigerator.

    b. Refrigeration units are designed to keep cold foods cold rather than to chill hot foods. They can take too long to cool foods to safe temperatures.

Another option is to pre-chill foods in a freezer for about 30 minutes before refrigerating.

Separate food items so air can flow freely around them. Do not stack shallow pans. Never cool at room temperature.

3. Stir frequently. Stirring accelerates cooling and helps to ensure that cold air reaches all parts of the food.

4. Measure temperature periodically. Food should reach a temperature of 70 F within two hours and 40 F within four hours. It's important to note that this time must be reduced if food has already spent time in the "temperature danger zone" at any other point in the preparation and serving process.

5. Tightly cover and label cooled foods. On labels, include preparation dates and times.

Be aware that although uncovered foods cool faster, they are at increased risk for cross-contamination. Be sure to store uncovered cooked and cooled foods on the upper shelves of the cooler, and cover them when they reach 45 F. Never store them beneath raw foods.

HACCP Step 8: Reheating

While assuming leftovers are safe might seem reasonable, it's not. In reheating and serving leftovers — just as in all phases of the food-preparation process — you must be careful to avoid contamination.

To safely reheat and serve leftovers, be sure to:

- Boil sauces, soups and gravies, and heat other foods to a minimum of 165 F within two hours of taking the food out of the refrigerator.
- Never reheat food in hot-holding equipment.
- Never mix a leftover batch of food with a fresh batch of food.
- Never reheat food more than once.

The Difference between Clean and Sanitary

Heat or chemicals can be used to reduce the number of bacteria to acceptable levels. They can also be used to reduce certain other harmful microorganisms.

Heat sanitizing involves exposing equipment to high heat for an adequate length of time. This may be done manually by immersing equipment in water maintained at a temperature of 170–195 F for at least 30 seconds, or in a dishwasher that washes at 150 F and rinses at 180 F.

For any method, it is important to check water temperature frequently. Thermometers and heat-sensitive tapes and labels are available for determining whether adequate sanitation temperatures have been achieved.

Chemical sanitizing can be accomplished by immersing an object in, or wiping it down with, bleach or sanitizing solution.

For bleaching, use ½ ounce or 1 tablespoon of 5 percent bleach per gallon of water. For using commercial products, follow the manufacturers' instructions.

Chemical sanitizers are regulated by the EPA, and manufacturers must follow strict labeling requirements regarding what concentrations to use, data on minimum effectiveness and warnings of possible health hazards.

Chemical test strips are available for testing the strength of the sanitizing solution. Because sanitizing agents become less effective as they kill bacteria and are exposed to air, it is important to test the sanitizing solution frequently.

Sanitizing Portable Equipment:

1. To properly clean and sanitize portable equipment, you must have a sink with three separate compartments: for cleaning, rinsing and sanitizing.
2. There should be a separate area for scraping and rinsing food and debris into a garbage container or disposal before washing, and separate drain boards for clean and soiled items.
3. Clean and sanitize sinks and work surfaces.
4. Scrape and rinse food into garbage or disposal. Pre-soak items, such as silverware, as necessary.
5. In the first sink, immerse the equipment in a clean detergent solution at about 120 F. Use a brush or a cloth to loosen and remove any remaining visible soil.
6. Rinse in the second sink using clear, clean water between 120 F and 140 F to remove all traces of food, debris and detergent.
7. Sanitize in the third sink by immersing items in hot water at 170 F for 30 seconds or in a chemical sanitizing solution for one minute. Be sure to cover all surfaces of the equipment with hot water or the sanitizing solution and keep them in contact with it for the appropriate amount of time.

8. If soapsuds disappear in the first compartment or remain in the second, if the water temperature cools or if water in any compartment becomes dirty and cloudy, empty the compartment and refill it.

9. Air dry. Wiping can recontaminate equipment and can remove the sanitizing solution from the surfaces before it has finished working.

10. Make certain all equipment is dry before putting it into storage; moisture can foster bacterial growth.

Sanitizing In-Place Equipment

Larger and immobile equipment should also be washed, rinsed and sanitized.

Use the following procedure:

1. Unplug electrically powered equipment, such as meat slicers.
2. Remove fallen food particles and scraps.
3. Wash, rinse and sanitize any removable parts using the manual immersion method described in steps 5 through 7 for sanitizing portable equipment.
4. Wash the remaining food-contact surfaces and rinse with clean water. Wipe down with a chemical sanitizing solution mixed according to the manufacturer's directions.
5. Wipe down all non-food-contact surfaces with a sanitized cloth, and allow all parts to air dry before reassembling. Sanitize cloth before and during by rinsing it in sanitizing solution.
6. Re-sanitize the external food-contact surfaces of the parts that were handled during reassembling.
7. Scrub wooden surfaces, such as cutting boards, with a detergent solution and a stiff-bristled nylon brush, then rinse in clear, clean water and wipe down with a sanitizing solution after every use.

A First-Rate Facility

Safe and sanitary food service begins with a facility that is clean and in good repair. The entire facility — work areas as well as equipment — should be designed for easy cleaning and maintenance.

It's important to eliminate hard-to-clean work areas, as well as faulty or over-loaded refrigerators or other equipment. Also get rid of dirty surroundings and any conditions that will attract pests.

Remember, the easier the workplace is *to* clean, the more likely it will *stay* clean.

Floors, Walls and Ceilings

Floors, walls and ceilings should be free of dirt, litter and moisture.

Clean walls regularly by swabbing with a cleaning solution or by spraying with a pressure nozzle. Sweep floors, then clean them using a spray method or by mopping. Swab ceilings, instead of spraying them, to avoid soaking lights and ceiling fans.

And don't forget corners and hard-to-reach places!

Ventilation

Good ventilation is a critical factor in maintaining a clean food service environment. Ventilation removes steam, smoke, grease and heat from food-preparation areas and equipment. This helps maintain indoor air quality and reduces the possibility of fires from accumulated grease. In addition, good ventilation eliminates condensation and other airborne contaminants. It also:

- Reduces the accumulation of dirt in the food-preparation area
- Reduces odors, gases and fumes

- Reduces mold growth by reducing humidity

To ensure good ventilation, be sure to:

- Use exhaust fans to remove odors and smoke.
- Use hoods over cooking areas and dishwashing equipment.
- Check exhaust fans and hoods regularly to make sure they are clean and operating properly.
- Clean hood filters routinely according to the instructions provided by the hood manufacturer.

Storerooms

Like all areas of the facility, storerooms must be kept clean and litter-free. To accomplish this, be sure to sweep and scrub walls, ceilings, floors, shelves, light fixtures and racks on a routine basis. Check all storage areas frequently — this includes your refrigerator and freezer as well as your dry-storage room. In checking storage areas:

- Look for damaged or spoiled foods, broken or torn packages and bulging or leaking cans.
- Remove any potentially spoiled foods immediately, and clean the area thoroughly.
- Make sure foods and other supplies are stored at least 6 inches from the walls and above the floor.

To avoid chemical contamination, store cleaning supplies and chemicals in a separate area away from food supply areas and other chemicals so they do not pose a hazard to food or people.

Bacteria

Bacteria are everywhere: in the air, in all areas of the bed-and-breakfast and all over one's body. Most bacteria are microscopic and of no harm to people. Many forms of bacteria are actually beneficial, aiding in the production of such things as cheese, bread, butter, alcoholic beverages, etc. Only a small percentage of bacteria will cause food to spoil and can generate a form of food poisoning when consumed.

Bacteria need food, water and warmth in order to survive. Their growth rate depends upon how favorable these conditions are. Bacteria prefer to ingest moisture-saturated foods, such as meats, dairy products and produce. They will not grow as readily on dry foods such as cereals, sugar or flour.

Bacteria will grow most rapidly when the temperature is between 85–100 F. In most cases, the growth rate will slow down drastically if the temperature is hotter or colder than this. Thus, it is vitally important that perishable food items are refrigerated before bacteria have a chance to establish themselves and multiply. Certain bacteria can survive in extreme hot and cold temperature ranges. By placing these bacteria in severe temperatures, you will be slowing down their growth rate, but not necessarily killing them.

The greatest problem in controlling bacteria is their rapid reproduction cycle. Approximately every 15 minutes, the bacteria count will double under optimal living conditions. The more bacteria present, the greater the chance of bacterial infection. This is why food products that must be subjected to conditions favorable to bacteria are done so for the shortest period possible.

Bacterial forms do not have a means of transportation; they must be introduced to an area by some other vehicle. People are primarily responsible for transporting bacteria to new areas. The body temperature of 98.6 F is perfect for bacterial existence and proliferation. A person coughing, sneezing or wiping their hands on a counter can introduce bacteria to an area. Bacteria may be transmitted also by insects, air, water and articles onto which they have attached themselves, such as boxes, blades, knives and cutting boards.

Dangerous Forms of Bacteria

The following section describes a number of harmful bacteria that may be found in a bed-and-breakfast. The technical names and jargon are given for your own information. The important points to retain are the causes and preventive actions for each.

Clostridium Perfringens

Clostridium perfringens is one of a group of bacterial infectious diseases that will cause a poisoning effect. These bacteria are extremely dangerous because they are tasteless, odorless and colorless, and, therefore, nearly impossible to detect.

Clostridium perfringens are usually found in meat or seafood that was previously cooked and then held at room temperature for a period of time. These perfringens are anaerobic; they do not need air in order to survive. They can thrive in masses of food or in canned foods in the form of botulism. In order to survive, the bacterium will form a spore and surround itself. The spore will protect the bacterium from exposure to the air and give it a much wider temperature range for survival than normal bacteria (65–120 F). These bacterial forms may survive through long periods of extreme temperature and then multiply when the conditions are more favorable.

Keeping cooked food consistently above 148 F or below 40 F eliminates clostridium perfringens bacteria.

Clostridium Botulism

This is another of the poisoning forms of bacteria. Botulism is a rare, infectious disease but it is far more lethal than the other types. Botulism exists only in an air-free environment like that of canned goods. These bacteria are most often found in home-canned goods; however, several national food packers have reported outbreaks in their operations.

Symptoms such as vomiting, double vision, abdominal pain and shock may occur anytime from three to four hours after ingestion, to eight days later.

Examine all canned goods closely before using. Look for dented, leaking cans and swollen cans or jar tops.

Staphylococci Bacteria

Staphylococci bacteria (Staph) are perhaps the most common cause of food poisoning. Staph bacteria can be found everywhere, particularly in the human nose. The bacteria by themselves are harmless. The problem arises when they are left uncontrolled to grow in food items. Food that has been left out, unrefrigerated, for just a few hours can produce the poisonous toxins of Staph bacteria.

Symptoms will appear two to six hours after consumption. Common symptoms are vomiting, muscle weakness, cramps and diarrhea. The sickness ranges from very severe cases — sometimes lethal — to a relatively mild illness. To prevent Staph poisoning, follow refrigeration procedures precisely. Only remove the refrigerated food items that you will be using right away.

Salmonella Infection

Salmonella infection is directly caused by the bacteria themselves, after consumption by a human. In certain cases, death has resulted; however, usually Salmonella cause severe — but temporary — illness. Symptoms are vomiting, fever, abdominal pain and cramps. Symptoms usually show up 12 to 24 hours after consumption and may last for several days.

Salmonella are found in the intestinal tract of some animals. They have been discovered in some packaged foods, eggs, poultry, seafood and meat. Thorough cooking and following refrigeration procedures can keep Salmonella growth to a safe limit.

Hepatitis, Dysentery and Diphtheria are some of the other infectious diseases that are bacterially derived.

Controlling Bacteria

The first step in controlling bacteria is to limit their access to the bed-and-breakfast. Make certain that all products entering the bed-and-breakfast are clean. Follow the prescribed bug-exterminating procedures to stop bacteria from being transported into the bed-and-breakfast. Keep all food products stored and refrigerated as prescribed. Clean up all spills as you go along, making the environment unsuitable for bacteria to live. Keep all food refrigerated until needed, and cook it as soon as possible.

The quality known as "pH" indicates how acidic or alkaline ("basic") a food or other substance is. The pH scale ranges from 0.0 to 14.0; 7.0 being exactly neutral. Distilled water, for example, has a neutral pH of 7.0. Bacteria grow best in foods that are neutral or slightly acidic, in the pH range of 4.6 to 7.0. Highly acidic foods, such as vinegar and most fresh fruits, inhibit bacterial growth. Meats and many other foods have an optimal pH for bacterial growth. On the other hand, some foods normally considered hazardous, such as mayonnaise and custard filling, can be safely stored at room temperature if their pH is below 4.6.

Lowering the pH of foods by adding acidic ingredients, such as making sauerkraut from cabbage or pickles from cucumbers, may render them non-potentially hazardous. This is not a foolproof prevention method, however. For example, although commercially prepared mayonnaise has a pH below 4.6, adding mayonnaise to a meat salad will not inhibit bacteria. The moisture in the meat and the meat's pH are likely to raise the pH of the salad to a point where bacteria can multiply.

Avoid Bacterial Cross-Contamination

One of the most common causes of food-borne illness is cross-contamination: the transfer of bacteria from food to food, hand to food or equipment to food.

Food to Food

Raw, contaminated ingredients may be added to foods, or fluids from raw foods may drip into foods that receive no further cooking. A common mistake is to leave thawing meat on a top shelf in the refrigerator where it can drip down onto prepared foods stored below.

Hand to Food

Bacteria are found throughout the body: in the hair, on the skin, in clothing, in the mouth, the nose, the throat, the intestinal tract and on scabs or scars from skin wounds. These bacteria often end up on the hands where they can easily spread to food. People can also pick up bacteria by touching raw food, then transfer it to cooked or ready-to-eat food.

Equipment to Food

Bacteria may pass from equipment to food when equipment that has touched contaminated food is then used to prepare other food without proper cleaning and sanitizing. For example, cross-contamination can occur when surfaces used for cutting raw poultry are then used to cut foods that will be eaten raw, such as fresh vegetables.

Coverings, such as plastic wrap and holding and serving containers, can also harbor bacteria that can spread to food. A can opener, a plastic-wrap box or a food slicer can also become a source of cross-contamination if not properly sanitized between uses.

Personal hygiene is the best way to stop bacteria from contaminating and spreading into new areas. Hands are the greatest source of contamination. Hands must be washed constantly throughout the day. Every time an individual scratches her head or sneezes, she is exposing her hands to bacteria and will spread it to anything she touches, such as food, equipment and clothes. Hand and nail brushes, anti-bacterial soaps and disposable gloves should be a part of every bed-and-breakfast, even if not required by law. Proper training and management follow-up is also critical.

Every employee must practice good basic hygiene:

- Short hair, and/or hair contained in a net
- Clean-shaven, or facial hair contained in a net
- Clean clothes/uniforms
- Clean hands and short nails
- No unnecessary jewelry
- A daily shower or bath
- No smoking in or near the kitchen
- Hand washing, prior to starting work, periodically and after handling any foreign object: head, face, ears, money, food, boxes or trash

An employee who has the symptoms of the common cold or any open cuts or infections should not go to work. By simply breathing, he or she may be inadvertently exposing the environment to bacteria. Although it is rarely practiced in the food industry, all employees should be required to have a complete medical examination as a condition of employment. This should include blood and urine tests. A seemingly healthy individual may unknowingly be the carrier of a latent communicable disease.

Are Your Hands Really Clean?

Hand washing is perhaps the most critical aspect of good personal hygiene in food service. Workers should wash their hands with soap and warm water for 20 seconds. When working with food, they should wash gloved hands as often as bare hands. Hand washing is such a simple — yet very effective — method for eliminating cross-contamination. Try the following exercise:

First, you'll need a fluorescent substance and a black light. Using these materials, you can show trainees the "invisible dirt" that may be hiding on their hands:

1. Have employees dip their hands in the fluorescent substance
2. Tell employees to wash their hands
3. Have employees hold their hands under the black light to see how much "dirt" is still there
4. Explain proper hand-washing technique
5. Have employees wash their hands again, this time using the proper hand-washing technique
6. Have employees once again hold their hands under the black light

Bugs, Insects and Animal Pests

Bug and insect infestation in a bed-and-breakfast is the result of poor sanitation practices. Aside from being a nuisance, they are a threat to food safety. Flies, cockroaches and other insects all carry bacteria, and many, because of where they get their food, carry disease. Bugs, insects and animals require the same three basic necessities of life as bacteria do: food, water and warmth. When healthful, thriving bugs and insects are visible; this is an indicator that proper sanitation procedures have not been carried out. Eliminate the environment that these pests need to live, and you will be eliminating their existence. Combining proper sanitation practices with periodic extermination spraying will stop any problems before they start.

To prevent the spread of flies in your establishment, keep all doors, windows and screens closed at all times. Ensure that garbage is sealed in airtight containers and is picked up regularly. All trash must be cleaned off the ground; flies can deposit their eggs on the thinnest scrap of food. Dumpsters must be periodically steam cleaned and deodorized. They should never contain any decaying food scraps.

All door jambs and building cracks, even the thinnest ones, must be sealed. Be cautious when receiving deliveries. Bugs may be in the boxes or crates. The greatest protection against cockroaches is your exterminator. Of course, the exterminator will be of little value if you do not already have good sanitary practices in place. Select an exterminator who is currently servicing other bed-and-breakfasts. Chemicals sprayed in a bed-and-breakfast must be of the non-residual type. These are safe and approved for use in food service establishments. Rodents are prolific breeders, producing as many as 50 offspring in a lifespan of one year. They tend to hide during the day, but they can be discovered by these telltale signs:

- Droppings
- Holes
- Nesting materials
- Gnawing
- Tracks on dusty surfaces

Animal pests, such as rats and mice, may be very serious problems for the bed-and-breakfast operator. These rodents can eat through a cement wall to gain access to your building. They are filthy animals that will eat any sort of garbage or decaying food available. Rats are infested with bacteria and, often, disease. They have been known to bite people, as have their fleas, which also spread their bacteria and disease. Rats and mice have evolved into creatures highly developed for survival. Once they have become settled in an area, they are very difficult to get rid of. They are prolific breeders and spread rapidly.

Rats and mice, like flies, are attracted to exposed garbage. They are extremely strong and can easily gain access to a building through a crack or hole no larger than a quarter. Ensure that your building's foundation is airtight. Keep all food products at least 6 inches off the floor; this enables the exterminator to get under the shelving to spray. Rat bait, a poisoning capsule resembling food, is particularly effective when spread around the building and dumpsters. As with any poison or chemical you use, make certain that it is labeled clearly and stored away from food-storage areas.

Kitchen Safety

By its nature, the food service environment is full of potential hazards to employees' safety. Knives, slicers, grinders, glass, hot surfaces and wet or greasy floors are only a few of the hazards food service workers face every day. Fortunately, most accidents also involve human error and, therefore, can be prevented.

Heat and Burns

There are many ways employees can get burned in a food service environment unless they're very careful. Burns can result from contact with hot surfaces such as grills, ovens, burners, fryers and other heating equipment. Burns can also be caused by escaping steam or by hot food or drinks that are splattered, splashed or spilled.

To prevent burns:

- Use thick, dry potholders or mitts, and stir food with long-handled spoons or paddles.
- Turn on hot-water faucets cautiously. Wear insulated rubber gloves for rinse water that is 170 F. Follow instructions for the use of cooking equipment — particularly steam equipment. Be sure all steam is expelled from steamers before opening the doors.
- Lift cooking lids and similar equipment away from yourself to avoid burns from steam.
- To avoid splattering and splashing, don't fill kettles too full. Also, don't allow food to boil over.
- Remember that oil and water don't mix, so be sure food is dry before you place it in a fryer.
- Point pan handles away from foot traffic, but also within reach, to avoid knocking over other pans.
- Do not crowd cooking surfaces with hot pans. Remove cooked foods from cooking surfaces immediately.
- Allow oil to cool and use extreme caution when cleaning fryers.
- Use caution when removing hot pans from the oven. Wear insulated gloves or mitts, and be certain no one is in the removal path.
- Do not wear clothing that may drape onto a hot spot and catch on fire.

Cuts

Just as they need to take precautions to prevent being burned, food service workers also need to be careful not to get cut. And it's not just knives that can cause trouble.

Workers can hurt themselves — or their co-workers — with the sharp edges of equipment and supplies or with broken glass. Nails and staples used in food packaging can also be dangerous.

To prevent cuts, take the following precautions:

- Use appropriate tools (not bare hands) to pick up and dispose of broken glass. Immediately place broken glass into a separate, clearly marked garbage container.
- Take care when cutting rolls of kitchen wrap with the cutter.
- Be careful with can openers and the edges of open cans. Never use a knife to open cans or to pry items loose.
- Use a pusher to feed food into a grinder.
- Turn off and unplug slicers and grinders when removing food and cleaning.
- Use guards on grinders and slicers.
- Replace equipment blades as soon as they are cleaned.
- Left-handed people need to take extra care when working with slicers and similar equipment. This is because the safety features on this equipment are typically designed for right-handed people.

In addition:

- Keep knives sharp. Dull blades are harder to work with and cause more cuts than sharp ones.
- Never leave knives or equipment blades in the bottom of a sink.

- Carry knives by the handle with the tip pointed away from you. Never try to catch a falling knife.
- Cut away from yourself on a cutting board.
- Slice, do not hack.

Also, when you're storing or cleaning equipment, be sure to:

- Store knives and other sharp tools in special places when not in use.
- Wash dishes and glasses separately to help prevent them from being crushed by heavier objects and breaking in the dishwasher or sink.
- Do not stack glasses or cups inside one another.
- Watch out for nails, staples and protruding sharp edges while unpacking boxes and crates.

Electrical Shock

Because of the variety of electrical equipment used in food service, electrical shock is a common concern.

To prevent electrical shock:

- Properly ground all electrical equipment.
- Ensure that employees can reach switches without touching or leaning against metal tables or counters.
- Replace all worn or frayed electrical cords.
- Use electrical equipment only when hands are dry.
- Unplug equipment before cleaning.
- Locate electrical switches and breakers to permit rapid shutdown in the event of an emergency.

Strains

Carrying equipment or food items that are too heavy can result in strains to the arms, legs or back.

To prevent strains:

- Store heavy items on lower shelves.
- Use dollies or carts when moving objects that are too heavy to carry.
- To move objects from one area to another, use carts with firm shelves and properly operating wheels.
- Don't carry too many objects at one time; instead, use a cart.
- Don't try to lift large or heavy objects by yourself.
- Use proper lifting techniques. Remember to bend from your knees, not your back.

Slipping and Falling

Anyone who slips and falls onto the floor can be badly hurt. Be sure your facility does not have hazards that put workers at risk.

To prevent slips and falls:

- Clean up wet spots and spills immediately.
- Let people know when floors are wet. Use signs that signal caution, and prominently display them. Wear shoes that have no-slip soles.
- Do not stack boxes or other objects too high. They can fall and cause people to trip.
- Keep items such as boxes, ladders, step stools and carts out of the paths of foot traffic.

Fires

More fires occur in food service than in any other type of operation. Fire extinguishers should be available in all areas where fires are likely, especially in the kitchen near grills and deep fryers. But be careful — don't keep extinguishers so close to the equipment that they will be inaccessible in the event of a fire.

All employees should be trained in avoiding fires as well as in the use of fire extinguishers and in evacuation procedures. Remember, always call the fire department first before using a fire extinguisher!

Choking

As kids, we probably all heard our parents say: "Don't eat so fast! Chew your food properly!" They may have added, "Don't talk while you're eating," and "Drink your milk carefully!"

It's good advice for children — and for adults. Anyone can choke on food if they are not careful. That's why an important part of food service safety is being alert to your customers.

Here's what to look for, and what to do:

- If a person has both hands to the throat and cannot speak or cough, it is likely he or she is choking.
- If this person can talk, cough or breathe, do not pat him or her on the back or interfere in any way.
- If this person cannot talk, cough or breathe, you will need to take action. Use the Heimlich maneuver, and call for help immediately.

All food service employees should be trained in the use of the Heimlich maneuver, and posters with instructions on how to perform it should be posted near the employee dining area.

Exposure to Hazardous Chemicals

Improper exposure to cleaning agents, chemical pesticides and chemical sanitizers may cause injury to the skin or poisoning. To protect workers from exposure to hazardous materials, special precautions need to be taken, including certain steps that are required by law.

For example, OSHA requires food service establishments to keep a current inventory of all hazardous materials.

Manufacturers are required to make sure hazardous chemicals are properly labeled and must supply a Material Safety Data Sheet (MSDS) to be kept on file at the food service facility. The MSDS provides the chemical name of the product and physical hazards, health hazards and emergency procedures in case of exposure.

Information about each chemical — including its common name, when it is used, who is authorized to use it, and information from the MSDS — must also be provided to workers.

To prevent improper exposure to hazardous materials, make sure:

- Only properly trained workers handle hazardous chemicals
- Employees have safety equipment to use when working with hazardous chemicals
- Employees wear nonporous gloves and eye goggles when working with sanitizing agents and other cleaners

Improper handling of food products or neglecting sanitation and safety procedures will certainly lead to health problems and/or personal injury. A successful bed-and-breakfast must develop a reputation for serving quality food in a safe environment. Should there ever be a question in your customers' minds as to the wholesomeness or quality of a product, the bed-and-breakfast will quickly lose its hard-earned reputation. The sanitation and safety procedures described in this section are very simple to initiate, but management must follow up and enforce them.

CHAPTER THIRTEEN

· · · · ·

Staff

According to the latest edition of PAII's *Statistics of Bed-and-Breakfast/Country Inns*, more than 70 percent of all inns have employees. Even if you don't start off with employees, as your business grows, you may find yourself with regular employees (as opposed to the temporary help you may hire for repairs, etc.). This chapter will help ensure that you're ready when you do need to start looking for, hiring and training employees.

Hiring Bed-and-Breakfast Employees

The key to hiring good, competent employees is to put aside personal prejudices and select one applicant over another only because you feel he or she will have a better chance of being successful at the job. What a potential employee is qualified and capable of doing is often quite different than what he or she actually will do. The purpose of this section is to provide the interviewer with the information necessary to determine if the applicant has the necessary qualities.

Key Points for Conducting Employment Interviews

Treat all applicants considerately and show a genuine interest in them, even if they have little or no chance of obtaining the job. Every applicant should be treated as a potential customer, because they are.

Make certain that you are on time and ready to receive the applicant. Arriving late or changing appointment dates at the last minute will give the applicant the impression that you are unorganized and that the bed-and-breakfast is run in the same manner.

Thoroughly know the job being offered. You cannot possibly match someone's abilities with a job you do not know or understand completely.

All interviews must be conducted in privacy, preferably in the interviewer's office. Interruptions must be kept to a minimum.

Make the applicant feel at ease. Have comfortable chairs and possibly beverages available. Speak in a conversational, interested tone.

Applicants will be full of questions about the job, its duties, the salary, etc. Newspaper advertisements tell only a little about the job and your company, so allow plenty of time for this important discussion.

Whenever possible, let the applicants speak. You can learn a great deal about them by the way they talk about themselves, past jobs, former supervisors and school experiences. Watch for contradictions, excuses and, especially, the applicant being on the defensive or speaking in a negative manner. Avoiding subjects is an obvious indication that there was some sort of problem there in the past; be persistent about getting the whole story, but don't be overbearing. Come back to it later if necessary.

Never reveal that you may disapprove of something an applicant has done or said; always appear open-minded. On the other hand, don't condone or approve of anything that is obviously in error.

Always ask a few questions they don't expect and aren't prepared for: What do they do to relax? What are their hobbies? What is the last book they read? Try to understand their attitudes, personalities and energy levels.

Perhaps one of the most useful things you can ask when interviewing prospective employees is: What were your favorite parts of your previous job? Look to see if the things they liked to do with previous employers fit with the things you'll be asking them to do for you. This is significant; it is important to cross-train employees to do as many jobs as possible, and it helps to know which of those jobs will be a good fit. Often in interviewing prospective food service employees, you'll get two types of applicants — those who say they prefer the "people part" of the job (talking to and serving customers, running the cash register) and those who like the "food part" of the job (chef, salad prep, line cook). Most applicants will be fairly honest about what they like to do.

Be sure to ask at least one behavior-based question; this will be very useful in getting at how an applicant responds in real-life work situations and how well he or she is able to handle them. For example: "What would you do if a customer complained that the 'soup just doesn't taste right'?" Or, "What would you do if your seemingly happy patron did not leave any tip at all?"

Unlawful Pre-Employment Questions

This section is not intended to serve on behalf of, or as a substitute for, legal counsel, or even as an interpretation of the various federal and state laws regarding equal and fair employment practices. The purpose of this section is only to act as a guide to the type of questions that may and may not be legally asked of a potential employee.

A thorough discussion of this subject with both the state and federal labor offices and with your lawyer would be in order. Standard employment applications may be purchased at your office supply store. Before you use these forms, let your lawyer examine one to make certain that it doesn't contain or insinuate any questions that might be considered illegal.

The Federal Civil Rights Act of 1964 and other state and federal laws ensure that a job applicant will be treated fairly and on an equal basis, regardless of race, color, religious creed, age, sex or national origin.

In order to support these regulations, you cannot ask certain questions of applicants in regard to the aforementioned categories. There is a fine line between what may and may not be asked of applicants. Use basic common sense in regard to the type of questions you ask and look up templates/Google anything if you have are uncertain about absolutely a question that you are thinking of asking. Any illegal question would have no bearing on the outcome of the interview anyway, so avoid questions that are related to, or might evoke an answer that infringes upon, the applicant's civil rights.

Age/date of birth is an area of great concern for establishments with liquor, wine or beer licenses. Age is a sensitive pre-employment question, because the Age Discrimination in Employment Act (**www.eeoc.gov/policy/adea.html**) protects employees age 40 years and older. It is permissible to ask an applicant to state his or her age if it is fewer than 18 years. If you need the date of birth for internal reasons, e.g., computations with respect to a pension or profit-sharing plan, this information can be obtained after the person is hired.

Drugs, smoking. It is permissible to ask an applicant if he or she uses drugs or smokes. The application also affords an employer the opportunity to obtain the applicant's agreement to be bound by the employer's drug and smoking policies. The application also affords an employer an opportunity to obtain the applicant's agreement to submit to drug testing.

Other problem areas. Questions concerning whether an applicant has friends or relatives working for the employer may be improper if the employer gives a preference to such applicants. Questions concerning credit rating or credit references have been ruled discriminatory against minorities and women. That shouldn't matter anyways since a person's financial history shouldn't have any bearing on their professional skills as your employee. Questions concerning whether an applicant owns a home have been held to be discriminatory against minority members as well since a greater number of minority members do not own their own homes. While questions about military experience or training are permissible, questions concerning the type of discharge received by an applicant have been held to be improper, because a high proportion of other-than-honorable discharges are given to minorities. The Americans with Disabilities Act prohibits general inquiries about disabilities, health problems and medical conditions. This might all seem like common sense to you, but it's important to spell all of these things out plainly because we now live in a world where people's constant access to the Internet leave you open to the potential of a misunderstanding between you and an applicant being seen by millions within a few days or maybe even a few hours (yes, it's that fast).

Here is a list of prohibited questions, some of which are obvious but used to illustrate the point:

- How tall are you, anyway?
- What color are your eyes?
- Do you work out at the gym regularly?
- Do you or anyone you know have HIV?
- Did you get any workers' comp from your last employer?
- How old are you, anyway?
- Have you been in prison?
- Are you really a man?
- Do you rent or own your home?
- Have you ever declared bankruptcy?
- What part of the world are your parents from?
- Are you a minority?
- Is English your first language?
- I can't tell if you're Japanese or Chinese. Which is it?
- So which church do you go to?
- Who will take care of the kids if you get this job?
- Is this your second marriage, then?
- Just curious: Are you gay?
- Are you in a committed relationship right now?
- How does your boyfriend feel about you working here?

Screening Potential Employees

Screening job applicants will enable you to reject those candidates who are obviously unsuitable before they are referred to a lengthy interview. This saves both the bed-and-breakfast and the applicants time and money. The preliminary screening can be done by an assistant manager or someone knowledgeable about the bed-and-breakfast's employment needs and practices. Potential job candidates may then be referred to the manager for intensive interviews. All applicants should leave feeling they have been treated fairly and had an equal opportunity to present their case for getting the job. As previously stated, this is an important part of public relations. Who knows — the applicant that just left may be your next customer.

Base your preliminary screening on the following criteria:

1. **Experience.** Is the applicant qualified to do the job? Examine past job experience. Check all references.

2. **Appearance.** Is the applicant neatly dressed? Remember, he or she will be dealing with the public; the way the applicant is dressed now is probably better than the way they will come to work.

3. **Personality.** Does the applicant have a personality that will complement the other employees' and impress customers? Is he or she outgoing, but not overbearing? Feel free to take extra time to discern a person's actual personality in case you are worried he or she may be pretending for the sake of the job.

4. **Legality.** Does the applicant meet the legal requirements?

5. **Availability.** Can the applicant work the hours needed? Commute easily?

6. **Health and physical ability.** Is the applicant capable of doing the physical work required? All employees hired should be subject to approval only after a complete physical examination by a mutually approved doctor.

Make certain the application is signed and dated.

All applicants at this point should be divided into one of the three following categories:

1. **Refer applicant.** Refer applicant to manager for interview and, if feasible, to the department head where the job is open.
2. **Reject.** Describe the reasons for rejection and place the application on file for future reference.
3. **Prospective file.** Any applicant who is not qualified for this position but may be considered for other areas of the bed-and-breakfast should be placed in a prospective applicant file.

What to Look for in Potential Bed-and-Breakfast Employees

Stability. You don't want employees to leave in two months. Look at past employment-sheet records. Stability also refers to the applicant's emotional makeup.

Leadership qualities. Employees must be those who are achievers and doers, not individuals who have to be led around by the hand. Look at past employment positions and growth rate.

Motivation. Why is the applicant applying to this bed-and-breakfast? Why the bed-and-breakfast industry in general? Is the decision career-related or temporary? Does the applicant appear to receive motivation from within or by a domineering other, such as a spouse or parent?

Independence. Is the applicant on his or her own? Does he or she appear to be financially secure? At what age did he or she leave home? And for what reasons?

Maturity. Is the individual mentally mature enough to work in a stressful environment? Will they be able to relate and communicate with other employees and customers who may be much older?

Determination. Does the applicant seem to always finish what he or she starts? Does he or she seem to look for, or retreat from, challenges? Examine time at school and at last job.

Work habits. Is the applicant aware of the physical work involved in bed-and-breakfast employment? Has the applicant done similar work? Does the applicant appear neat and organized? Look over the application; is it filled out per the instructions? Neatly? In ink? Examine past jobs for number and rate of promotions and raises.

The Final Selection and Decision

Reaching the final selection, to whom to offer the position, is often a difficult choice. You may have many applicants who are qualified and would probably become excellent employees, but which one do you decide upon? Always base your choice on the total picture the applicants have painted of themselves through the interviews, résumés and applications. Gather advice from those who interviewed or had contact with the individuals. Not only will this help you reach the correct decision, but will also make the rest of your staff feel a part of the management decision-making team. Whomever you select, he or she must be someone you feel good about having around, someone you hopefully will enjoy working with and who you feel will have a very good chance of being successful at the job.

When you offer him or her the job, make certain the applicant fully understands the following items before accepting the position:

Salary. Starting pay, salary range, expected growth rate, the day payroll is issued, company benefits, vacations, insurance, etc.

Job description. List of job duties, hours, expectations, etc.

Time and date of, and to whom he/she should report, on the first day of work.

Rejecting Applicants

Rejecting applicants is always an unpleasant and difficult task. The majority of the applications will be rejected almost immediately. Some applicants will ask the reason for rejection. Always be honest, but use as much tact as possible in explaining the reasoning behind the decision. Avoid a confrontation, explaining only what is necessary to settle the applicant's questions. Usually it will be sufficient to say, "We accepted an applicant who was more experienced," or "…who is better qualified."

As mentioned before, some applications may be transferred into a "prospective file" for later reference. Inform the applicant of this action, but don't give the impression that he or she has a good chance of being hired, nor state a specific date when you will be looking for new employees.

Employee Handbook/Personnel Policy

Federal law mandates that all employers, regardless of size, have written policy guidelines. Employee handbooks/policy manuals are used to familiarize new employees with company policies and procedures. They also serve as guides to management personnel. Formally writing down your policies could keep you out of court; prevent problems and misunderstandings; save time spent answering common questions; and look more professional to your employees.

Explaining and documenting company policy to your employees has been proven to increase productivity, compliance and retention. Detailed in the following chart are some common areas to be covered.

Lack of communication, along with inadequate policies and guidelines, have been cited as major factors in workplace legal disputes. Failure to inform or notify employees of standard policies has resulted in the loss of millions of dollars in legal judgments. Simply not being aware that their actions violated company policy has been an effective defense for many terminated employees. Most important is to have the employee sign a document stating he or she has received, reviewed, understands and intends to comply with all policies in the manual.

If you have ever written a policy document before, you know how time consuming it can be. Even if you were a lawyer, it would likely take you 40 hours to research and write a comprehensive employee manual. To pay someone to draw one up for you can cost thousands of dollars. Atlantic Publishing (**www. atlantic-pub.com**) has put together a standard employee handbook guide for the food-service industry. All you have to do is edit the information. The template contains all of the most important company handbook sections, and it's written in Microsoft Word so that customizing and printing your manual will be as easy as possible.

Topics to Be Covered in Employee Handbook

- Absenteeism and Punctuality
- Acts of Misconduct
- Affidavit of Receipt
- Availability for Work
- Benefits Eligibility
- Benefits Program
- Bereavement Leave
- Bonus Plan
- Break Policy
- Communications
- Company Property
- Confidentiality of Company Information
- Conflicts of Interest

- Criminal Convictions
- Disciplinary Guidelines
- Educational Assistance
- Employee Conduct
- Employee Discounts
- Employee Relations
- Employment Classification
- Employment of Relatives
- Employment References
- Equal Employment Opportunity
- Family Leave of Absence
- Harassment
- Holidays
- Hours of Work
- Insurance
- Insurance Continuation
- Job Abandonment
- Jury Duty
- Mandatory Meetings
- Medical Leave of Absence
- Military Leave
- Neatness of Work Area
- Office Equipment
- Orientation
- Other Forms of Separation
- Outside Employment
- Overtime
- Payroll
- Performance-Based Release
- Performance Reviews
- Personal Appearance
- Personal Mail
- Personal Telephone Calls
- Personnel Files
- Pre-Tax Deductions
- Problem Resolution
- Recording Time
- Rehiring Former Employees
- Reimbursable Expenses
- Safety
- Salary and Wage Increases
- Searches
- Severe Weather
- Social Security
- Solicitations and Contributions
- Standards of Conduct
- Substance Abuse
- Suggestions
- Termination Procedures
- Tools and Equipment
- Travel Expenses
- Unemployment Compensation
- Use of Company Vehicles
- Vacation
- Violence and Weapons Policy
- Voluntary Resignation
- Workers' Compensation
- Work Performance
- Workplace Monitoring

Personnel File

Once the applicant is hired, an individual personnel file should be set up immediately. It should contain the following information:

- Application
- Form W-4 and Social Security number
- Name, address and phone number
- Emergency phone number
- Employment date
- Job title and pay rate
- Past performance evaluations
- Signed form indicating receipt and acceptance of Employee Handbook/Personnel Policy Manual
- Termination date, if applicable, and a detailed account of the reasons for termination

Training

Getting employees to do things right means taking the time to train them properly from the start so that they understand what needs to be done, how to do it and why it should be done that way. Effective training, however, involves more than simply providing information. Training is not a problem, and it cannot be "solved" and then forgotten. Managers and supervisors at every level must soon realize that training is a continual process, as is learning; it must never stop.

The most effective training technique is interactivity. Get people to stand up and do things. Show them how to set a table, look for lipstick on a glass, wash their hands properly, use a thermometer, wash a dish, make a martini, garnish a plate, etc. Let the employees participate.

Most managers and supervisors think of training as teaching new employees *skills,* such as dish washing or bartending. Training needs to be far more than that; management must look beyond its own interests. As mentioned before, we must start to consider the employees' interests, goals, needs and desires if we are to become successful.

The employee must know not only their job and how to perform it, but how their performance affects others in their jobs in other parts of the bed-and-breakfast. They must visualize their position as an integral part of an efficient machine, not as a separate, meaningless function.

Telling an employee that his or her position and performance is crucial to the bed-and-breakfast's success and *showing* the reasons why are two entirely different things. The importance of performing his or her job in the manner in which he or she was trained must by physically demonstrated to the employee, as well as the ramifications of varying from these procedures.

Orientation and Instruction

A complete orientation of the trainee to his or her new job and new company is an intricate part of the training process. The entire orientation will take less than 30 minutes; unfortunately, however, it is rarely done. There is no excuse for not giving the new employee a good introduction before he or she starts the actual training. Described below are some basic orientation practices:

1. Introduce the new employee to yourself and the company.
2. Introduce the new employee to all of the other employees.
3. Introduce the new employee to their trainer and supervisor.
4. Explain the company's employee and personnel policies. Present him or her with the Employee Handbook/Personnel Policy Manual.

5. Outline the objectives and goals of the training program:
   a. Describe the training, where and how it will take place.
   b. Describe the information that will be learned.
   c. Describe the skills and attitudes that will be developed.

6. Set up a schedule for the employee. It should include:
   a. The date, day and time to report to work during training.
   b. Who will be doing the training and who the supervisor is.
   c. What should be learned and accomplished each day.
   d. The date when the training should be completed.

At this point the trainee may be presented to the trainer. Ideally, the employee's regular supervisor does all of the training. The trainer must be a model employee who is thoroughly knowledgeable about and experienced in the job. The trainer must be able to communicate clearly and have a great deal of patience and understanding.

The trainee must be taught the how, why, when and where of the job. This is best accomplished by following the trainer's example and methods. After confidence is built, the employee may attempt to repeat the procedure under the watchful eye of the trainer.

The trainer must gauge how fast the trainee is learning and absorbing the material against the time schedule set up by the manager. Daily written or oral reports should be presented to the manager on the trainee's progress and needs and placed in their employee file. Compare the trainee's production to that of an experienced worker. Written and practical tests can be given to evaluate how much material is being absorbed and utilized. Add new material when the old material has been assimilated. Relate the old material to the new as you continue to build towards training the employee.

Once the employee has completed the training, the trainer or supervisor should prepare a final written report and evaluation. This report should describe the strengths and weaknesses of the trainee, their knowledge of the job, quality of work, attitude and a general appraisal of the employee. After the manager reviews this report, all three parties should meet to discuss the training period. The employee should be congratulated on successfully completing the training program. A review of the final report would be in order and then filed in the employee's personnel file for future reference. Ask the employee's opinion on the training program; he or she may have some thoughts on improving it. This same question should be presented to the employee after two weeks of work. Find out if the training program adequately prepared the trainee for the actual job.

Outside Help in Training

When training sessions involve several people or even the entire staff, it is a good idea to bring in outside help for your meetings. These people are experts in their fields. Often just a phone call is enough inducement. Reward these people for their time and effort with a complimentary gift certificate.

There are great resources for outside-training information available to assist in your training programs: videos, posters, books, software, etc. One great source for all these products is Atlantic Publishing (**www.atlantic-pub.com**).

Outside Help: Speakers and Subjects

- **State Liquor Agent** – Liquor laws, compliance, etc.
- **Health Department Inspector** – Health and sanitation practices/ requirements.

- **Wine Distributors** – Wine tasting, promotion, etc.
- **Red Cross Instructor** – Basic first aid, the Heimlich maneuver to stop choking and C.P.R. procedures.

Evaluating Performance

Evaluating each employee's job performance is a crucial element in developing a structured work environment and sound employee relations. Every employee must be aware of his or her strengths and which areas of his or her job performance need improvement. Quarterly or periodic one-on-one evaluations help break down the communication barriers between management and employees. Many of an employee's work-related problems, thoughts and ideas can be revealed in the evaluation session. However, remember to keep in mind that evaluations are only a part of the communication process and should not be considered as a substitute for daily communication. Management must always be available to listen. Communication is an ongoing and continual process.

See the following example of the **Employee Evaluation Form**.

EMPLOYEE PERFORMANCE EVALUATION FORM

NAME: _____ POSITION: _____

INTERVIEWER: _____ DATE: _____

LAST EVALUATION DATE: _____ SALARY: _____

For each of the following categories grade the employee's performance on a sliding scale of 1 to 10 (see scale below). The overall grade is the average of all scores plus the interviewer's comments.

1-2 poor   3-4 below average   5 average   6-7 above average   8-9 very good   10 exceptional

KNOWLEDGE OF JOB
procedures, paperwork, skill, function
RATING: _____
Comments: _____
_____
_____

QUALITY
up to specification, accuracy, consistency
RATING: _____
Comments: _____
_____
_____

ATTITUDE
towards work, management, other employees, customers
RATING: _____
Comments: _____
_____
_____

LEADERSHIP
ability to give direction
RATING: _____
Comments: _____
_____
_____

RELIABILITY
dependable, on time, follows through on assignments
RATING: _____
Comments: _____
_____
_____

PRODUCTIVITY
volume, utilization of time
RATING: _____
Comments: _____
_____
_____

APPEARANCE
uniform, neat
RATING: _____
Comments: _____
_____
_____

SERVICE
alert, fast
RATING: _____
Comments: _____
_____
_____

OVERALL RATING: _____

SALARY ADJUSTED: ☐ YES ☐ NO

NEW SALARY: _____

Recommendations: _____
_____
_____

Items to be followed up on: _____
_____
_____
_____

Consider these points prior to filling out the evaluation forms:

Know the employee's job description thoroughly. You are evaluating how well the employee meets the job requirements; you are not comparing against other employees nor evaluating the employee according to what you see as their potential.

Always conduct the evaluation in private, with no interruptions. Schedule each evaluation far enough apart so that there is plenty of time to discuss everything in one sitting.

Don't let just one incident or trait — positive or negative — dominate the evaluation. Look at the whole picture over the entire time since the last evaluation.

Evaluations should balance positive and negative attributes, they should never be one-sided. A totally negative evaluation will almost never motivate a poor employee. Bring out some of their positive contributions, and describe in detail what changes are needed. A completely negative evaluation will only scare the employee. Should a totally negative evaluation be warranted, it is probable that the employee should have been terminated long ago.

Review past evaluations, but don't dwell on them. Look for areas where improvement or a decline in performance has taken place.

Always back up your thoughts and appraisals with specific examples. Allow plenty of time for the employee's comments: remember, you could be wrong. If examples or circumstances that were never mentioned before come out in the evaluation, you are guilty of allowing the communication process to deteriorate.

Don't cover too much material or expect the employee to make a drastic change overnight. An evaluation is only part in a series of continuous steps to direct the employee.

Begin the evaluation with the employee's positive points and then direct the discussion to areas that need improvement.

Certain personality traits and deficiencies may not always be changeable. Don't overemphasize them, but show how they might affect the employee's job performance and the performance of others.

Finish the evaluation on a positive note. The employee should leave with a good feeling about his or her positive contributions to the bed-and-breakfast and know precisely what and how to improve on his or her weaknesses.

After the evaluation, make certain that you follow up on the thoughts, ideas and recommendations that were brought out during the evaluation. Without a follow-up, the evaluation is of little value.

Evaluations are confidential. File them in the employee's personnel file only if no one else has access to them there.

The Decision to Terminate an Employee

There comes a time when an unsatisfactorily performing employee, after being evaluated and given a fair opportunity to correct his or her deficiencies, must be terminated. Discharging an employee is always a difficult and unpleasant task, but it must be done for the good of the bed-and-breakfast. Although it may be an unpleasant experience, it is far worse to let the employee stay on. Before long, the entire staff's morale will drop, causing a decrease in productivity.

The decision as to whether an employee should be terminated or retrained is difficult and often prejudiced by your inability to examine the entire picture of the employee's performance. The final decision to discharge an employee should be reached after carefully weighing the pros and cons — never in anger or when tired or under stress. Ask the employee's supervisor for an evaluation of the situation and the employee. Examine the employee's training, supervision and past evaluations. Make certain the employee has been given a fair opportunity to prove himself. Also be certain that neither you nor any member of your management staff has in any way contributed to, caused or perpetuated the problem.

Immediately after reaching your decision to terminate, set up a meeting with the employee. Don't let more than 24 hours go by; you don't want this information to leak out.

The employee's supervisor should be present during the exit interview. He or she will be able to add support and witness the action. This is important, as the employee may use some legal means to gain a settlement. Conduct the exit interview in a private room with no interruptions. Should the employee disagree with your reasoning or points, give him or her the opportunity to discuss them, but make sure you back up everything you say with proven facts and statements. Remain seated and calm during the proceedings; don't get up quickly or move suddenly. Absolutely never touch the employee, except when shaking hands. These actions may be misinterpreted and lead to a confrontation.

Fill out a report on the termination proceedings, and file it in the employee's personnel file. This report will be important should the employee decide to challenge the action. Develop a plan to fill the vacancy as soon as possible. Keep in mind that it will take several months before a new employee can be brought up to full productivity and that, after training, he or she may not work out at all.

Although nothing can fully prevent a former employee from filing a lawsuit, there are ways to decrease the likelihood of litigation: Be honest with the employee about his or her performance and the reason for the termination, treat employees consistently and aggressively investigate claims of discrimination. Above all, document the chances you've given employees to improve prior to your decision to terminate them. If a termination is challenged, and there are no records of the problems cited as reasons for termination and indicating opportunities given to correct these problems, there could be a problem. Keep in mind your notes don't have to be very detailed, but a dated description of a problem or of the employee's progress that is slipped into a personnel file helps dramatically.

Other employees always perceive the termination of an employee as a threat to their security. You may even be looked upon as unfair or exceedingly harsh. Sometimes an explanation is needed to soothe the other employees; in most cases, though, the reasons will be obvious to them and they will be on your side. Still, and again, *document everything.*

Index